MW00424260

NETROOTS RISING

NETROOTS RISING

How a Citizen Army of Bloggers and
Online Activists Is Changing
American Politics

Lowell Feld and Nate Wilcox

Foreword by Markos ("Kos") Moulitsas Zúniga

Westport, Connecticut
London

Library of Congress Cataloging-in-Publication Data

Feld, Lowell.

Netroots rising : how a citizen army of bloggers and online activists is changing American politics / Lowell Feld and Nate Wilcox ; foreword by Markos ("Kos") Moulitsas Zúniga.

p. cm.

Includes bibliographical references and index.

ISBN-13: 978–0–313–34660–6 (alk. paper)

1. Internet in political campaigns—United States. 2. Political campaigns—United States. 3. Internet—Political aspects—United States. I. Wilcox, Nate. II. Title.

JK2281.F39 2008

324.70285'4678—dc22   2007048264

British Library Cataloguing in Publication Data is available.

Library of Congress Catalog Card Number: 2007048264
ISBN: 978–0–313–34660–6

First published in 2008

Praeger Publishers, 88 Post Road West, Westport, CT 06881
An imprint of Greenwood Publishing Group, Inc.
www.praeger.com

Printed in the United States of America

The paper used in this book complies with the Permanent Paper Standard issued by the National Information Standards Organization (Z39.48–1984).

10   9   8   7   6   5   4   3   2   1

Contents

FOREWORD

These are crazy times in politics.

Things used to be fairly predictable for political professionals. Sure, their lives were hectic dealing with impossible campaign schedules and the demands of modern political campaigns, but they always knew what to expect. Sure, uncertainty has always been a hallmark of every campaign, but at least we were familiar with the roles the various actors played: On the inside, every campaign had a candidate, a media consultant, a communications director, a pollster, a field director, and a finance (fundraising) director. On the outside, every campaign had to deal with their opponent, the media, the volunteers, the donors, and the voters.

Everyone had his or her role, and everyone was expected to play it. Voters, for example, were supposed to passively absorb thirty-second television spots, read the direct mail in their mailboxes, and then, maybe, turn out to vote. Volunteers? They could lick envelopes at campaign headquarters or make phone calls. Any and all other talents they might have had were considered irrelevant and unwanted. And so on.

And that system might have continued on had the Democratic Party "professionals" enjoyed even the tiniest measure of success. Yet the opposite was taking place; conservativism was so ascendant, and so self-assured in the face of Democratic incompetence, that then–House Majority Leader Tom DeLay crowed about a "permanent Republican majority" after the 2004 results had been counted. The progressive movement then faced what was to be its nadir—an ascendant Republican Party holding the White House, the Senate, the House, the Supreme Court, and a majority of state legislative seats and state houses.

Fortunately, a frustrated group of political partisans started organizing. Fed up by the ineffectiveness of a moribund Democratic Party and the rise of the conservative juggernaut, they decided that the old rules weren't doing anyone any good, much less the country they loved so dearly. With the availability of the Internet, the party finally had a medium that allowed for coordination and aggregation of their efforts. No longer were they isolated political junkies in a sea of "blue" in Berkeley, California, or a sea of "red" in Tulsa, Oklahoma. With geographic barriers erased, these new activists started coming together: They started organizing.

The aforementioned political professionals viewed these early Internet activists as a strange breed, like nothing they had ever seen before. Many of the professionals dismissed the activists as young, "far-left," and politically naïve— that is, people who refused to play their proper roles, meddling in business better left to those who knew what they were doing and had the proper credentials. The "mainstream" press was even more dismissive, sneering at the impudent upstarts.

I was one of those barbarians at the gate when I started the Daily Kos blog. I was a 1980 war refugee from El Salvador, a U.S. Army vet, a Juris Doctor from Boston University, and a low-level and unremarkable project manager at a San Francisco web development firm. My background was colorful by any measure, but nothing in it provided me with the proper "credentials" to comment on our nation's politics. I didn't have the pedigree to be "heard," and the media and political gatekeepers worked to marginalize me and my new allies in the nascent but growing netroots.

But it didn't matter. The floodgates were open, and the technology allowed us to easily (and gleefully) crash those gates. Thousands of newly minted netroots activists poured into the breech, ignoring the sneering and nay-saying from establishment forces, and decided to wage political war on their own terms.

And it was glorious. Aggressive, in the face of a timid, risk-averse Democratic Party. Fun, in the face of the tedious Robert's Rules of Order. Innovative and entrepreneurial, unlike the stultified party establishment stuck in the past.

As with any movement, heroes have emerged from the unlikeliest places to secure our victories—and not just against the Republican machine, but against an entrenched Democratic establishment. You'll read about many of these heroes in this book. But it's hard to overlook the contributions by the authors themselves. Nate Wilcox was an early ally, even though he came from the dreaded world of the political consultant. I doubt anyone in the consulting world today understands the netroots ethos and culture so thoroughly, and can navigate that world as effortlessly and effectively as he does. Lowell Feld has become a key and important figure not just in a couple of hard-fought, high-profile Democratic victories in Virginia, but also in the overall revitalization of his state's Democratic Party. Lowell's greatest accomplishment was in 2006, when his seemingly quixotic Draft James Webb effort ended up defeating the Republican 2008 presidential front-runner, George Allen, and helping Democrats take back control of the U.S. Senate.

Yet in spite of their successes, Nate and Lowell are but two in a progressive army that numbers hundreds of thousands to millions of committed activists, all working for a new generation of leadership to shake up moribund party

establishments everywhere from Washington, D.C., to state capitals and city
halls.

The story isn't that certain leaders have emerged to shake up the world, but
that in this new progressive movement, anyone can be a leader and shake up
the world.

And this book will prove that.

Markos ("Kos") Moulitsas Zúniga
Berkeley, California

PREFACE

BACKGROUND

As the twenty-first century dawned, the gulf between the American people and its political leadership had never been wider. In each election for forty years, an ever-smaller percentage of the population turned out to vote. Between 1960 and 2000, voter turnout fell from 63 percent of the voting-age population to just 51 percent. The United States had become a nation of political consumers, passively watching campaigns and candidates on television. At the same time, the quality of news coverage was bottoming out into the sensationalistic babble of twenty-four-hour cable news. Nonstop "missing white girl" coverage and the "shark attack summer" before September 11, 2001, represented prime examples of this phenomenon.

These disturbing trends reached their nadir in December 2000, with the presidential election being decided by an ideologically divided Supreme Court in favor of George W. Bush. Despite having received half a million fewer votes than Al Gore, the newly elected President Bush claimed to possess a broad mandate to govern from the far right. Following the 9/11 attacks, Bush scorned the rare opportunity to unify America, instead opting to pursue a radical authoritarian agenda that combined xenophobia, ultranationalism, and an unprecedented expansion of presidential power.

Just as things bottomed out, thousands of citizen activists across America tapped into a powerful new means of communicating, informing, and organizing—the Internet. This latest evolution in communications technology empowered citizen activism just as broadcast and cable television had weakened it. From 1998 to the end of 2002, a nascent netroots revolution bubbled beneath the surface as progressives began blogging about politics and joining MoveOn, the first important online progressive organization. MoveOn had begun in 1998 with a simple online petition opposing the impeachment of Bill Clinton, and by 2002, it had grown to include several hundred thousand people united by their opposition to invading Iraq. But it wasn't until early 2003 that the online revolution really exploded with the insurgent presidential campaigns of Howard Dean and Wesley Clark.

In the early 2000s, the Democratic Party establishment abandoned its base and rolled over in support of George W. Bush's invasion of Iraq. In fact, the front-runners for the 2004 presidential nomination unanimously supported the war until Howard Dean began to speak out against it. The response to Dean's declaration that he was from the "Democratic wing of the Democratic Party" was immediate and dramatic, propelling a long-shot challenger to the head of the pack within a few months. A second 2004 grassroots explosion was triggered by efforts to draft General Wesley Clark to run for president by Democrats who opposed the war but doubted that Dean could win. The story of the Clark-for-president netroots movement starkly illustrates the (still unresolved) clash between a rising netroots and an entrenched class of paid political "professionals."

Neither of the two national netroots candidates won the Democratic Party's presidential nomination in 2004, but the netroots movement they energized continued to grow in the years that followed. Eventually, like a steadily rising tide breaching the floodwalls, the netroots rose from complete outsiders to a crucial force in the decisive Democratic victories of 2006.

The authors of this book were active in the early rise of the netroots— Lowell in his work for Wesley Clark and Nate in his work for Howard Dean. Like millions of other Americans, they have remained committed to achieving positive political change in the United States. This book centers on a series of campaigns in which the authors were involved as volunteers, consultants, or bloggers.

BIOGRAPHIES

A political junkie from a young age, Lowell Feld was mesmerized by the Watergate scandal at the age of thirteen and campaigned in Newington, Connecticut, for Gerald Ford in 1976. In high school, Lowell joined the Teenage Republicans and participated in Senator Lowell Weicker's one-week, Washington, D.C., summer internship program. In 1980, Lowell cast his first presidential vote for John Anderson, the independent from Illinois. After Reagan's election and the rise of the religious right, Lowell left the Republican Party.

Lowell received his bachelor's degree in international relations and psychology from the University of Pennsylvania in 1984, then studied the Middle East at George Washington University and Tel Aviv University. After receiving his master's degree, Lowell worked for the U.S. Energy Information Administration as an international oil markets analyst. He married, traveled with his wife, and largely avoided politics.

The 2000 election fiasco shook Lowell out of his apolitical lethargy. Watching a bunch of Republican hired goons steal the election from Al Gore was one of the most discouraging and frustrating things Lowell had ever seen. The 9/11 attack on the Pentagon hit close to home for Lowell, who lived in

Arlington and worked in downtown D.C. The attacks on New York City, where Lowell was born and lived until he was six years old, horrified him as well.

A few months after the invasion of Iraq in March 2003, Lowell volunteered for the Draft Wesley Clark movement and the Clark for President campaign. Lowell ran two websites: Environmentalists for Clark and Hispanics for Clark. After Clark's loss, Lowell approached the Kerry campaign but was told they were "all set." Nonetheless, Lowell volunteered for Kerry, despite the fact that he expected Kerry to lose to George W. Bush and Karl Rove's swiftboating minions.

In 2004, Lowell watched his presidential candidate, Wesley Clark, crash and burn. Lowell turned to volunteer work in support of John Kerry's campaign for president. Kerry's loss to Bush in November 2004 further depressed Lowell. The prospect of four more years of Bush/Cheney and a Congress controlled by the likes of Tom DeLay was a bitter pill to swallow.

In 2005, after watching John Kerry get "swiftboated," Lowell decided to "think globally, act locally," launching a Virginia-focused Democratic political blog called Raising Kaine with the intent of helping elect Democrats in Virginia, first and foremost Tim Kaine as governor. During 2005, Lowell worked to build Raising Kaine into a site that could help elect Democratic candidates and promote Democratic values in his state. The rise of state-level blogging and netroots activism was evident in 2005 as U.S. House of Representatives candidate Paul Hackett came close to a miraculous upset of Republican Jean Schmidt in an August special congressional election in Ohio, while Tim Kaine went on to victory in Virginia.

As the 2005 election wound to a successful conclusion, Lowell pondered who could compete against Senator George Allen in 2006. Soon, Lowell found himself corresponding with Ronald Reagan's former Navy Secretary James Webb, who had become a Democrat and was now considering a run for U.S. Senate from Virginia. In late December 2005, Lowell co-founded the Draft James Webb movement. Lowell quit his Energy Department job in March 2006, devoting himself to full-time politics. He joined the Webb campaign as its netroots coordinator in July 2006. Today, Lowell consults, blogs, and writes books like this one.

Nate Wilcox spent his twenties playing punk rock in Austin, Texas, bars before deciding in 1997 to get a job and return to college. He landed a $5 per hour internship at a powerhouse public affairs firm, Public Strategies Inc. (PSI). The job entailed clipping out news stories related to the firm's clients from every major newspaper in Texas and from two national papers. Supplemented with stories downloaded from the Associated Press and *New York Times* terminals, the clips were assembled into booklets that were faxed to agency clients around the world. For the time, this was considered high tech.

Nate built a simple website to post the news stories he was clipping from newspapers. He built a similar site for one of the firm's clients and then organized his fellow interns to build a public website for another client. Soon, PSI was charging clients tens of thousands of dollars for technologically simple websites built under Nate's direction.

Not long afterward, Nate found himself directing the company's new online division. Consulting with clients like Firestone, Southwestern Bell, Fannie Mae, and Texas Utilities, Nate learned the art of the modern communications campaign: polling, message development, crisis management, press relations, direct mail, television advertising, and mobilizing citizens to lobby their legislature. Working at a firm where such spin doctors as Paul Begala and Mark McKinnon influenced public opinion on behalf of massive corporations was like peeking behind the curtain and seeing the Wizard of Oz for what he was—a charlatan with a knack for self-promotion, who overawed and misled the gullible, and used "magic" to make himself seem bigger and more powerful than he was.

In 1998, Nate helped give a presentation to the Texas Democratic Convention on using the Internet for politics. The idea was greeted with a chorus of complaints that "poor people don't have computers" and "this stuff will never make a difference in an election." Most of the people in the packed Alamodome basement viewed the Internet as a threat to the Democratic Party's grassroots efforts.

Even worse, it seemed as if almost everyone else in Texas had turned Republican. Democrats on the ballot in 1998 actually competed to be the strongest backers of George W. Bush. Garry Mauro, the hapless Democratic nominee for governor, stood alone as his down-ballot comrades ran ads showing them standing side by side with Bush and even calling themselves "Bush Democrats." Rumor had it that Democratic Lieutenant Governor Bob Bullock, the most powerful elected official in the state (because of the unique structure of the Texas constitution), had cut a deal to support Bush right there in the PSI offices. Just weeks before the election, when Bullock endorsed Bush over his fellow Democrat Garry Mauro, those rumors seemed to be confirmed.

The contested 2000 national election and the *Bush v. Gore* Supreme Court ruling shocked Nate, who had not been a strong Gore supporter. But the absolute kicker was Enron. The collapse of the giant Texas company and the disappearance of billions of dollars in a matter of weeks convinced Nate that the people in charge of America had no idea what they were doing. He had personally seen leading players in the Bush administration takeover emerge from the same ethos as the bosses of Enron and knew them to be frauds of the same magnitude.

After months of self-reflection, Nate decided to trade the lucrative world of corporate public affairs for an uncertain career as a Democratic operative. He signed on with the Tony Sanchez for Governor campaign on the afternoon of September 11, 2001. The momentous events of that morning had dramatically brought home to Nate the life-and-death stakes of politics in the new millennium. Though everyone involved in Sanchez's tactically innovative (and extraordinarily expensive) 2002 campaign worked hard to defeat Rick Perry,

Bush's handpicked successor as governor of Texas, they were met with a crushing defeat at the polls.

Nate understood that the old top-down politics and the Democrats' desperate attempt to blur the differences between the parties would never work against Karl Rove's Republican campaign machine. Unemployed following Sanchez' defeat, Nate evolved into an online activist, first launching an online petition that organized Texas Democrats who opposed Tom DeLay's 2003 congressional redistricting power grab and then working as a volunteer for the Howard Dean campaign. Around this time, he turned down a lucrative offer to work for Joe Lieberman's presidential campaign, preferring poverty to compromise. Those efforts brought him to the attention of many Democrats who wanted to use the Internet more effectively, and he consulted for numerous campaigns in the 2004 cycle, building websites, managing e-mail campaigns, and conducting online fundraising.

Following the 2004 campaign, Nate took the lessons he learned fighting for Howard Dean and used them to help Richard Morrison, a thirty-seven-year-old first-time candidate, give Tom DeLay his toughest-ever electoral challenge. Morrison lost, but the scare he gave DeLay was critical in the majority leader's eventual downfall. In both cases, initial defeat begat lessons learned, and the trajectory of the netroot's influence steadily climbed.

In 2005, Nate was recruited by Jerome Armstrong, one of the founders of the progressive blogosphere and a key consultant for the Howard Dean campaign, to work as online communications director for former Virginia Governor Mark Warner's political action committee (PAC). Warner was considering a 2008 presidential bid and wanted to make aggressive use of the Internet in his campaign. After moving to Virginia in 2006, Nate met co-author Lowell Feld, serving as a sounding board and sympathetic ear as Lowell worked on his first political campaign—to elect Jim Webb and defeat George Allen, then a leading Republican candidate for president in 2008. In the process of that election, the netroots movement won one of its biggest victories ever. U.S. Senator-elect Jim Webb later praised netroots as "a tremendous help to my campaign and a huge inspiration to me personally," declaring, "I am where I am in large part because of their support."[1]

IMPORT AND INTENT

These stories were made possible in part by the Internet, one of the most powerful technological advances in history. During the past several years, the Internet increasingly has served as a catalyst to activism for millions of previously passive people, uniting them and enabling a new wave of citizen activism in America. Bloggers play a key role in our story, but the book is not only about bloggers. It is also about the netroots movement defined much more broadly—that is, the citizen activists using online tools such as Yahoo! groups, blogs, Meetups, instant messaging, and e-mail to organize on-the-ground activities (such as canvassing, flyering, and block-walking) that are as old as American democracy itself.

We are under no illusion that ours are the most important stories of the emerging netroots; they are simply the stories we know best. We have been blessed with the opportunity to play a small role in a large movement that has made a big difference for American democracy. Hundreds of thousands of equally committed activists and candidates have contributed as much time and effort, or more.

Above all, we want these stories to inspire more citizens to become involved in their democracy, and to prove the truth of Howard Dean's rallying cry, "You've got the power!"

ACKNOWLEDGMENTS

Many individuals assisted us in this project. Thanks to the following, who agreed to be interviewed or who otherwise provided input: Chris Ambrose, Jerome Armstrong, Ben Barnes, Pete Brodnitz, Matt Browner-Hamlin, Trei Brundrett, Eric Burns, Debby Burroughs, Eric Byler, Josh Chernila, Adrienne Christian, John Cobarruvias, Rick Cofer, Yosem Companys, Lori Baldwin Coppinger, Tim Craig, Steve D'Amico, Stan Davis, Kyle DeHaas, Mary Detweiler, Lee Diamond, David Donnelly, Abbi Easter, Kelly Fero, Donnie Fowler, Jr., Marc Greidinger, Conaway Haskins, Jon Henke, Corey Hernandez, Jeff Hewitt, John Hlinko, Andy Hurst, Larry Huynh, Aldon Hynes, Waldo Jaquith, Steve Jarding, Bob Kerrey, Barbara Kreykenbaum, Charles Kuffner, Byron LaMasters, John Lebkowsky, Vince Leibowitz, Fred Lewis, Dan Lucas, Susan Mariner, Glen Maxey, Richard Morrison, Karl-Thomas Musselman, Ellen Nagler, Mike Nicholson, Annabel Park, Betty Parrott, Ralph Parrott, Todd Phelan, Aziz Poonawalla, Andrew Resnick, John Rohrbach, Kodi Sawin, Antonia Scatton, Matt Singer, Glenn Smith, Jim Spencer, Joe Stanley, Matt Stoller, Tim Tagaris, Ben Tribbett, Jessica Vanden Berg, and Jim Webb.

Thanks to everyone who read drafts of our book, including James Boyce and Lisa Sockett. Along with Lowell's wife, Lisa was one of the people who encouraged Lowell to write a book on the Jim Webb campaign.

Thanks to Bill Kloman, an editor from the old school who epitomizes professionalism (and patience).

Thanks to Jerome Armstrong for his invaluable advice and assistance on the book writing process in general and on the netroots movement in particular. Jerome is not known as "the Blogfather" for nothing. He is also a good friend.

Big thanks to Markos Moulitsas Zúniga for writing the foreword and for his consistent encouragement of this project.

Of course, thanks to our wives, Rosa Theofanis and Kelly Brown, who were endlessly and selflessly supportive and encouraging throughout the process. Without them, this book would never have been written.

INTRODUCTION

It's the story of people standing up and making themselves heard. It's the story of how to engage those Americans in a real dialogue, how to reach them where they live, how to stop *selling* to them and start *listening* to them, how to make better use of the most revolutionary idea to come along since the first man learned to light a fire.

No, I'm not talking about the Internet. Or computers. Or telecommunications.

I'm talking about democracy.

Joe Trippi, *The Revolution Will Not Be Televised*

During the last decades of the twentieth century, politics was largely a commercial, mass media phenomenon. Candidates were foisted upon voters by small cabals of political insiders, financial backers, and campaign "experts." The tools of mass marketing were used to "sell" those candidates to the voters, just like one would sell a bar of soap or a car. In contrast, in the first decade of the twenty-first century, hundreds of thousands of citizen activists are now taking advantage of newly available communications tools to revolutionize American politics.

In 1965, a graduate student at Louisiana State University, Raymond Strother, wrote a thesis, "The Louisiana Political Candidate and the Advertising Organization," predicting that "the campaigns of the future would abandon grassroots organization and embrace media."[1] Strother went on to make his prediction a reality. Over the next four decades, Strother worked as a political media consultant for an all-star list of candidates including Bill Clinton, Gary Hart, and Lloyd Bentsen, becoming one of the leaders of a generation of consultants that established the media model of campaigns.

Strother's formulation was right for his day, but that day is over. We contend that the campaigns of the future will merge dynamic grassroots organization with more targeted paid media. In fact, we believe they already are doing this, with several examples of political campaigns in recent years being outspent but still emerging victorious. In part, that was the result of tapping into the power of ordinary people doing extraordinary things. This book tells the stories of just a few of the hundreds of thousands of citizen activists who have seized on the Internet's fast communication possibilities to rescue the Democratic Party—and, more broadly, our democracy—and to lead its return to power from the bottom up.

THE DECLINE OF PUBLIC JOURNALISM AND
THE RISE OF THE BLOGOSPHERE

In his 2007 book, *The Rise of the Blogosphere*, City University of New York Professor Aaron Barlow notes that the rise of the blogosphere cannot be separated from "the failures of professional, commercial journalism." Barlow points to the media's "fixation on themselves and the inside-the-beltway struggles that fascinate them so." Barlow blames the glorification of "objective journalism" and its detached "don't let your feelings show" attitude for alienating the public and causing people to lose faith in the traditional press. Barlow believes that this "objective journalism" came at the expense of "public journalism," with reporters acting as "the public's adjutants" and conveying "the information needed for resolution of the questions the public is addressing." This vacuum opened up a huge space for "citizen journalism," including blogs, to rush in. Traditional media increasingly became corporatized, centralized, conflict averse, advertising revenue driven, detached, complacent, shallow, lazy, dispassionate, and, ultimately, unaccountable.[2]

The coup de grâce for the mainstream media was its nearly complete failure to do its job leading up to September 11—"shark attacks" were the big story in the summer of 2001, with nary a mention of Al Qaeda or Osama bin Laden. Continuing this passivity, the mainstream media largely accepted the Bush administration's arguments regarding the "war on terror," "homeland security," and the supposed threat posed by Iraq in the run-up to war with Iraq in March 2003. The tragic consequences of the disastrous Iraq War would provide a huge motivation for progressive citizen journalists to take matters into their own hands. That it would succeed to such a degree, and so quickly, is nothing short of amazing.

What effect will this have on American democracy? In February 2006, Lakshmi Chaudhry wrote in the journal *In These Times* that the netroots movement was acting as a check on mainstream news coverage. As Chaudhry explained, "this 'we can fact-check your ass' credo has not been merely to put journalists on notice, but to change the way public knowledge is produced on a daily basis." Chaudhry added an important point, that "[a] news article is now merely the beginning of a public conversation in the blogosphere, where experts, amateurs and posers alike dissect its merits and add to its information, often keeping it alive long after journalists have moved on."[3]

WHO ARE THE NETROOTS?

Whatever its size, the influence of the netroots is larger than its numbers tend to indicate. Daily Kos, the largest and most influential Democratic blog, receives around 500,000 visits per day, far fewer than the tens of millions who watch a weekly episode of *American Idol* or *Monday Night Football.* Influence can't be measured by raw numbers alone, however.

Malcolm Gladwell's excellent book, *The Tipping Point: How Little Things Can Make a Big Difference,* argues that three types of people play outsize roles in influencing others—"connectors," "mavens," and "salesmen."[4]

That's the progressive blogosphere in a nutshell—knowledgeable people with wide social circles who are skillful at persuading others. In other words, the bloggers are mavens whose influence far exceeds their relatively small numbers. The political operatives are connectors who use e-mail and websites to turn isolated individuals into an organized political force. The netroots and grassroots foot soldiers are the salespeople of the movement, carrying the message offline to their real-world friends and neighbors. Of course, most netroots activists play multiple roles as different opportunities arise. In this book, we will talk about some of the everyday extraordinary people who have affected the political process. People like ...

Trei Brundrett

A hip-hop DJ and computer programmer, the twenty-seven-year-old Trei Brundrett's decision to attend a June 2003 Austin rally for Howard Dean sparked a political obsession that led him to the blazing, late-summer heat of Albuquerque and the freezing January rain of Iowa to campaign for Dean. He went on to spend 2006 working full time in politics as a web developer.

Debby Burroughs

A self-described "ordinary citizen, wife, mother, and nurse" in her late fifties, Burroughs lives in Richmond, Virginia. Following the Bush-Gore electoral fiasco of 2000, the terrible 9/11 attacks, and the misguided March 2003 invasion of Iraq, Burroughs became inspired by General Wesley Clark to try to make a difference. Burroughs became a leader in the Draft Wesley Clark movement and the Clark for President campaign in Virginia. In 2006, Burroughs was a star volunteer for Jim Webb in his upset victory over George Allen. Burroughs says she gets involved with a political candidate only if "properly inspired," and then she gives an all-out effort.

Eric Byler

Byler is a thirty-five-year-old Asian American who has written and directed independent films like *Charlotte Sometimes*, *Americanese*, and *My Life,*

Disoriented. In September 2006, Byler flew to Virginia from Los Angeles to volunteer for Jim Webb's Senate campaign. Byler produced several popular videos, including "Generation Webb" and "Real Virginians for Webb." Byler also assisted in the effort to turn out Asian Americans for Webb.

Stan Davis

A sixty-year-old Lakewood, Colorado, man who suffered a debilitating stroke in 1999, Davis spent three and a half years in an assisted living center near Denver, where his major activities were walking thirty feet to take meals and watch "unmitigated trash on television." In early 2003, Davis heard about the Draft Wesley Clark movement, started spending twenty hours per day reading and sending Clark-related e-mails, and eventually became moderator for the national Draft Clark Yahoo! group. According to Davis, the Clark campaign saved his life.

Waldo Jaquith

A twenty-eight-year-old blogger in Charlottesville, Virginia, Jaquith hiked most of the Appalachian Trail, ran (and lost) for Charlottesville City Council, has ridden a unicycle, juggled, and won two VH1 Music Awards for "Coolest Fan Website." In addition, Jaquith is considered to be the father of the Virginia Democratic blogosphere. In 2005, Jaquith played a major role in helping elect Tim Kaine as governor of Virginia. Jaquith is a technological whiz who created a bill-tracking system for the Virginia General Assembly and a blog aggregator for Virginia political blogs. By any standards, Jaquith is extraordinary.

Glen Maxey

The fifty-six-year-old former state legislator from Austin, Texas, had just retired from politics when he got involved in the Howard Dean campaign. The first openly gay state legislator in Texas history, Maxey had served ten years in the Texas House of Representatives, evolving from laughingstock to power player in the process. In early 2003, Maxey thought he was at the beginning of a cushy career as a lobbyist. Instead he became a volunteer organizer for Howard Dean, beginning an adventure that would lead him to form the largest-ever organization of Texas progressives and also to come within a hair's breadth of being elected state chair of the Texas Democratic Party. In the summer of 2007, Maxey announced his candidacy for Travis County tax assessor-collector.

Annabel Park

Park is a thirty-nine-year-old Korean American woman who left her job and friends in Los Angeles to volunteer for the Webb campaign. Park was a force of nature during the Webb campaign, spurring Korean American support for Webb and founding "Real Virginians for Webb" in response to George Allen's disparaging remark ("Let's give a welcome to macaca here")[5] to another young Asian American (and native Virginian) named S. R. Sidarth.

Aziz Poonawalla

In September 2002, Poonawalla—a twenty-seven-year-old doctoral student at the University of Texas Graduate School of Biomedical Sciences in Houston at the time—started a website called Dean Nation. The objective was to support an obscure former governor of Vermont, Howard Dean, for the 2004 Democratic presidential campaign. Poonawalla's blog helped launch a netroots movement that would help upend Democratic politics in coming years.

Greg Priddy

This brilliant thirty-something former U.S. government contractor was heavily involved in both the Wesley Clark and Jim Webb campaigns. In early February 2006, Priddy found himself sitting in Jim Webb's writing office, filling out the paperwork to file Webb as a U.S. Senate candidate, and discussing how Webb might run a Howard Dean–style netroots campaign. Today, he is a senior energy analyst for a leading consulting firm.

Melissa Taylor

The Philippine American and owner of an import-export business became passionate about Howard Dean in 2003. Never previously political, Melissa traveled from Houston to New Hampshire to campaign for Dean, then spent 2004 working as the volunteer coordinator for Richard Morrison's long-shot challenge to Tom DeLay in Texas. Taylor is now the director of party administration for the Democratic Party in Harris County, Texas.

Chapter 1

DOING EVERYTHING WRONG

From today's vantage point, the 2002 campaigns look like a different political era. Back then, paid television ads were the main weapon in a candidate's communications arsenal. Pundits chattering on network and cable news channels set the tone and selected the topics. They decided what was appropriate and what was out of bounds, with ordinary citizens largely unable to counter or contradict them. And, overall, the media accepted the slander that they had a "liberal bias," bending over backward to prove that they didn't.

In 2002, progressive grassroots activists were marginalized on the Democratic side, where Bill Clinton's strategy of blurring distinctions between himself and his conservative opponents (also known as "triangulation") remained the model. Democratic candidates sought opportunities to disagree with their own base to demonstrate that they were reasonable centrists, not captive to the left wing of their party. Essentially, Democrats tried to be "Republican-lite," nearly unanimous in their support of President Bush's aggressive foreign policy and differing only around the edges on domestic policy.

In 2002, Republicans held a large advantage on the Internet, where sites like the Drudge Report, Free Republic, and Instapundit echoed the top-down talking points doled out by Karl Rove and Congressman Tom DeLay, the House majority leader. This model had first been put into practice during the Clinton impeachment battle of the late 1990s, when Matt Drudge consistently broke salacious, poorly sourced stories that the press would then report as having "come off the Internet." Free Republic, a large online community of rabid right-wingers, proved its worth during the 2000 election Florida recount. The slogan "Sore/Loserman" for Gore/Lieberman first appeared on Free Republic, suggested by a Republican activist. Within days, "Sore/Loserman" signs were appearing at rallies in Florida, garnering major coverage on cable news.

In addition to Free Republic, Instapundit—produced by Tennessee law professor Glen Reynolds—became the leading pro-war blog. Reynolds represented a new breed of citizen activists who used blogs to express their political opinions. The initial wave of political bloggers was overwhelmingly composed of conservatives who had become politically active in the aftermath of

September 11. Together, they helped create a thunderous chorus of support for President Bush's relentless push to invade Iraq.

In 2002, campaign contributions to Democrats came almost exclusively from large donors writing $2,000 checks after being cultivated by candidate phone calls and at fancy high-dollar events. Small donors were the nearly exclusive province of Republicans. To reach these people, Republicans had developed databases of supporters who would reliably respond to inflammatory fundraising letters with a $25 or $50 check. In contrast, Democrats had grown increasingly reliant on "soft money"—that is, corporate contributions that could not be used directly by campaigns but could be spent freely by the political parties and special interest PACs (political action committees). Democrats underinvested in their grassroots efforts relative to the Republicans, while simultaneously lacking the inclination to finance an expensive direct mail donor cultivation effort.

The 2002 passage of the McCain-Feingold campaign finance reform law, with its ban on soft money, threatened to cripple the Democratic Party. With the law's new fundraising restrictions in place, most political analysts believed the Republicans would maintain a large financial advantage over Democrats for the rest of the decade. At the same time, the media climate gave Republicans another clear advantage over Democrats. In 2002, just months after September 11, cable networks competed with each other to demonstrate the most ardent support for George W. Bush, with few if any dissenting voices featured. Most newspapers weren't much better.

BIG PLANS, BAD MODEL

Democrats began planning for the 2002 midterm campaign cycle long before the events of September 11, 2001. Ironically, this placed Democrats at a serious electoral disadvantage, because their strategies were almost all based on ones that had worked during the Clinton era, a time of relative peace and prosperity. As it turned out, 2002 was not the year to campaign on health care, corporate crime, or nuanced distinctions between the parties.

The most aggressive and ambitious Democrats in 2002 were in Texas. For the first time since 1994, George W. Bush was not on the ballot in the Lone Star state, and Democrats launched a concerted effort to test the Republican bench. The 1990s had been a long decade for Texas Democrats. Beginning on a high note, with liberal icon Ann Richards's upset win for governor in 1990 over a Republican multimillionaire (Clayton Wheat Williams, Jr.), the rest of the decade saw Democrats drummed out of one office after another in the state. This included Ann Richards herself, as the tough-talking, motorcycle-riding, gun-toting grandma ran into the fearsome combination of George W. Bush and Karl Rove. Richards once had enjoyed approval ratings in the 70 percent range, but in 1994, she was soundly beaten by Bush.

It's hard to believe in retrospect, but George W. Bush generally governed Texas from the center, forming close alliances with Democrats. In 1998, Democrats fortunate enough not to be running against Bush tried to run alongside him. Democratic State Comptroller John Sharp, for instance, prominently featured Bush in several ads for his lieutenant governor's bid. The name of the game was to blur the distinction between the parties. Unfortunately it didn't work out, as Texas Democrats lost races for governor (George W. Bush over Garry Mauro), lieutenant governor (Rick Perry over John Sharp), and attorney general (John Cornyn over Jim Mattox).

One thing lacking for the Democrats in 1998 had been a well-funded Hispanic high up on the ticket. In that year, there were more than 900,000 registered Hispanic voters in Texas who had never voted. John Sharp was confident that if a Hispanic ran for governor in 2002, the excitement of seeing one of their own at the top of the ticket would draw Texas Hispanics into the voting booths in record numbers.

Sharp first approached Henry Cisneros, the former mayor of San Antonio and Clinton administration official. For several years in the late 1980s and early 1990s, Cisneros had seemed like a sure shot to be Texas's first Hispanic governor. But the Republican takeover of Texas and the illness of Cisneros's son had gotten in the way. Cisneros had made a return to public service as secretary of Housing and Urban Development in President Bill Clinton's cabinet, but he resigned in 1996 under a cloud of scandal related to payments to a mistress.

Despite these problems, Cisneros remained the most high-profile Hispanic politician in the state and a natural choice for Sharp to approach about the 2002 Texas gubernatorial race. Sharp and his advisors met with Cisneros and laid out the plan, which started with registering the 900,000 Hispanics who had never voted. The theory was that this could constitute a demographic tidal wave, and that if Democrats fielded a diverse and well-funded team of candidates, led by Cisneros at the top of the ticket, they could revolutionize Texas politics.

After Sharp had rhapsodized for an hour or so, Cisneros said, "That sounds great, John. Would I win?" Sharp couldn't resist making a joke, and said, "No, but I would."[1] Not surprisingly, Cisneros begged off and Sharp and his team had to look elsewhere.

Billionaire oilman and banker Tony Sanchez was an unlikely choice to seek the Democratic nomination for Texas governor in 2002. For one thing, Sanchez had strongly backed George W. Bush since the mid-1990s, eventually becoming one of Bush's top fundraising "pioneers." Sanchez and his business partners were second only to Enron in the amount of money raised for Bush's 2000 presidential campaign. In addition, Sanchez was a quiet, retiring man, used to meeting with small groups in big boardrooms.

Despite these problems, Sanchez agreed to meet with John Sharp and Sharp's political consigliere, Kelly Fero, in March 2000. Fero outlined the plan, much the same plan that he and Sharp had given Cisneros a few months earlier. "Tony looked like a deer in the headlights at that first meeting," Fero recalls. "He had a real 'Why me?' expression in his eyes."

A week later the trio met again. "Already by that second meeting," Fero says, "it was pretty amazing. The 'Why me?' look had turned into a 'Why *not* me?'"

A POLITICAL *TITANIC*

With Sanchez openly considering the 2002 Texas governor's race, consultants and power brokers were sucked instantly into his orbit. The sheer size of Sanchez's personal wealth pulled the Democratic establishment toward him like a black hole that swallows light and matter. Among those who descended on Sanchez were former Bill Clinton advisor Paul Begala, former Texas lieutenant governor Ben Barnes (then a powerful lobbyist in Washington), Ann Richards's advisor George Shipley, pollsters Fred Yang and Paul Maslin, and media consultant Jim Mulhall.

Also signing on with Sanchez was Nate Wilcox. Joining his first political campaign after years in the lucrative world of corporate public affairs, Nate was hopeful that his expertise in online communications could help the Democrat, Tony Sanchez, win office.

A culturally traditional Catholic, Sanchez was opposed to the death penalty and abortion, but he was in favor of tax increases if necessary to balance the budget. After a few months of smoothing and polishing at the hands of his new Democratic brain trust, Sanchez reversed his positions and emerged as prochoice, prodeath penalty, and committed to solving Texas's fiscal woes with a good "scrubbing of the budget"—and with no mention of tax increases.

One of the new Sanchez consultants was Glenn Smith, a longtime member of the Austin press corps who had managed Ann Richards's tough primary win in 1990. Smith believed that modern database and Internet technologies held enormous political potential. For his part, Sanchez had been one of the first investors in Blockbuster Video, a pioneer of database-driven retailing, which Blockbuster had used to practically clear the country of mom-and-pop video stores. Each Blockbuster outlet was so completely programmed from home base that a new store could be opened anywhere in the country within forty-eight hours by filling a tractor trailer with the store's inventory, decorations, equipment, and supplies—down to the rolls of toilet paper for the restroom. Smith's vision of a huge voter database, enhanced with consumer marketing data used to deliver perfectly targeted messages to voters, clicked immediately with Sanchez. In the spring of 2001, Smith set about implementing that vision.

The Sanchez campaign mounted an ambitious grassroots outreach program. Its advanced technological strategies—including large voter file databases augmented with consumer marketing data, door-to-door canvassers able to record data on PalmPilots for instant uploading to the system, and use of paid staffers to contact voters rather than volunteers—would be expanded on by progressives in 2004, most notably by the group America Coming Together.

But for all of its desire to innovate, the people who ran the Sanchez campaign resolutely refused to open communications channels that would engage voters in a true dialogue. For all its online innovation in 2002—e-mail fundraising appeals, aggressive online advertising, and even a video game that mocked the opponent—the campaign failed to attempt a truly interactive, netroots strategy, such as the one Howard Dean's presidential campaign would successfully use just a year later. Whereas the Dean campaign would launch a blog that would allow Dean's supporters to post comments, the Sanchez campaign, with its traditional emphasis on controlling its message, never seriously considered running such a truly open, participatory, netroots campaign. Within the campaign, disagreements emerged about the best way to target voters, persuade them, and get out the vote. But nobody debated the essential nature of political campaigns as top-down affairs run by big inside players who used slick marketing to sell candidates as merchandise to be consumed by voters.

Thus, despite tens of millions of dollars poured into slick television ads, Tony Sanchez never managed to connect with voters. (In fairness to Sanchez and his campaign team, the Texas political terrain had changed dramatically after September 11, and it is doubtful that anything they might have done differently would have changed the outcome of their race.) In late August 2002, Republican Rick Perry's campaign fired off a fatal shot, a series of ads that linked a Sanchez-owned savings and loan with the laundering of drug money in the 1980s. The ads all but accused Sanchez of murdering a Drug Enforcement Agency agent who had been killed in Mexico by the same gang that, years earlier, had used Sanchez's business to launder money. The vicious Republican attack ads hit a raw nerve with white voters in Texas. Despite an extensive outreach program by the Sanchez campaign that resulted in a voter turnout spike along the Mexican border and in certain inner-city areas, a suburban Republican voting surge more than made up the difference. On November 5, 2002, Tony Sanchez lost to Rick Perry by more than 800,000 votes out of 4.6 million cast, despite the fact that the Sanchez campaign spent at least $69 million (and as much as $100 million according to some accounts) on the race.

A SIGN OF THINGS TO COME

For Nate Wilcox, the Sanchez loss had been a bitter pill to swallow. Although Nate's work on the campaign garnered extensive coverage in media outlets—including the *New York Times* and CNN and online magazines such as *Slate* and *Salon*—and won numerous awards, he had gotten into politics to win elections, not prizes. The Sanchez campaign had made an unprecedented commitment to technology and had spent a tremendous amount of money, but it hadn't helped.

Even as Texas Democrats in 2002 were mounting the most expensive political failure of the new century, a much more modest campaign in Massachusetts pointed toward the future. In January 2002, former Clinton Secretary of Labor Robert Reich launched a long-shot grassroots campaign for governor of Massachusetts. An outspoken old-school progressive, Reich had no intention of running a "modern" consultant-driven campaign. Instead of spending his time shuttered in a room making fundraising calls to donors, Reich had the radical notion of talking to voters about his ideas. The Reich grassroots strategy was the kind of campaign that traditional political consultants laughed at, confident as they were in their ability to launch a last-minute media blitz that would overwhelm anything in their way.

One thing was quite different about Reich's campaign from similar efforts even a few years previously: the Internet. By 2002, the Massachusetts progressives who Reich stirred up with his uncompromising rhetoric of economic fairness and political empowerment were able to coordinate their efforts online. A spontaneous network of websites, online groups, and e-mail lists sprung up around the state and made it dramatically easier for Reich's supporters to organize themselves. Unfortunately for Reich's political aspirations, it was still a bit early in the development of the netroots; a year later, as both the Howard Dean and Wesley Clark campaigns would discover, online organizing would upend the Democratic presidential race—at least for a while. Still, Reich surprised observers with an unexpected second-place finish in a crowded field that included candidates who spent far more money on broadcast media.

DEAN NATION

At that time, few people were aware that the Internet was fueling a grassroots explosion that would dramatically change American politics. One of those people who was aware was a Portland State graduate student named Jerome Armstrong. In June 2002, Armstrong met Vermont governor and potential presidential candidate Howard Dean. Armstrong's blog, MyDD, had focused on politics since mid-2001. During the first half of 2002, the site increasingly turned its attention to Governor Dean's possible presidential candidacy. Armstrong brought printouts of his blog to show Dean, and the two men discussed the potential uses of e-mail, blogs, and the Internet.

According to Armstrong, Governor Dean's "receptivity and sense of intuitive understanding" of the ideas he presented was highly encouraging. Armstrong pressed ahead with his blogging on behalf of a possible Dean candidacy. On July 31, 2002, Armstrong wrote a prescient post detailing ways that Dean could use the Internet to become more than a footnote in the polls:

Here's what Dean could do to transform his weakness into his strength. Exploit the [I]nternet. His current website is sparse, not updated, and not very interesting. What he needs to develop is a website that gravitates the online discussion of 2004 toward him. A practical, user-friendly site, that sticks content to the user and sparks online debate. What I have in mind is a professional-looking campaign news-weblog that posts all the Dean and related press headlines with the ability for users to comment, with moderators in place to keep the discussion from being freeped.

Jerry Brown was nearly able to upset Bill Clinton through using a 1-800 number for fundraising and setting up a national grassroots organization. The money and organization is right here on the net for Dean to get, it's just a matter of him putting a few things in place to set it rolling in that direction. McCain pulled in millions overnight from online contributions after his NH win, Dean could bring in even more than McCain.[2]

By late summer 2002, Armstrong's site had become the main online meeting place for Dean supporters. Blog commenters included Joe Drymala and Mathew Gross, who would later work on the Dean campaign as speechwriter and online communications director, respectively. Reflecting on that summer and fall, Armstrong wrote in June 2006, "the task of serving as what was seemingly the organizational nexus of the Howard Dean campaign became overwhelming."[3] In the absence of any official Dean campaign website, Armstrong found himself fielding a high volume of e-mail. Much of it came from people who thought he was an official representative of the campaign. Some of them even complained, "Can't you create a better official website?"

Not all of the visitors to MyDD were political naifs, however. Future Dean for President campaign manager Joe Trippi had been "lurking" (reading but not commenting) on the blog for some time. When Trippi first e-mailed Armstrong, the graduate student's initial response was a curt, "What do you want?" Soon, however, Armstrong softened his stance: "Oh, *that* Joe Trippi. Sure, give me a call."

Armstrong had previously written a post calling Trippi "an idiot for not seeing the potential of Dean online."[4] In actuality, Trippi had several years' experience in nascent online communities. He had contacted Armstrong both because he wanted to clear things up and also to pick Armstrong's brain for ideas related to the campaign.

"Starting a separate blog seemed like a solution, but doing so alone seemed crazy," Armstrong recalls, and it was too early to expect the Dean campaign to officially launch its own blog. Fortunately, a twenty-seven-year-old political neophyte and doctoral student from Houston named Aziz Poonawalla launched a group blog focusing on the Dean campaign. According to Armstrong, that blog, Dean Nation, "took over … the [I]nternet presence of Howard Dean's campaign."

Armstrong and Poonawalla were joined by Anna Brosovic, a twenty-eight-year-old systems administrator living in the Dallas-Fort Worth area. Together, the three activists brought enormous idealism and energy to their collective effort. As Poonawalla noted in early 2003, "This blog is the purest expression of the principles of free speech and democracy that I have ever been involved with."[5] Over the winter of 2002–2003, momentum built rapidly, with site traffic growing from a few hundred visitors a day to a few thousand.

As 2002 moved into 2003, nobody—not even the few thousand people known as the "evangelizing netroots"—could have imagined that they represented the start of a netroots movement that would help upend Democratic politics in coming years.

Dirty Tricks and Cheap Shots

While Democrats began to exploit new online possibilities and searched for a winning campaign strategy, Republicans settled on a proven formula for success: combine vicious last-minute media attacks with dirty tricks on the phones and in the mail boxes of voters. Just as Republican Rick Perry successfully linked Tony Sanchez with drug dealers and cop killers in the 2002 Texas governor's campaign, that same year Georgia Republicans launched a last-minute barrage of scurrilous attack ads against incumbent Senator Max Cleland, a decorated veteran who had lost three limbs in Vietnam. The ads, which somehow managed to link Cleland to Osama bin Laden and Saddam Hussein, had a direct and dramatic impact on the race. Released in an atmosphere of supine corporate media credulity, they helped Republican challenger Saxby Chambliss overcome a ten-point deficit in the polls to beat Cleland on Election Day, 53 percent to 46 percent.

The anti-Cleland ads hit just one year after the 9/11 attacks, at a time when Americans remained deeply frightened, although if asked, they might not have admitted it. The Bush administration's drumbeat-and-demagoguery approach to building public support for the 2003 Iraq invasion had proven successful to a significant extent. The first progressive blogs had garnered audiences only in the hundreds, far short of what was needed to provide a significant counterweight. In stark contrast, today's leading progressive blogs receive hundreds of thousands of visits per day and have achieved a significant degree of influence. In 2002, however, the deceptive narrative imposed by the Bush administration, permitted in part by the complicity of the corporate media, went largely unchallenged—with disastrous results.

In addition to Bush administration scare tactics, another favorite weapon in the Republican campaign arsenal during the 2002 elections was automated "robo-calls." Typically, the calls would be sent out in the final days of a campaign, often late at night and often falsely purporting to be from Democrats. Voters would awaken to a recorded message, usually something outrageous or frightening, intended to make Democratic voters reconsider voting at all.

Most of these programs remain in the shadows of history, visible if at all only as expenditures in campaign finance reports. One of the most egregious of these programs, however, a Republican effort to sabotage Democratic get-out-the-vote (GOTV) efforts in New Hampshire, is well known. Resulting in felony convictions for multiple Republican operatives and donors, the Republicans had attempted to jam the Democrats' phone lines on election day. The sabotage was obvious and easily detected. Unfortunately for New Hampshire Democrats, however, the election was long since lost by the time the wrongdoers were brought to justice. In years to come, progressive bloggers would prove highly effective in monitoring and disclosing these dirty tricks. But in 2002, the blogs were just getting started and had only a fraction of the influence that they hold today.

In the end, the Democrats lost a net total of two seats in the U.S. Senate in 2002, with Republicans gaining control of that chamber by a fifty-one to forty-eight margin (with one independent, Jim Jeffords of Vermont). Democrats lost seats in Georgia (Cleland), Missouri (Jean Carnahan), and Minnesota (Paul Wellstone, who died tragically in a plane crash during the campaign). In the House of Representatives, Democrats fell from 212 to 204 seats, whereas Republicans increased from 221 to 229 seats. It may not have been a landslide victory for the Republicans, but it was certainly not good news for the Democrats.

BIG FAILINGS AND BIG PLANS

In Texas, Democrats spent almost $100 million during 2002 and lost every statewide race. Tom DeLay had formed a political action committee, Texans for a Republican Majority (TRMPAC), which had spent $1.6 million to dramatically affect twenty-two state legislative races. In contrast to the Sanchez statewide broadcast television blitz, DeLay's TRMPAC spent its money strategically and flooded the state representative races with inflammatory mailers and radio spots. TRMPAC not only ensured that Republicans achieved a majority in the Texas State Legislature, but also ensured that the "right" Republicans were elected. Moderate Republicans were systematically targeted and beaten in the primaries. DeLay and his team wanted to ensure that their man, Tom Craddick, would be elected speaker of the Texas House. DeLay and Company had big plans—both for Texas and for America.

Chapter 2

HOWARD DEAN AND THE KILLER DS

During the 2002 election cycle, a moribund national Democratic establishment was crushed by a Republican Party that aggressively capitalized on the nation's post–September 11 anxiety. Essentially, the Democratic campaign model of the 1990s remained in full effect: move to the middle politically, distance oneself from the Democratic base (a la Clinton's June 1992 "Sister Souljah moment"), and run media-driven campaigns in which fundraising was the candidate's major task and grassroots activists were considered menial laborers, but not much more. That may have worked for Bill Clinton, but it wasn't working for the Democratic Party as a whole. Corporate scandals—the hot topic in the spring and summer (the U.S. Department of Justice confirmed in early January 2002 that it had begun a criminal investigation into Enron's bankruptcy filing of December 2, 2001)—were driven from the front pages and television screens by misleading cries and alarms of imminent danger from Iraq. On November 5, 2002, Republicans gained eight seats in the House and two seats in the Senate.

THE DEMOCRATIC WING OF THE DEMOCRATIC PARTY

As 2003 began, Democrats were feeling demoralized, ready for someone—anyone—to lead them out of the political wilderness. On March 15, 2003, former Vermont Governor Howard Dean spoke out clearly and forcefully at the California Democratic Convention. Declaring that he was from the "Democratic wing of the Democratic Party."[1] Dean tapped into what people were feeling, and the reaction was electrifying. Democrats had gone over a decade without any "red meat"—the kind of confrontational, bold, and proudly partisan language that speaks to the most deeply held passions of party loyalists. Activist, antiwar Democrats had been looking for someone to articulate and lead their opposition to President Bush's march toward war with Iraq, and now they had that leader in the person of Howard Dean.

In the spring of 2003, as Dean spoke out against the Iraq War (which had begun on March 20), he was filling a huge void in the body politic and on the progressive side of the political spectrum. Despite an orchestrated, post–September 11 campaign of fear and lies by the Bush administration, large antiwar rallies had been held across the country in the months leading up to the invasion of Iraq. The rallies had no impact whatsoever on Bush's decision to invade Iraq, further frustrating and angering antiwar Democrats. Thus, when Howard Dean stood up to Bush on Iraq, it sparked a movement that the Democratic Party hadn't seen in some time and one they didn't know how—or weren't prepared—to handle.

Under the innovative leadership of campaign manager Joe Trippi, the Dean campaign used the Internet to channel that activist energy into a potent force. Chris Bowers, one of the most prominent progressive bloggers in America, calls the Dean campaign "the defining moment for the blogosphere, the netroots and the contemporary progressive movement."[2] By generating a strong response from small donors, a revival of volunteer activism, and a muscular rebuttal to the Republican agenda, Bowers believes that Howard Dean and his online supporters "put the netroots on the map as a force with which to be reckoned."[3]

THE REPUBLICAN WING OF THE REPUBLICAN PARTY

Around this same time, the majority leader of the U.S. House of Representatives, Republican Tom DeLay, prepared to execute one of the most audacious power grabs in U.S. political history. Already, the power behind the chair of Speaker Dennis Hastert, Congressman DeLay had invested millions of dollars of political action committee (PAC) money to successfully affect the outcome of the Texas legislative elections in 2002. In 2003, DeLay would call in his chips, pressuring the twenty-two newly elected state representatives and his ally, Tom Craddick, the new speaker of the Texas House, to undertake an unprecedented mid-decade redrawing of the state's congressional district boundaries. By this innovative means—many would say sneaky, unethical, even illegal—DeLay intended to flip up to ten seats in the U.S. House of Representatives from Democratic to Republican control. DeLay's objective was nothing less than the installation of what he called a "permanent Republican majority" in America.[4]

Tom DeLay's plans led inevitably to Austin, the surprisingly liberal capital of Texas. There, resistance to DeLay and support for Howard Dean would soon awaken a sleepy Texas Democratic Party. This scenario certainly didn't look likely following the Democrats' crushing defeat at the polls the previous November both nationally and in Texas. DeLay's TRMPAC had poured millions of corporate dollars into twenty-two state legislative races, giving Republicans their first majority in the state legislature since the 1800s.

Texas Republicans felt so cocky that the Texas Association of Businesses sent out a mailer the day after the elections bragging that they had "blown the doors off the 2002 elections."[5] At the time, few people noticed that the invitation to the Tom Craddick announcement they were promoting said, "Paid for by Texans for a Republican Majority PAC." Even fewer could imagine the significance those words would take on over the next couple of years.

A REAL RED FLAG

As they compared notes, two Austin attorneys—Fred Lewis and Chris Feldman—were beginning to realize that something big and bad had happened in the 2002 elections. What they discovered was disturbing from the perspective of free speech and democracy. In the run-up to the elections, Lewis had noticed a suspicious pattern in the mailings he had received from the Texas Association of Businesses and from former Travis County Commissioner Todd Baxter about the record of Democratic incumbent Ann Kitchen (Lewis's state representative). Baxter was running against Kitchen. According to Lewis, "on Monday, you'd get a piece from the Texas Association of Businesses on education and how horrible Ann Kitchen was on education and how great Todd Baxter was. On Tuesday, you'd get a mailer from Todd Baxter talking about how great he was on education. Either it was an incredible coincidence or they were coordinating." Kitchen, who was defeated in her reelection bid, suspected that the business association mailers had been printed with corporate money, which is illegal in Texas. Kitchen also believed the mailers may have been coordinated with Baxter.

Lewis and Feldman investigated and discovered that the Texas Association of Businesses had sent out a newsletter shortly after the election, bragging about their "issue ads."

"That was a real red flag," Lewis recalled. "You can use corporate money for advocating, for example, that you want deregulated utility rates and that's fine, but you can't use corporate money in the state of Texas to influence an election." Feldman told Lewis that he thought there had been a deliberate conspiracy to funnel huge amounts of corporate money into Texas legislative races. Lewis at first thought Feldman was crazy, but mounting evidence unearthed by Feldman indicated something strange had taken place in Texas during 2002.

In February 2003, Feldman discovered that TRMPAC had kept two very different sets of books: one as a Texas state PAC that filed with the Texas Ethics Commission, the other as a 527 organization that filed with the Internal Revenue Service (IRS). The report TRMPAC filed with the Texas Ethics Commission declared hard money contributions and expenditures. "Hard money" is raised according to campaign finance rules and can be used for electioneering or given to campaigns. But TRMPAC had included much more interesting information in its filings with the IRS. Lewis recalls that TRMPAC "had filed all their contributions, including corporate ones, with the IRS." But "with the Texas Ethics Commission, they had filed only their hard money, individual contributions, and expenditures." As a result, according to Lewis, "nobody in Texas knew they were raising corporate money; the reports were on the web with the IRS, but nobody knew to look." Now, people were looking.

MEETING UP FOR DEAN

In January 2003, Dean bloggers Jerome Armstrong, Anna Brosovic, and Aziz Poonawalla began pushing Meetup, a company that allows people with shared interests to meet and discuss their views, on Dean Nation as well as on MyDD. Meetup had not been designed with politics in mind, but Jerome Armstrong and the other Dean Nation bloggers quickly understood the potential. On February 5, 2003, the first Dean Meetup was held in New York City and a few other cities across the country.

DavidNYC, a prominent Daily Kos blogger, described the scene:

On a chilly (but not bitter) winter night, fifteen New Yorkers of all stripes crowded into a tiny bar in lower Manhattan for the very, very first Dean Meetup ever. Perhaps a couple of hundred other Americans were doing the same thing in different spots around the country.

We were from Brooklyn, Queens and Manhattan; we were young and not so young; we were black, white and Asian; we were gay, we were straight—in other words, we were a quintessentially New York crowd. And above all, we were excited about this guy named Howard Dean, who was running for president and saying the kind of things we had all been longing to hear.

What struck me most—what surprised me most—was that I alone among this group had previously worked on a political campaign. Fourteen other people who had never been directly involved in politics before were showing up to help a guy who was at 1 percent in the polls. It was really quite remarkable, and it pointed to one of the Dean campaign's greatest strengths and most lasting legacies: Howard Dean helped bring legions of new people into the political process. And it started on Day One.[6]

Dean was so impressed, he reportedly exclaimed, "Look at the power of the net!"[7] A month later, Howard Dean's campaign manager, Joe Trippi, decided to have Dean drop by the second Meetup in New York City. In just a month, the Meetup had grown tenfold, with more than 500 supporters meeting the candidate at the Essex Club on March 5, 2003. Just ten days later, the campaign exploded as Dean gave his famous, "Democratic Wing of the

Democratic Party" speech at the California Democratic Party Convention. With that speech, Dean engaged the imagination of hundreds of thousands of Americans who were opposed to the imminent invasion of Iraq. Equally significant, Dean seized the leadership mantle of progressive Democrats that had been vacant since the devastating loss of Minnesota Senator Paul Wellstone in an airplane crash the previous fall.

It was around this time that Glen Maxey, a former Texas state representative, essentially appointed himself as Texas coordinator for the Dean campaign. According to Maxey, he would call the Dean campaign and they'd say, "We're not going to do anything about Texas for six months." Maxey told them he was worried about Texas *today*. He volunteered to be the Dean coordinator in Texas, adding that "you can fire me when you find one." Then, he "just went out and did it."

Meanwhile, Jerome Armstrong—the only one of the three Dean Nation blog founders not from Texas—moved to Vermont and become a consultant for the Dean campaign. Armstrong had been speaking with Joe Trippi since December 2002. At that time, Armstrong had written a blog post attacking Trippi's conventional strategy for Dean, arguing instead for a strategy centered on the Internet. Once in Vermont, Armstrong initiated a large-scale Google advertising campaign that swelled the online ranks of Dean's supporters. Armstrong put his own blog, MyDD, on hiatus for the duration of the campaign. Markos Moulitsas Zúniga, Armstrong's business partner, placed a disclaimer on his Daily Kos blog that informed readers his company (Armstrong Zúniga) was working for Dean. Over the next few months, Daily Kos traffic swelled as the Dean movement picked up momentum. Another former writer at MyDD, Matthew Gross, became a full-time staffer for the Dean campaign and launched the official Dean blog, Blog for America.

Following Armstrong's departure and the launch of the official Blog for America site, the two Texans—Poonawalla and Brosovic—continued their work on Dean Nation. Their grassroots status left them free to offer constructive criticism of the candidate and the campaign, as contrasted with what Poonawalla called the "boosterism" of Blog for America. Despite its willingness to criticize—or perhaps because of it—the Dean Nation blog proved to be a strong asset to the Dean campaign. One of the blog's key achievements was raising more than $40,000 for the campaign, an early sign of the potential for netroots fundraising.

The first Dean Meetup in Austin took place in March 2003 and was led by Glen Maxey. A veteran of many campaigns, including Ann Richards's victorious 1990 gubernatorial run, Maxey gave the Austin for Dean effort a laser-like focus on effective organizing that few other Dean Meetups could rival. Immediately, Maxey put people to work collecting petition signatures to get Dean on the Texas Democratic presidential primary ballot. December 2, 2003, was the first day candidates were allowed to file for the 2004 Texas Democratic presidential primary, which was scheduled for March 9. Glen Maxey and a swarm of Dean activists reported first thing that morning to Texas Democratic Party headquarters with a huge stack of more than 20,000 petition signatures— far exceeding the 5,000 minimum—to put Dean on the ballot. Meanwhile, the online tools that enthusiastic and talented Dean supporters were developing made it even easier to build a statewide Texas political organization, easier than Maxey had ever realized it could be before his involvement with the Dean campaign.

The few experienced political operatives paying attention to the Dean campaign were struck by the Texas Dean supporters' success, especially compared with other recent attempts at organizing Texas Democrats. Longtime Texas Democratic activist Susan Morris later commented in the *Texas Observer* that she was "used to walking into events for Ron Kirk or Tony Sanchez and knowing everyone in the room."[8] In contrast, Morris says, at a Dean event in Austin, Kirk and Sanchez people "were just hanging around the perimeter, going, 'How did they get 400 people to come to a political meeting?'"[9]

What was taking place in Texas was a microcosm of what was happening all over the country in the Dean movement. Texas was certainly important for Dean—hosting several of Dean's largest rallies, raising significant amounts of money, and contributing a large number of activists. In part, this response was due to the fact that Democrats in red states like Texas responded strongly to Dean's in-your-face rhetoric, which gave them the courage to stand up and openly identify themselves as partisan Democrats for the first time in years. This phenomenon would recur again and again in coming years, with the netroots demonstrating a disproportionate impact on campaigns in Republican-dominated areas like Ohio, Montana, and Virginia.

One aspect of the Dean movement was unique to Texas, however—Glen Maxey's leadership, which kept the movement focused on achieving tangible political goals like signing up supporters and registering voters. It's often said among veterans of Texas for Dean that if there had been fifty Glen Maxey's around the country, Howard Dean would be president today. Maxey provided the kind of energy that left people scratching their heads and wondering how he got 400 people to come to a political meeting.

DELAY VS. THE DEANIACS

In early 2003, Texas Democrats were about to receive another big jolt of energy, this time inspired not by idealism but by anger. In November 2002, Republicans had gained control of the Texas Legislature for the first time in 130 years. Within a few months, rumors began to circulate that the new speaker of the Texas House of Representatives, Tom Craddick, would try to push through an unprecedented second-in-a-decade congressional redistricting.

The governor, lieutenant governor, and speaker all denied any such plans. But by the final days of the session, it became clear that Tom Craddick, egged on by Tom DeLay, intended just such an extraordinary move.

Veteran Democratic strategist Kelly Fero recalls that Texas Democrats were "slow to adjust" to a possible redistricting push. But Craddick, DeLay, and Governor Rick Perry had been working on their strategy for months. According to Fero, the Democratic leadership was "caught flat footed," while "a handful of Internet activists kick-started the opposition" to the redistricting scheme. Fero says, "It was outside the ability of the Democratic officials to imagine that this was really going to happen and ... that there was anything they could do to stop it."

In May 2003, inspired by the impact the Dean bloggers were having on both the local and national political scenes, Nate Wilcox launched a website, SaveTexasReps, to focus opposition on the redistricting and to provide Texas Democrats with up-to-date information. Other grassroots activists, such as Alfred Stanley of Austin, 2002 congressional candidate John Courage, and John's wife Zeda True-Courage, also initiated grassroots efforts to bolster the Democratic caucus. But it was not until Wilcox started collecting petition signatures from Texans opposed to the redistricting that the antiredistricting movement really started to heat up.

Several Texas Democratic politicians supported SaveTexasReps. For instance, Congressman Chris Bell's office contributed toward the costs of the effort, while Lloyd Doggett's and Martin Frost's congressional offices provided helpful background information and inside gossip. Embattled Democrats in the Texas House of Representatives were quick to notice the groundswell of support. They began to lay plans for a cunning counterstroke as the 2003 session wound to a close and as DeLay's minions ratcheted up their efforts. With only a few days left before the legislature adjourned for the year, the Republicans made it clear that they would press ahead. Rumors that they intended to carve liberal Austin into three separate congressional districts were particularly infuriating.

As the activists used the Internet to build a chorus against redistricting, more than fifty Democrats suddenly broke quorum. In mid-May 2003, two chartered buses carried many of these Democrats north to Ardmore, Oklahoma, with the rest trickling in by twos and threes. Former Speaker Pete Laney even flew a couple of the more rebellious Democrats in his small private plane. Nobody knew at the time that a furious Tom DeLay had personally contacted the Department of Homeland Security and ordered them to track down Laney's plane.

By leaving the state, the Democrats had put themselves beyond the reach of the Texas Rangers, who otherwise could have compelled their attendance in the legislature. This made a quorum impossible and effectively blocked DeLay's redistricting effort for a time. Glenn Smith, a veteran reporter and former campaign manager for Tony Sanchez, called the escape of the so-called

Killer Ds "the only instance I've seen in over thirty years under that big pink dome where Democrats actually pulled off something that required both courage and solidarity."

Not surprisingly, the story drew tremendous national news coverage. The attention caused the number of signatures on Wilcox's antiredistricting website to spike through the roof. In the end, the Killer Ds managed to run out the clock on the regular 2003 legislative session. At that point, they believed they had won the fight. But like a horror movie in which the monster keeps coming back to life, Tom DeLay succeeded in pressuring Governor Perry into calling not just one but three special sessions that year.

DEAN DOES IT BIG IN TEXAS

As the standoff in the Texas Legislature continued, the Texas Deaniacs had less than two weeks to help Glen Maxey prepare for Howard Dean's first visit to Texas as a presidential candidate. The Dean visit was to feature a rally on June 9, 2003, which would test Maxey's organizational abilities. In May, Dean had drawn 1,500 to a rally in Seattle; Maxey's goal was to match that. Volunteers made phone calls, handed out fliers at grocery stores and street fairs, posted announcements in laundromats and on lampposts, and used the Internet to promote the rally every way possible.

On June 9, Howard Dean spoke to a packed fundraiser at a house on the wealthy west side of Austin. Dean then rushed to the east side of town for the public rally. Nobody anticipated the huge crowd that awaited Dean there. Just a year earlier, the Sanchez campaign had spent more than $10,000 trying to build a crowd for the Democratic nominees for governor, attorney general, and railroad commissioner. Even though that rally was held just a few weeks before the hotly contested elections, the Sanchez campaign barely managed to persuade 150 people to show up. In contrast, the former governor of Vermont, who was registering in the single digits in the national polls at the time, inspired 3,200 people to come out nearly a year and a half before the November 2004 election. Wilcox was thrilled at the success and saw that positive political change really was possible in America.

At the rally, State Representative Eddie Rodriguez—one of the Killer Ds—drew an enthusiastic ovation from the fired-up crowd when he took the stage to introduce Howard Dean. The sudden explosion of energy from Texas Democrats had everyone feeling euphoric. Just eight months earlier, the Democrats' multiethnic dream team (Hispanic American Tony Sanchez for governor and African American Ron Kirk for U.S. Senate) was crushed in the 2002 election. Now, Texas Democrats were feeling energized and optimistic, organizing both online and in the "real world."

Many of the people attending the Dean rally had never been to a political event. Some, like graphic artist Marla Camp, law firm administrator Fran

Howard Dean gives the thumbs-up in San Antonio, Texas, August 25, 2003. Courtesy of Karl Thomas Mussleman.

Vincent, and book editor Teri Sperry, would become committed activists in coming years. University of Texas Democrat Byron LaMasters attended the rally, writing about it on his blog. Soon, he and several other students would launch the Burnt Orange Report, a community blog that would become a hub for Texas Democrats.

Another Austin resident at the rally was Trei Brundrett, a local computer programmer who had volunteered briefly on the Bill Bradley for President campaign in 2000. Brundrett had drifted away after not getting much positive feedback and had remained uninvolved in politics until the Texas redistricting drama caught his attention. Brundrett was also alarmed at the threat of losing his popular congressman, Lloyd Doggett.

"The redistricting thing lit a fire under me," Brundrett recalls. "After seeing regular people stand up and speak out at the hearings, I knew I wanted to get involved in the process." Then, Brundrett read an article in the *Austin Chronicle* that said Howard Dean was coming to town. At the rally, Brundrett stood close to the stage and afterward managed to meet Governor Dean. Brundrett was particularly impressed by the passion and excitement of an older Hispanic veteran who was also meeting the candidate for the first time.

At home, Brundrett researched Dean on the Internet. Having just set up his own blogging platform, the fact that Dean's campaign had a blog impressed Brundrett greatly. The next night at dinner, Brundrett told his wife Danielle that Dean was the candidate who would fight the Republicans and that he wanted to be part of it. Brundrett sent an e-mail to Glen Maxey and quickly received an encouraging response. This meant a lot to Brundrett. As he became increasingly involved in the campaign, he grew impressed by Maxey's approach to participatory democracy: "If you have a good idea, you're in charge of making it happen."

Brundrett's first campaign activities consisted mostly of reading Blog for America and contributing comments to the conversation. Soon, however, he was hosting house parties, contributing money, and working on the Dean for Texas website.

PUTTING UP A FIGHT

The infusion of energy, new volunteers, and optimism into the Texas Democratic Party was much needed. Texas Democrats were finally starting to put up a fight, but first they were in for a series of defeats. The series began with the three special sessions that Governor Perry had called to ramrod redistricting through the state legislature. There was no way more than fifty of the Killer Ds could break quorum for an entire one-month session. The financial costs alone were prohibitive to the citizen legislators, who received only nominal salaries. But DeLay didn't get his way just yet. On July 28, just before Governor Perry was to call a second special session, eleven Democratic state senators headed to New Mexico for a month in exile, once again throwing a wrench into DeLay's plans.

Wilcox assisted the redistricting rebels by putting up a website for the Democratic House Caucus (with just three days' notice) on which they could publicize their story and raise money. Wilcox was called into a meeting with two leaders of the House caucus, Representatives Pete Gallego and Trey Martinez-Fisher, fully expecting it would focus on ways to promote the site and build on the momentum of the Killer Ds. Instead, Wilcox found himself in the middle of an amateurish good-cop, bad-cop routine, with the cerebral Gallego asking questions about access to the site's data and the blustering Martinez-Fisher barking threats. The two officials claimed to be angered because Wilcox had access to the data collected on the site he had built for them. At the time, perhaps fifteen e-mail addresses had been entered in the database.

Martinez-Fisher boasted to Nate Wilcox that he had told other Democratic state representatives that he would "kick your [Nate's] ass." The much smaller Wilcox, shocked, reacted like the true child of a rough-and-ready oil town saying, "Have you ever been to West Texas? 'Cause you're fixing to visit it. Where I come from if you threatening somebody, you'd better be ready to fight."

Gallego managed to restore calm—not that anyone had been particularly alarmed by the threats of the five-foot-five-inch-tall Internet specialist. As the meeting concluded, Martinez-Fisher patted Wilcox on the shoulder and said, "It's not that we don't want you to make a living, we just don't want to see you driving around in a Hummer." In the end, the state representatives announced they would not be paying for their website, but that Wilcox could make amends by sending an e-mail on their behalf to his burgeoning antiredistricting e-mail list.

The petty and bullying attitude of the two state representatives stood in sharp contrast to the strong support and guidance that Wilcox was receiving from operatives at higher levels of the party. Matt Angle, chief of staff for Congressman Martin Frost, was generous with advice and even managed to funnel some financial support to Wilcox's efforts. It was at Angle's urging that Wilcox posted his antiredistricting petition online. Kelly Fero, key advisor to newly elected state party chair Charles Soechting, also played a key role, feeding Nate stories and news clips on a daily basis and serving as a sounding board for strategic ideas.

"HOW TO COVER YOUR SPAMMING ASS CORRECTLY"

As the redistricting drama played out, Howard Dean's candidacy was growing fast nationally. In Texas, the number of Dean supporters attending Dean Meetups continued to increase. By the end of June 2003, Dean's online fundraising had shattered all records, defying the expectations of the political cognoscenti and propelling Dean to the front of the presidential pack. Reviewing a presentation from Dean's national fundraising team that showed donations spiking, Glen Maxey told a group gathered in his office, "I just don't see how we [can] fuck this up."

No sooner had those words been uttered than the enthusiastic local organizers began making mistakes. One was that they became too enamored of the Internet, sending annoying spam e-mails to Texas voters. In July 2003, Wilcox started reading online complaints about these e-mails and wondered whether the Dean people were using Tony Sanchez's mailing list from the 2002 gubernatorial campaign. Lists like that often get passed around after campaigns end. Sometimes, people misuse them, perhaps failing to realize that e-mail isn't the same as traditional direct mail and that it's all but useless to take an e-mail list from one campaign and apply it to another. That technique doesn't work and it certainly annoys people.

Maxey quickly posted an apology and a promise never to spam again. Techies who had threatened to turn on the campaign applauded Maxey's forthright response. One even wrote a blog post entitled, "How to Cover Your Spamming Ass Correctly." The incident drew national press coverage but hardly slowed the Deaniacs' momentum. In July 2003, the national Dean campaign put their Meetup power to work in Iowa. National campaign manager Joe Trippi called on everyone attending a Dean Meetup anywhere in the country to write a letter to an Iowa caucus voter extolling Dean. The campaign provided address information, as well as stamps, envelopes, pens, and paper. Hundreds of Dean supporters from the Austin area sat down at picnic tables at the huge Scholz's Beer Garden, wrote their letters, and presented them to Maxey for delivery to Iowa.

ENOUGH IS ENOUGH

Meanwhile, in DeLay's home district, a thirty-seven-year-old environmental trial lawyer, husband, and father of four, Richard Morrison, could no longer stand being represented in Congress by Tom DeLay. According to Morrison, the son of a successful and politically well-connected trial lawyer, "I had looked around and called around and begged everyone I could think of to run against DeLay. No one would even give it a second thought." DeLay had not faced a serious challenge since his first reelection campaign in the 1980s. In 2000, DeLay's Democratic opponent had raised less than $10,000 and had received a paltry 36 percent of the vote. DeLay's 2002 challenger, a local lawyer named Tim Riley, had upped the ante to almost $200,000, but still had received only 35 percent of the vote.

As of early 2003, all conventional political signals indicated that Tom DeLay was invulnerable. Richard Morrison knew that as well as anyone. As Morrison said in 2003, "These folks out here in Sugar Land—there's a real hard-core 40 percent that wouldn't even consider voting for a Democrat, another third that are Democrats but don't always vote, and maybe just maybe there's another bunch that would be open to voting for change if they just understood how little Tom DeLay really cared about them and their problems." But as the melodrama of DeLay's congressional redistricting power play slogged forward through the spring and summer of 2003, Morrison decided to take the plunge. If no one else would do it, he would run against DeLay himself.

At the August Dean Meetup in Austin, Glen Maxey had more local concerns. Maxey urged Dean supporters in his group to attend the "Enough Is Enough" rally, scheduled for August 9, to oppose redistricting. Maxey had several complementary goals in mind: (1) demonstrating that Deaniacs were good Democrats who opposed DeLay's redistricting scheme as much as anyone; (2) raising the Dean supporters' profile with Texas Democrats, who would be coming in from across the state; and (3) recruiting active Democrats to the burgeoning Dean for President movement.

The Dean supporters who turned out in force that early August day were only one of many factions opposing DeLay. Byron LaMasters counted forty buses from around the state bringing thousands of protesters—a few Republicans but overwhelmingly Democrats—from as far away as Lubbock and Brownsville. LaMasters estimates that the crowd included some 4,000 hardy souls, braving humidity and 100-degree heat to voice their opposition to Tom DeLay's odious power grab.

Despite their strong support for the united Democratic Party effort to oppose DeLay's redistricting plan, Texas Dean supporters put their presidential candidate first. When Congressman Martin Frost, whose people were leading the antiredistricting effort, joined a group of conservative congressional Democrats criticizing Dean on the Iraq War, he received hundreds of angry phone calls at his district office. The Frost team was alarmed that a significant number of the calls from Dean supporters, including Dean Nation blogger Anna Brosovic, were coming from within the congressman's own district. Frost chief of staff Matt Angle was so concerned that he placed an angry phone call to Glen Maxey in Austin. "Call your people off, Glen," Angle warned. Angle probably did not expect Maxey's response: "Sorry Matt, I couldn't if I wanted to. Those folks read what your guy said on the Internet and they posted your office number up without anybody telling them to. This isn't what you're used to; this is truly bottom-up activism."

MOVEON MOVES IN

A week after the antiredistricting rally, a new force entered the fray in the form of MoveOn.org. The organization had formed during the late 1990s controversy over the Clinton impeachment. At that time, California software designers Wes Boyd and Joan Blades had sent out a single-sentence e-mail to about 100 friends, calling for Congress to censure President Clinton and to "move on." Within a few weeks, hundreds of thousands of people had signed their petition. Boyd and Blades sent follow-up e-mails to the petition signers to keep them informed about the impeachment and soon found themselves heading up a major political organization, formed entirely online. By 2003, MoveOn had more than 2 million members nationwide and had held its own online presidential primary in June 2003 (Howard Dean won a plurality but not a majority of the votes).

In August 2003, an e-mail sent to MoveOn's national list raised more than $1 million in just a few days to support the eleven Texas Democratic senators who had fled to New Mexico. Tony Sanchez's former campaign manager

Glenn Smith had been one of the few in the Texas Democratic establishment aware of and sympathetic to MoveOn, and had spent months cultivating the group's co-founder, Wes Boyd. Smith's efforts had seemingly paid off handsomely for Texas Democrats.

But when those same Texans found out that MoveOn would be using the money to launch a national media blitz aimed at Hispanics in key swing states, they couldn't help but feel a bit carpetbagged. In particular, the eleven state senators who had spent a month away from their homes and jobs—some were ill but were far from their doctors—had to have been a bit miffed at MoveOn's priorities. Others who had hoped that MoveOn would invest the money in grassroots infrastructure were equally frustrated. The only tiny bright spot for Texas Democrats who had watched the money roll in was MoveOn's inclusion of a Texas antiredistricting petition buried in the footnotes of one of its e-mails. Demonstrating MoveOn's power, that footnote alone helped double the Save Texas Reps antiredistricting list in one day.

Despite the grassroots energy, Internet fundraising, and bold tactics of the Democrats in the legislature, Tom DeLay eventually got his way. In August 2003, at the end of the special session, one Democratic senator broke ranks and returned to Austin. From that point, it was just a matter of getting the Republicans to agree among themselves how to slice up the state. That proved harder than anyone expected, and before all was said and done, DeLay himself was forced to travel to Austin to crack heads and cut deals. Despite having no constitutional role in the Texas legislative process, DeLay was able to force through the legislature the radical, partisan redistricting that he had bought and paid for with corporate money. Mission accomplished.

Wilcox was outraged at the stunning and blatant antidemocratic misbehavior of elected officials in Texas. Combined with ready access to the means of communicating his displeasure, Wilcox was impelled to take action. As a citizen and as a person of conscience, Wilcox felt that he needed to do whatever he could to put things right. Wilcox's story was repeated across fifty states by thousands of citizens like him. This outpouring of activist energy would build the netroots into an explosive and revolutionary political phenomenon. Ordinary American citizens, concerned and angered at what was happening in their country, now had the means and motivation to do something about it.

As Tom DeLay was busy getting his way on redistricting, Glen Maxey's Texas volunteers were finding ways to affect the early state presidential caucuses and primaries. In September 2003, a contingency of Texans for Dean was sent to New Hampshire. Billed as Dean's Texas Rangers, the volunteers went door to door, with their efforts heavily promoted to the press. At the time, it seemed like an innovative way for volunteers from big states with late primaries to leverage their passion and affect the process in small states with early primaries. Since Dean's defeat, it has become conventional wisdom that out-of-state canvassers can do more harm than good, especially if locals feel they are being invaded by "foreigners" who don't understand or care about local issues and concerns. This critique has been widely cited as a reason for Dean's failure in Iowa. Dean veterans like Joe Trippi and Jerome Armstrong disagree that bringing in out-of-state supporters was in and of itself a bad idea and instead lay the blame at the feet of a poorly organized campaign that didn't utilize personal resources effectively.

I'M NOT CRAZY

Meanwhile, in September 2003, Richard Morrison finally found a political consultant who took his embryonic candidacy against Tom DeLay seriously. Morrison had called virtually every Democratic political operative in the Houston area, but none had expressed interest. Through an old friend in Austin, Morrison came in contact with a young operative who knew the Internet and was willing to take on the daunting, seemingly hopeless, task of challenging DeLay. Six months earlier, Nate Wilcox would have written off a campaign against DeLay as a waste of time and money. But the groundswell against Texas redistricting, combined with the Dean campaign, had demonstrated to Wilcox that change was possible. More practically, Wilcox knew that any Democrat who could mount a serious challenge against DeLay in his home district would have the potential to raise lots of money, and lots of hell, on the Internet.

A few weeks later Wilcox met Morrison. The first thing Morrison said to Wilcox was, "I'm not crazy, I know I'm not going to win." He'd been reading up on Newt Gingrich and saw a possible model there. "Gingrich didn't win his first time out," Morrison reasoned. "But, he let people know who he was and what he was all about. Then the second time he ran he won. That's how DeLay is going to get beat." Morrison and those around him knew it would take a good deal of money to give DeLay a real challenge—Tom Riley's $200,000 in 2002 had not made a dent. The long-term strategy was to raise money online, nationally, and across Texas from people who were outraged by DeLay's antics. But to get to a point at which the campaign could garner national attention would require seed money, and that proved even harder to raise than expected.

One problem was that Representative Nick Lampson, a four-term congressman whose district had been gutted by DeLay's redistricting efforts, had been traveling the area and musing publicly about challenging DeLay. Every prominent Democratic donor that Morrison called had heard the Lampson rumors and preferred the idea of supporting a sitting congressman against DeLay than a complete unknown like Morrison. Raising funds was not going to be easy.

MORRISON WOWS THE DEANIACS

Meanwhile, as the Dean campaign's momentum built nationally, the campaign continued to keep an eye on Texas. Shortly after Dean had secured the

Richard Morrison speaking at a Democracy for Texas rally in Austin, Texas, August 22, 2004. Glen Maxey is seated in the foreground. Courtesy of Trei Brundrett.

backing of two of the most important labor unions in the country, SEIU and AFSCME,[10] he came to Houston for a mass rally. The union endorsements were the first sign that elements of the Democratic establishment were willing to bet on Dean and his outsider campaign. Dean's appearance in Houston gave Richard Morrison's quixotic campaign against Tom DeLay an early boost, because Morrison had the opportunity of introducing Dean at the Houston event. Glen Maxey had helped get Morrison on the bill, providing a priceless opportunity for the largely unknown candidate to speak to more than 10,000 Dean supporters.

The conventional wisdom for Democrats running in conservative congressional districts (such as rural Texas) called for avoiding national Democratic candidates—particularly "liberals" such as Howard Dean—like the plague. For that reason, the most prominent Texas Democrat at the Dean rally was Congresswoman Sheila Jackson Lee, from one of the most reliably Democratic districts in the country. Democrats like Nick Lampson, Chet Edwards, and Houston Mayor Bill White were nowhere to be seen. Morrison, however, couldn't afford to pass up the opportunity. Any attention to his fledgling campaign was a godsend, and he needed to take advantage of Dean's appearance.

Morrison and Wilcox showed up at that Dean event with stacks of printed fliers that they put on all the seats. The fliers had pictures of Morrison, his wife, and their four kids dressed all in white T-shirts and holding hands. True, it was laid on a bit thick, but the campaign needed to let people know that Morrison was a good guy, as different from Tom DeLay as possible. Wilcox had never seen Morrison speak to a crowd and had no idea how he would perform. Morrison, an unassuming guy one-on-one, got up and blew the crowd away. People were pumping their fists in the air and hollering by the time he finished. It was just a short speech to introduce himself, get some cheap applause at DeLay's expense, and talk up Dean to his hometown crowd, but Morrison nailed it like a seasoned pro.

Morrison had received his first standing ovation as a candidate, but it wouldn't be his last. One of those applauding Morrison's speech was local activist John Cobarruvias of the Bay Area New Democrats (BAND). Cobarruvias and his BAND team would become the heart of Morrison's volunteer activists in the eastern part of the district (Clear Lake, near NASA headquarters). This is a prototypical example of the way the Dean netroots movement would affect American politics more broadly than just the 2003–2004 presidential race. A significant percentage of the citizens who first became politically active because of Howard Dean would later employ their energies and skills on state and local campaigns just like Richard Morrison's.

DEAN CRUISES INTO 2004

By the end of 2003, Howard Dean's online legions had propelled him to front-runner status among the Democratic presidential candidates as the first votes neared. Dean's amazing online fundraising prowess, his strong standing in the polls, and his passionate netroots supporters had caused even Beltway insiders to start taking him seriously. All Dean had to do was get past Iowa.

For veteran political organizers like Glen Maxey who were working to elect Howard Dean, the power of the Internet continued to amaze. As Maxey recalls,

> When [Dean campaign manager Joe] Trippi asked if I could fill two airplanes to Iowa and one to New Hampshire with Texas Rangers, the young Deaniacs in my office were ecstatic. I was, however, terrified. What a logistical nightmare to take 450 volunteers across the country by plane, stay in volunteers' homes, and not lose the luggage or my mind. But then it happened. Magically, by e-mails and website signups, we organized the entire thing in a matter of less than ten days. And I began to wonder why I was paying for a phone line at my desk. Contrary to every organizational nightmare I'd ever organized before, I had not made a single phone call.

By late 2003, it seemed that almost anything was possible. Heading into the first caucus of the 2004 election year with strong leads in the polls and in fundraising, the Deaniacs were feeling confident that Iowa would be the first stop on the way to the White House. Little did they know.

Chapter 3

ACTIVISTS BUILD A MOVEMENT, INSIDERS KILL IT

O ver an illustrious military career that began during the Vietnam War, Wesley K. Clark rose to the rank of four-star general, led NATO forces in Europe, and fought an air campaign in Kosovo that achieved victory without the loss of a single American soldier. After his retirement in May 2000, Clark wrote a book (*Waging Modern Wars*), started a business venture (Wesley K. Clark & Associates), appeared frequently as a television commentator on military and foreign affairs, and played a lot of golf. General Clark may not have thought about running for president of the United States, but by late 2002, other people were beginning to think about it for him.

JOHN HLINKO FEELS A DRAFT

One of those people was a uniquely talented individual named John Hlinko, who boasted of being a standup comedian, a published economist, and an "activist agitator." Hlinko also ran Extreme Campaigns, a small political consulting firm that specialized in technology and marketing. In the fall of 2002, Hlinko started looking at potential Democratic candidates for president. The choices at that point included former Vermont Governor Howard Dean; U.S. Senators John Kerry of Massachusetts, John Edwards of North Carolina, Joe Lieberman of Connecticut (Al Gore's 2000 running mate), and Bob Graham of Florida; and Congressman Dick Gephardt of Missouri. None of these possibilities impressed Hlinko as an obvious choice to defeat George W. Bush in 2004, particularly given his belief that impeccable national security credentials would be required in the first post–September 11 presidential election.

Then, as Hlinko puts it, "One guy with the first name 'General' caught my attention, big time." Hlinko started paying attention to Clark, asking people about him, and becoming increasingly enthusiastic. Hlinko was convinced that Clark should be the next president. The question was how to convince Clark.

In February 2003, Hlinko had dinner with his girlfriend (now wife), Leigh Stringer. Joining them were his friend Dave Wallace, a Washington public relations professional; and Samer Shehata, a professor at Georgetown University. Hlinko was surprised to discover that Wallace and Shehata had also become independently interested in Wesley Clark. "If three people with different backgrounds and different political viewpoints had all become intrigued, and had done so at a time when Clark's name recognition was still quite low," Hlinko reasoned, "there was an appeal that clearly could 'go viral.'" A few weeks later, over lunch at a D.C. Italian restaurant, Hlinko and Wallace talked it over and decided to start a draft. Joining them was Hlinko's brother-in-law Josh Margulies, a Republican. In mid-April 2003, Hlinko, Margulies, and Wallace launched a website called DraftWesleyClark, hosted at first on Hlinko's Extreme Campaigns site.

Jason McIntosh of Draft Clark 2004, a rival draft group formed in May, credits Hlinko's early involvement as "crucial," although he also notes that "the actual first draft site, draftwesleyclark.us, was started back in January of '03." On April 13, Daily Kos founder Markos Moulitsas Zúniga endorsed Wesley Clark's candidacy on Daily Kos and launched his own Draft Clark site, DraftClark. According to Zúniga's business partner Jerome Armstrong,

> On the very same day, John Hlinko launched DraftWesleyClark.com. Our relationship with them was cordial from the beginning. If there was going to be a Clark candidacy, we'd need all the help we could get, was our feeling. The Draft Clark effort gained momentum throughout the month of April, and by mid-May, we were told, a decision would be made. At the same time, [Dean campaign manager Joe] Trippi began e-mailing and calling to re-connect. Though still open to working with the Dean campaign, we began to see the larger picture at this time, of the prospects of utilizing the internet in campaigns beyond Dean or Clark.

Armstrong asserts that the Draft Clark movement began on Daily Kos with a series of favorable posts by Moulitsas. In the end, however, Moulitsas and Armstrong decided not to wait for Clark to make a decision about whether to run. Instead, they joined up with Howard Dean, who was surging in the spring of 2003 and grabbing the imagination of netroots activists everywhere with his tough talk about President Bush, the war in Iraq, and the importance of representing the "Democratic wing of the Democratic Party." For the rest of 2003, Moulitsas's working relationship with the Dean campaign reinforced the existing perception among Clarkies that Daily Kos was hostile territory for their candidate.

ORDINARY PEOPLE DOING EXTRAORDINARY THINGS

In early June 2003—one month after George W. Bush had erroneously declared "mission accomplished" in the Iraq War—a sense of foreboding engulfed Lowell Feld. The Democratic field at the time had not inspired him with either confidence or enthusiasm. Lowell had nothing against Howard Dean, but he didn't see any way that someone who could be labeled as a "Vermont liberal" with no national security credentials could win a national election in the harsh, post–September 11 national political climate.

On June 15, Lowell watched Wesley Clark on *Meet the Press*, after which he excitedly told his wife, "This is the guy who's going to beat Bush!" Lowell ran to his computer and typed the words "Wesley Clark" into Google. To his amazement, he discovered a Draft Wesley Clark movement has already begun, along with a gathering called a Meetup (what's a "Meetup"? he wondered). The next one, in fact, was scheduled in three weeks at a Washington, D.C., bar, Stetson's.

About 50 people attended the event, including reporters and a camera crew from CNN. Lowell was excited at the prospect of finally doing something to help defeat George W. Bush and change the future for the better. Hlinko led the Meetup with his usual corny but endearing enthusiasm. Cleverly, Hlinko led a toast to General Clark at 20:04 military time (get it? 2004!), with a glass of *draft* beer. Hlinko spoke about creating the Draft Wesley Clark movement from nothing in just two months, certainly an impressive accomplishment. And Hlinko talked passionately about getting the kind of president we had been promised as kids. General Clark's friend (and former executive director for the National Summit on Africa), Colonel MacArthur DeShazer, spoke of Clark's intellectual prowess, his steely character, and his deep concern for the country's future. Lowell was excited.

Many other people around the nation were becoming similarly excited about Clark as well. They were attending Meetups for Clark. They were joining Yahoo! groups, a free online service enabling people with a shared interest— be it gardening, sports, or politics—to organize, share information, and plan activities. Among other things, Meetups and Yahoo! groups helped to combat the "bowling alone" phenomenon—that is, the tendency of people in contemporary society to go their own ways and not to interact, as described by Robert D. Putnam in his influential 1995 essay and 2000 book. In sum, Meetups and Yahoo! groups were powerful new tools for citizen activism.

Stan Davis, a 56-year-old Colorado man who had nearly died of a stroke in 2002 and was retired for medical reasons, had also seen Clark's June 15 *Meet the Press* interview. Clark's persona and message excited Davis, who registered on both major Draft Clark websites. On July 7, after attending the first Denver Draft Clark Meetup, Davis joined the only existing Yahoo! group for Clark. Davis ultimately became moderator of the largest national Clark Yahoo! group (Clark 2004), as well as one of Clark's most passionate netroots supporters.

Another early Clark adopter was Debby Burroughs of Richmond, Virginia, a self-described "ordinary citizen, wife, mother, and nurse" who became an

Draft Clark group in front of the New Hampshire for Clark office, summer 2003. (Susan Putney is pictured in the front row, third from the left; Matt Stoller is third from the left, back row.) Courtesy of Brent Blackaby.

important Draft Clark grassroots leader in Virginia. For Burroughs, Clark represented a strong, credible candidate who was not a run-of-the-mill politician. Along with many thousands of other supporters, Burroughs saw Wesley Clark as fitting the bill for an electable antiwar candidate.

But why Clark and not Dean? For many Clark supporters, it came down to his electability. Many Clark supporters looked at the "Deaniacs" as backing a candidate who effectively expressed their anger but who would likely lose to Bush in a McGovern-like landslide. In the summer of 2003, the conventional wisdom among netroots Democratic activists was that Dean would be the Democratic nominee in 2004. Many "Clarkies" believed that a Dean nomination would hand the White House back to Bush and Company on a silver platter.

Clark supporters mainly included people like Stan Davis and Debby Burroughs, proud Americans who previously had not been politically active, but who became so in 2003. These citizen activists were energized in part by the terrible events of September 11, in part because of the Iraq War, and in part by their outrage at the Bush-Cheney-DeLay radical right-wing agenda. More broadly, these were ordinary Americans who were finding new ways to express their opinions, both online and in the "real world," that previously had not been available. As Stan Davis likes to say, the Draft Clark movement was "ordinary people doing extraordinary things."

John Hlinko with fiancee Leigh Stringer in front of the Clark04 bus. Courtesy of John Hlinko.

GRASSROOTS IN ACTION

One such ordinary person doing extraordinary things in early 2003 was Susan Putney, an advertising vice president from Dover, New Hampshire, now a legend among Clark supporters. That spring, however, Putney was simply a regular citizen with no formal campaign experience. In April 2003, Putney spoke with John Hlinko, who had just started Draft Wesley Clark. There weren't many Clark supporters at that point, which to Putney meant that they could be "as creative as [they] wanted" to be.[1]

Putney developed a "campaign in a box," which included laptop presentations, brochures, and biographies that could be printed out and distributed to fellow draft people. Putney went around New Hampshire giving her presentation on Wesley Clark to anyone who would listen, including state representatives and senators, encouraging them to stay neutral until Clark entered the race. Putney did whatever she could to get attention for Clark—staffing phone banks, videotaping Clark's New Hampshire visits, marching in parades, organizing rallies, and standing on street corners holding signs in below-zero temperatures.

In May 2003, Putney, along with John Hlinko of Draft Wesley Clark and Jason McIntosh of Draft Clark 2004, helped produce a radio spot about General Clark entitled, "Dream Candidate." Putney was also involved, along with McIntosh and Brent Blackaby, in forming the Draft Clark 2004 PAC, the goal of which was develop infrastructure and coordinators across the country.

On May 12, 2003, Putney personally delivered the first 1,000 "please run" letters, originally posted on the Draft Wesley Clark website, to General Clark during his first visit to New Hampshire (on a trip Clark insisted was "strictly business"). The letter at the top of the stack was from a young Navy sailor named Dave Montoya (who later became an important volunteer on the Webb for Senate campaign in 2006). While on board the USS Abraham Lincoln returning from the Persian Gulf after the start of the Iraq War, Montoya had written to General Clark and urged him to run for president. Montoya urged the general to "carry his vision to the American people." When Putney showed Montoya's letter to Clark, she saw his eyes moisten. When Clark finished, he took Putney's hand and said, "These are amazing, I'm very moved … but I'm not a candidate." According to Putney, "When the press asked Clark what he thought about receiving 1,000 e-mails, he remarked he did not know about the draft until just now, and he couldn't help but be moved looking at the letters."[2]

NOT JUST A *LITTLE RASCALS* EPISODE

The August 4 Meetup at Stetson's in D.C. was significantly larger than July's Meetup, so John Hlinko broke the attendees into several subgroups. John asked Lowell to lead a breakout session on Media Attention, which led to a photo of Lowell appearing in *Newsweek*'s online edition. One idea that came out of Lowell's breakout session was to do a heavy push on Hispanic outreach. A couple weeks later, Lowell and his techie friend Eric Grim simultaneously launched two websites, Hispanics for Clark and Environmentalists for Clark.

The month of August was a blur of activity, with thousands of people across the country working hard in their interest areas, and with a decision by General Clark drawing near. The Draft Wesley Clark group continued to focus on marketing, "media buzz," and public outreach, while the Draft Clark 2004 group moved full speed ahead on planning a "ground game" and building technical tools that would be needed if and when Clark declared for president.

Behind the Draft Clark effort were a number of visionaries and clever marketers. John Hlinko was one of those people. Wisely, Hlinko saw the draft's main value as "providing a platform for making potential supporters aware of General Clark, and giving the media a reason to cover and showcase him." Hlinko bristles when the draft is referred to as amateurish, unsophisticated, or "just an Internet thing." To the contrary, Hlinko argues, the Draft Clark effort was a "multi-faceted, multi-media campaign, which succeeded not so much because of tens of thousands of e-mail addresses in a database, but because we got tens of millions of people to see news coverage of it on CNN, ABC, NBC, etc." In Hlinko's opinion, if the draft had existed only in cyberspace, the media would never have provided significant coverage. And without media coverage, the draft "would have failed like so many other aborted draft efforts." But the press coverage was due to Hlinko's impressive public relations skills as much as anything else.

Hlinko explains that the draft wasn't just "a spontaneous outpouring of people on the net or a *Little Rascals* episode where the kids all get together on the spur of the moment to build a new playhouse." Instead, Hlinko describes the draft as "a serious campaign conducted by a heck of a lot of very serious, talented, creative, hardworking people." And, Hlinko adds, "Without those people putting in a heck of a lot of time, the draft would have failed."

Whether the draft movement was a serious campaign or a *Little Rascals* episode, it was wildly successful. Draft organizers talk about how it developed into a "perfect storm," with all the elements coming together in a nearly optimal fashion. Hlinko believes that such a movement never could have succeeded in the pre-Internet era, and that is almost certainly correct. As Hlinko puts it, "There was simply no way pre-Internet to recruit, engage, and mobilize so many citizens so quickly, at such a low cost." But with the Internet allowing people to connect across large distances in real time and essentially for free, the entire campaign paradigm had shifted. Essentially, the rise of the netroots had transformed the way citizen activists engaged in American politics.

Among other accomplishments, the draft raised about $2 million in pledges for a potential Clark campaign, and it did so primarily in two months (July and August). It boosted Clark from relative obscurity to first place in some polls by the time he announced for president in September 2003. Hlinko says that DraftClark, and Daily Kos (before Moulitsas joined Dean) "were extremely important in energizing the netroots, and in getting other blogs and major media to cover us." Hlinko believes that "the Yahoo! groups were a great, easy means of letting the most enthusiastic supporters swap ideas, encourage each other, and come up with plans for building more and more buzz." And Hlinko feels that competition between different groups of Clark supporters (for example, Draft Clark 2004 and Draft Wesley Clark) "spurred everyone to work that much harder."

Larry Huynh, a talented young leader in Draft Clark 2004, agrees with Hlinko with regard to the power of the Internet as a transformative political organizing and motivational technology. According to Huynh, if people anywhere in the country can meet and exchange ideas as they never before had been able to do (and at essentially no cost), the potential for enhanced citizen activism increases geometrically. In the case of the Draft Clark campaign, Huynh points out that by the time the campaign started, the draft groups had gathered databases of some 70,000 names—an impressive accomplishment for a low-budget, grassroots-netroots operation in just a few months' time.

The utility of those databases is a separate question. Yosem Companys—Wesley Clark's national advisor on Hispanic and Latino issues, and currently a doctoral candidate in management science and engineering at Stanford University—says that when the draft databases were submitted to the campaign, they "lacked even the most basic demographic information," with numerous e-mail addresses "no longer functional." In contrast, John Hlinko says that his Draft Wesley Clark group "actually collected the e-mails and related data in a very robust database system." Hlinko asserts that the 50,000 e-mails turned over to the campaign were "definitely used" to generate "at least $1 million in short-term donations."

This sort of quibbling about the quality of supporter data is a typical feature of political campaigns. And as much as political operatives may obsess about the critical importance of lists, the harried atmosphere of political campaigns encourages sloppy data management. To political operatives whose success hinges on immediate results, the value of an e-mail list is measured by the response the campaign gets when it hits "send" on an e-mail blast, not on the nitty-gritty details of the data quality. By this standard, there seems little doubt that receiving Hlinko's list allowed the Clark campaign to communicate with several thousand committed supporters.

BUILDING A COMMUNITY

The netroots effort to draft Wesley Clark was highly effective during the summer of 2003. Again, it's important to emphasize that "netroots" doesn't mean a bunch of disembodied electrons or even people sitting in their underwear in basements, munching on nacho chips. To the contrary, it means citizen activists—real people—using the Internet to gather information, to organize with other like-minded folks across the country, to plan events, to raise money, and to make the case for their candidate. Much of the actual activity takes place in person, not online.

In many ways, the Clark Meetups served as a bridge between the virtual and real worlds. Yosem Companys, who currently is studying (as part of his doctoral thesis at Stanford) the emergence of the 2004 Draft Clark movement, notes that Clark Meetups were "valuable and effective" as a means for "building commitment" and "providing a mechanism by which people could meet face-to-face and create trust." That's important, given the relative anonymity of the online world. And then, Companys adds, the trust gained from meeting in person "could be taken back to online relationships."

During the Clark draft, those online relationships took place to a great degree in the Yahoo! groups. In 2003, if you wanted online functionality, Yahoo! groups were about the only game in town. This included the ability to make groups public or private, to post files and photos, to approve or reject members, and to "moderate" the forums to keep things focused and civil. Aside from the public Yahoo! groups, whose membership reached into the thousands, private groups also formed. For instance, the Clark Action Team allowed local, regional, and national leaders to hold focused (and private) discussions on tactics and day-to-day organizing essentials. The Yahoo! groups, like any other tool, were far from perfect, but it is hard to imagine how the Draft Clark effort could have functioned without them.

How do people find each other and build community online? According to Yosem Companys, "People joined the Clark groups to talk about General Clark and found like-minded people." Companys notes the "empowering" nature of this, "especially when you feel frustrated with events in the world and don't know many people around you who feel the same because they do not openly express the same sentiments." This is yet another characteristic of the blogosphere—that is, someone can find political soul mates they never knew existed, sometimes half a world away.

Political scientist Robert Dahl was the first to note in 1970 that face-to-face meetings are constrained by the problem of time, distance, and numbers. The Internet, in contrast, reduces both the temporal and spatial constraints by enabling people to talk to hundreds of others from the comfort of their own homes. The power potential inherent in this phenomenon is enormous; once people find each other online, they can then combine their talents and energies in ways that would have been nearly impossible just a few years earlier using the existing means of communication—that is, fax, phone, and regular old "snail mail."[3]

According to Companys, "When someone in the online group feels empowered and energized, that energy and sense of empowerment is likely to spread." You "tackle something larger, you accomplish that, and the outcome again is recognized by the group." Of course, the contrary is true as well: If significant political or personality differences emerge within online groups, this can lead to schisms, hard feelings, and a loss of effectiveness. By the end of the Clark campaign, several rival, national pro-Clark Yahoo! groups (led by particular personalities with particular styles) were at odds, sometimes clashing with each other.

The leadership of charismatic individuals over the Internet should not be discounted merely because participants are not communicating in person.

Most Clark activists had never met John Hlinko, yet he was highly influential nonetheless. As Companys notes, Hlinko's "zany ideas created excitement and built momentum because they typically and surprisingly worked so well." For instance, Hlinko's brainstorm of handing out "Clark Bars" along with Clark literature worked well; who could refuse a free candy bar, even one that tasted like "chocolate covered barley," as Hlinko disparagingly described it? Interestingly, Clark Bar manufacturer NECCO rejected a proposal by Lowell Feld and John Hlinko to churn out a batch of special, limited edition "Clark for President" bars. They said they didn't want to get involved in politics.

Among the charismatic leaders of the draft was Stirling Newberry, the self-styled Draft Clark philosopher king. Newberry's near-daily treatises explained what the Clark campaign stood for and how it differed ideologically from those of other candidates—not to mention his theories on life and the universe. These treatises became required reading for many Clark 2004 Yahoo! group members during the summer and early fall of 2003. True, Newberry's points often went over his readers' heads, but those who made the effort found Newberry's ideas thought provoking, if not mind boggling.

Another type of leadership was provided by technologically talented people such as Larry Huynh, Josh Lerner (a friend of General Clark's son Wesley, Jr.), Andrew Hoppin, Ellen Nagler, and Denyse Rackel. Companys notes that these were some of the people who "created the technical infrastructure without which the Clark groups could not have succeeded." Companys adds that "the techies are pragmatists" who, by building the needed technical infrastructure, enable the "writers" to "spend their time preaching the gospel of their preferred candidate or cause with missionary zeal in the streets of cyberspace and the virtual communities that constitute it."

With regard to the demographics of Clark's citizen activists, Companys's research found that "the typical draft leader was that of an educated, well-spoken, politically connected and technologically savvy young person from a major city, often a graduate from an Ivy League institution." More information on demographics comes from a January 2004 Bentley College study of the Clark Meetups. The Bentley study found that most attendees were "Caucasian, middle aged, middle income professionals," almost all of whom reported that they used the Internet "several times a day." The Bentley study also discovered that "about half of Clark attendees were already involved in the campaign before they decided to attend a Meetup," but that Meetup attendees said "they would become more involved in the campaign and more supportive of their candidate as a result of the Meetup experience."[4]

One question from 2003 is why Wesley Clark became—along with Howard Dean—the netroots candidate (as opposed to John Kerry, for instance). Draft Clark leader Matt Stoller believes "Clark got in because people said, 'We need someone in there who's against Iraq but who isn't Howard Dean.'" But it wasn't just anti-Dean sentiment. As Clark's Oklahoma primary campaign manager Jessica Vanden Berg points out, Clark had net-roots appeal as an "insurgent," as an "authentic candidate," and as someone who was providing "leadership from places other than what is normally offered."

CLARK DECLARES, THE PROFESSIONALS DESCEND

In the end, the draft succeeded almost beyond anyone's wildest dreams. On September 17, 2003, Clark declared his candidacy for president, and the Draft Clark people were ecstatic. Susan Putney described the moment as an emotional one: "Our dream was becoming a reality, [proving that] a few con-cerned citizens ... on a grassroots movement could indeed change the world."[5] Aside from the excitement and emotion, the Draft Clark effort had produced impressive results: more than 80,000 names of supporters, hundreds of coordi-nators across the country, more than $2 million in campaign pledges, and offi-ces in several states, including New Hampshire, the site of the nation's first primary.

The efforts by the netroots throughout the spring and summer of 2003 had the potential to compensate for Clark's late entry into the race. At least in theory, Clark would not be forced to start his campaign from scratch. As Clark's first campaign manager, Donnie Fowler, Jr., explains, "In many ways, General Clark would not have been able to do what he did out of the gate without the netroots, without the two draft movements, without their creativ-ity and their commitment." Fowler adds that the day Clark announced, "he did not have a headquarters, a campaign manager, even a checking account; literally, what he had was his background, his charisma, and these two draft movements."

The need to make up for lost time was particularly important because Clark faced a formidable field of opponents for the nomination—Howard Dean, John Kerry, John Edwards, Dick Gephardt, and Joe Lieberman. That was a tall order, even for a brilliant, charismatic four-star general who had won a war. Also, with the first Democratic caucuses and primaries just four months away, there wasn't much time to get a serious campaign up and run-ning. The ace card appeared to be the netroots, that is, if General Clark and his advisors were prepared to run a different type of campaign from the tradi-tional, top-down, pollster- and consultant-driven effort.

Unfortunately, at the point when Clark declared his candidacy—and shot to the top of at least one poll—troubling signs began to emerge. Several of the leading draft people began to notice that the netroots activists were not being integrated with the traditional Washington political professionals who had descended on Clark campaign headquarters in Little Rock like locusts. Key campaign positions appeared to be going to the "same old, same old"—former staffers to Bill Clinton, Al Gore, and Terry McAuliffe—and not, for the most part, to leaders of the draft. That might not have been a problem if the professionals had appreciated and understood how to run a netroots-style campaign. Sadly, this didn't turn out to be the case.

Looking back, John Hlinko reflects that "while some of the professionals were certainly good people with a willingness to teach *and* learn, others had absolutely no clue about the benefits that the grassroots had already brought, and could continue to bring." True, this was "a new paradigm for a campaign." But, as Hlinko points out, "there will always be some who … stubbornly cling to the paradigm they've been using, even if it's completely outdated." In the case of the Clark campaign, Hlinko laments, although the draft "showed up with tens of thousands of volunteers, $2 million in pledges, an astonishing amount of media coverage, and more momentum than any of the declared candidates … some of the professionals seemed to think we had nothing of value."

Clark had spoken eloquently about the need for a new style of politics in this country and a different kind of campaign. Instead, the Clark campaign's first moves in the weeks after his announcement appeared to reflect "old politics" at its worst. General Clark came into the campaign with a huge head of steam, a prototype campaign created without spending a penny, a quick jump to the top of the polls, and a great chance to be the Democratic nominee. Within a few weeks, however, the professional campaigners had managed to undo what people like John Hlinko and many others had built up during the summer.

How did they manage this? One clue was in their treatment of the grassroots effort, including the websites that had sprung up like wildfire. For instance, on September 24, links to Lowell's Environmentalists for Clark and Hispanics for Clark sites were removed, along with nearly all other grassroots websites, from the Clark campaign site's home page. This led to a decline of 96 percent in visits to Hispanics for Clark, from 1,439 on September 23 to just 54 on September 26. This was not an isolated incident, and obviously it did not bode well for integrating the netroots into the Clark campaign.

On October 5, Ellen Nagler, the leader of the Santa Barbara for Clark movement, and one of the brightest political people in the Clark movement— her campaign experience dated back to Bobby Kennedy in 1968—wrote to Lowell in an instant message chat that "the Clark Movement is being systematically excluded." Nagler complained that Digital Clark (an online repository for radio and television interviews with Clark) "is gone" and that "for days, if you clicked on the [popular] Clark Tribune newsletter on the main site you got redirected to the main campaign press page." Nagler expressed her belief that the campaign professionals viewed the draft people as "mavericks" or even "unruly children" who needed to be "brought under control or sent away from the table if we misbehave."

Sadly, Nagler's frustration was all too typical of the discussion among netroots leaders at the time. For instance, a key Virginia grassroots leader who later joined the Clark campaign as a paid staffer, Chris Ambrose, says that soon after Clark declared, things started to fall apart between the grassroots and the professionals. According to Ambrose, this occurred because of a combination of "bad organization, bad management, too much of a reliance on the traditional, old way of doing things." Ambrose says that "whether they felt threatened or just didn't get it, I don't know." Perhaps it was both.

DONNIE FOWLER DEPARTS

It wasn't just the netroots that was having problems with the Clark campaign. On October 7, Donnie Fowler, Jr., resigned as Clark's campaign manager, after just a few weeks on the job. Fowler, who had been described as "one of the young, rising stars of the Democratic Party," complained, among other things, about "widespread concerns that supporters who used the Internet to draft Clark into the race [were] not being taken seriously by top campaign advisers." Fowler does not blame General Clark for this turn of events. To the contrary, Fowler says that Clark "always embraced the netroots, understood their power, what they had done for him and what they were capable of doing for him, and he always respected them." In contrast, Fowler says that around a half dozen top campaign professionals—"largely D.C. establishment types" who "didn't understand" the netroots—"wanted control of the campaign" and believed that the netroots people were "a bunch of kooks."

Fowler attempted to persuade other top campaign officials that the netroots had "created a candidate that is not a blue-suit politician," and that "if you pull General Clark to a blue-suit politician and away from this organic, up-from-the-grassroots candidate, fresh-faced, fresh ideas, you're going to ruin his chances." Fowler even proposed having a "separate line on the campaign flow chart for the netroots, for the Draft movement," but he was met with a stone wall of opposition from campaign chairman Eli Segal and others who Fowler calls "bandwagon hoppers." Fowler believes that Segal "didn't understand" the draft and felt that it "should be on the finance team" (because supposedly it was good only for raising money).

General Clark, meanwhile, was "on the road and not in Little Rock to manage this situation," which regardless is "not the candidate's job." Unfortunately, this allowed the Clark campaign's Washington insiders—who Fowler says viewed the netroots with utter disdain, as "loose cannons" who they'd never worked with before—to win the battle. According to Fowler, these people embodied "a lot of fear, a lot of ignorance … and prejudice" against the netroots. In Fowler's view, this attitude "at the end of the day was why the netroots was rejected. It wasn't only about the netroots, it wasn't only about the Internet, it wasn't only about new technology. It was a broader disease that still curses a lot of the Democratic Party."

In contrast to the "fear and ignorance" that characterized much of the campaign leadership, Fowler was a big supporter of the netroots, arguing tirelessly that it was like a "wild, raging river" that could be harnessed to the campaign's advantage. Trying to stop up that river, in Fowler's view, was "even worse than letting the river run wild." Ironically, a product of this establishment—Donnie, Jr., the son of legendary South Carolina Democratic powerbroker Donnie Fowler—turned out to be the one Clark campaign manager most sympathetic to the netroots. Perhaps it was Fowler's technology background in Silicon Valley, or perhaps it was just that he was more open to new ideas and new ways of doing things. Whatever the reason, Fowler was a big proponent of integrating the netroots into the campaign. But he was outnumbered, outgunned, and ultimately—despite General Clark personally attempting to talk him out of leaving—out of the campaign.

No question, the loss of Fowler was a significant one for both the Clark campaign and the Draft Clark movement. John Hlinko, who by this point had been hired onto the Clark campaign but was feeling underutilized, believed that Fowler "clearly understood the power" of the netroots and the technology needed to make it work at "peak efficiency." Hlinko recalls Fowler "talking in 2003 about using Treo smart phones in the field for real-time data collection, analysis, etc." Hlinko argues that Fowler understood "the importance of keeping the movement fun, of keeping an insurgent flavor."

Unfortunately, according to Hlinko, others in power "totally did not get it, nor did they have any desire to figure it out." Hlinko admits that "we had our share of difficult people in the grassroots as well." But overall, Hlinko believes that "a lot more of the grassroots folks were willing to work collaboratively with and learn from the professionals than vice-versa." As a consequence, the Clark campaign "lost a lot of momentum in those early, critical weeks—the time when the momentum mattered the most." In Hlinko's view, the departure of Fowler—"a champion of the grassroots/netroots"—from the Clark campaign was "a sign that we [the netroots] would not be playing a serious leadership role."

DISCONTENT IN THE RANKS

Other signs abounded. Around this time, Matt Stoller's relationship with the Clark campaign went from bad to worse. Stoller, a 2000 Harvard graduate who is now one of the most prominent national bloggers, was then running The Clark Sphere, United for Clark, and the popular Clark Tribune, a daily e-newsletter. Stoller, an important figure in the Draft Clark movement, was frustrated at what he was seeing both with the so-called professionals as well as with the rivalries and turf battles in the draft movements. Still, although Stoller had a bad feeling that the Clark campaign would be a "disaster," after Clark declared his run for the presidency on September 17, Stoller quit his job and went to Little Rock with the intent of helping to elect Clark. Instead, Stoller says that "they wouldn't even let me in the office." Apparently, because

Stoller was a blogger, people felt he might leak inside information from the Clark campaign.

Even worse, Stoller believes that he was perceived by many at the Clark headquarters as having been critical of the Clark campaign, first and foremost for "cutting out" the netroots. Although Stoller feels that his criticism was always "constructive," apparently it wasn't appreciated by several powerful people at Clark's headquarters. In sum, Stoller wasn't trusted (John Hlinko says that Stoller "tick[ed] off some campaign folks with what he wrote, but I felt he got a lot more grief than he deserved"). Stoller left Little Rock after a week or two without making any headway, feeling that the campaign was explicitly trying to "crush the grassroots."

In late September, Stoller told *Wired* magazine that "a movement is a movement, and it can't be controlled through top-down hierarchical methods."[6] In early October, Stoller was even more frustrated, accusing the Washington insiders of "systematically dismantl[ing] the Draft Clark movement" and instead "running a traditional campaign."[7] In November, Stoller shut down the Clark Tribune, and by the end of 2003, he put his efforts toward writing on a blog completely unrelated to the Clark campaign. Needless to say, this was not a good sign for the Clark campaign or its relationship with the netroots.

Meanwhile, on October 8, Stoller's ally Stirling Newberry published his infamous "Open Letter to the Clark Movement." The letter began, in typically melodramatic Newberry style, "By the time you read these words, the bell will be tolling for Wesley Clark's candidacy." Newberry then proceeded to blame "[m]any people intimately connected with the Draft movement" for "inflating their accomplishments, and working to fragment the movement, so that they could get jobs in the campaign." According to Newberry, "by lying about their accomplishments, [they] undercut the very credibility of the people who were fighting for the Draft movement." According to Newberry, the result was that "the Draft movement is on the outside looking in—with its most vocal supporter resigning from the campaign, and the positions of others left in doubt—and its most eloquent spokespeople cut out of the process entirely." But Newberry saved his most potent venom for the Clark campaign itself, calling it "nothing more than the Gore campaign with a better candidate." Newberry even criticized General Clark himself: "Either he will show he can take charge, or he will be forever branded a tool of insiders, unable to understand the enormity of the task."[8]

Newberry's letter caused a major storm within the Clark movement, generated tremendous vitriol toward Newberry himself, and began a bitter controversy which, in many ways, has not been resolved to this day. Many Clark supporters resented not only the content of the letter and some of its implications, but particularly the fact that Newberry had gone public with his complaints. Yet Donnie Fowler says that Stirling Newberry—as polarizing as he was brilliant—actually was right to complain about the way the netroots was being treated: "Once the traditionalists got firm control over the budget, which is what it comes down to, and the schedule, and they did it in a few weeks after the announcement, that was the point of no return." Fowler adds that the vicious response to Newberry's letter came about because "some of the people who were running the communications operation are killers, and their first instinct is to kill."

The day after Newberry's letter appeared, campaign spokesperson and Draft Wesley Clark veteran Maya Israel "dismissed the criticisms as invalid and said Newberry had been disgruntled with the campaign two days into Clark's candidacy."[9] Israel added that out of 200 or so Draft Clark grassroots people across the country, only "four or five [were] disgruntled."[10] That seems highly improbable. Although most of the Clark grassroots did not share Newberry's intense anger at the Clark campaign, it is highly unlikely that the "disgruntled" numbered only "four or five."

On September 25, for instance, Markos Moulitsas Zúniga had commented on Daily Kos that while he had "nothing against Clark"—and was in fact "an early supporter"—he had "everything against [Clark's] organization."[11] Moulitsas wondered, incredulously, why "the Clark campaign is fueling this hostility by systematically dismantling the sites that collectively formed the backbone of the Draft movement's effective netroots effort, dissing the people [who] built them."[12] These were good questions, questions that many other Clark supporters and outside observers shared.

NO RESPECT

The arrogance and disdain that Donnie Fowler and others described was apparent in Virginia. There, the grassroots was working hard to collect petition signatures for Clark, but it was getting little respect from the Little Rock professionals. According to Virginia grassroots leader Chris Ambrose, "We had collected probably 80 percent of the signatures we needed to get Clark on the ballot in Virginia, when the Clark campaign people told us that they were going to 'bring in paid people and take care of the whole thing.'" Ambrose recalls that "their basic attitude was almost like, 'you're dismissed,'" as if "they didn't want the signatures we had collected!" With the filing deadline just a few weeks away, however, there was no way the Clark campaign was going to get the job done. So, "they got back to us a few days later and said, 'Okay, you saved us a lot of money, thanks.'" But, in Ambrose's opinion, that response came only because "they had no other choice."

Another Virginia grassroots leader, Abbi Easter, describes the attitude of Little Rock professionals toward the Virginia volunteers as "very condescending and patronizing." Unfortunately, this type of attitude appears to have been endemic to the Clark campaign. Dozens, perhaps hundreds, of variants of this same story have emerged from across the country.

Larry Huynh, the Draft Clark 2004 leader who had joined the Clark campaign to handle e-mail solicitations, maintains a more positive view of the campaign. According to Huynh, despite certain "unavoidable" problems, the campaign also did "new and innovative" things like implementing a Call from Home program to get out the vote and launching the Clark Community Network website. The latter effort was coordinated by one of the earliest political bloggers, Cameron Barrett, and was significant for being one of the first sites developed using "Scoop" technology. Scoop is an open-source software package that allows for the development of collaborative, self-policing online communities. Unlike online forums that rely on vigilant moderators to control obnoxious, off-topic, or abusive "troll" behavior by members, Scoop enables members to "troll rate" people and, essentially, as in the television show "Survivor," vote them off the virtual island. True, "troll rating" can be abused as well, with people occasionally punishing others simply because they disagree—not for being disagreeable. Two of the most popular national liberal blogs, Moulitsas's Daily Kos and Armstrong's MyDD, each are based on Scoop.

Huynh argues that "things were going well leading up to Iowa," with Clark "surging in New Hampshire" and raising a great deal of money. For instance, Huynh notes that in the fourth quarter of 2003, Clark raised $10 million, including $3 million online. According to Huynh, another $2 million came in over the Internet in January 2004. Thus, despite complaints from the netroots about being excluded or not properly utilized, the Clark campaign was succeeding in certain ways, perhaps because of the innate appeal of its candidate and his message.

Still, the discontent among many in the Clark netroots remained and even intensified as time went by. On November 28, Ellen Nagler wrote to Lowell that "Clark deserved a really good campaign … [but] he didn't get one." In Nagler's view, Clark had "listened to the wrong people." Nagler's frustration poured out:

> We were this close, Lowell. This close. Another week or two and we'd have had the community software up and running, and of course Clark Tribune and Digital Clark. It has taken them months to reconstruct what we had almost finished. Instead, they dismantled the whole structure, made the people behind it either persona non grata, or marginalized them so much that they've walked away, evaporated.

What happened? How could the netroots not have been integrated into the Clark campaign, which seemed like such a "no brainer" in August and early September 2003? According to John Hlinko, it was not "necessarily a result of anything nefarious … or any kind of grand conspiracy against the grassroots." However, "there were people who viewed us as a hindrance, and who tried to shove us to the side due to their own selfish interests." Hlinko adds, "we in the draft hurt ourselves because there was some divisiveness ... and we were more easily viewed as troublesome, to be ignored." Finally, because it was all brand new, Hlinko believes that "there simply was no rulebook for how to integrate that movement."

Jason McIntosh of Draft Clark 2004 concurs: "The people in charge, the ones that were calling the shots, for various reasons, made just absolutely horrendous decisions, and were not good leaders or motivators."

Yosem Companys points to the top-down versus bottom-up culture clash: "Professionals are trained in perfectly calibrating the message and controlling every aspect of the campaign, while grassroots organizers are all about openness and participation." This divide is, of course, common in political campaigns, especially high-profile and high-pressure presidential campaigns. But the problem appears to have been magnified in the Clark case by the fact that the draft people had worked independently for months before Clark's official announcement. Making matters worse, Clark's late start meant that time was extremely limited before the first primary. In either case, Companys observes, "It's not easy to tell people who are used to working independently to start following orders and toeing the line."

Despite all the tensions and difficulties, the grassroots—and the Clark campaign in general—certainly had its successes. According to Howard Park, a grassroots Clark leader in the D.C. area, "led by Chris Ambrose, northern Virginia developed an especially strong grassroots campaign, collecting 10,000 signatures, all from volunteers, to qualify for the ballot." In addition, according to Park, Northern Virginia Clark supporters ran a successful phone bank, "with more than 140 volunteers, ranging in age from 17 to 83." In addition, busloads of Clark supporters from the region traveled to New Hampshire in the weeks leading up to that state's January 27, 2004, primary.[13]

Ultimately, Companys believes, both "the professionals and the grassroots have important roles to play in politics," but they need to respect what each brings to the table. According to Companys, "The professionals need to learn that they are living in a brave new world where information is free and perfectly mobile and where control is no longer the name of the game." And the volunteers need to recognize that "the expertise of professionals in political, field, finance and media work is not easily supplanted by grassroots organizers."

"NO CONFIDENCE IN LITTLE ROCK"

Virginia grassroots leader Abbi Easter recalls that the Virginia Clark volunteers had "no confidence in Little Rock," creating an "almost completely dysfunctional relationship between Little Rock and the grassroots in Virginia." Debby Burroughs, another Virginia grassroots star for Clark, says that the grassroots "got the candidate where they wanted him—to run." Then, once Clark was there, "the professionals were brought in and those who had worked so hard to bring Clark's name to the forefront, to raise pledges, and to build a national following were dumped." Burroughs feels that the grassroots were "discounted as amateurs with little to offer" and that this "created a lot of resentment and frustration."

The situation was especially frustrating for Clark diehards, who "believed in him wholeheartedly as the person who could be what this country needed." In contrast, according to Burroughs, "The professionals did not know the candidate, and to them, this was another job." Even worse was the campaign's decision—with just three months to go before the first primary—to bring in a "completely new team" and "let the volunteers go." According to Burroughs, "all momentum [in Virginia] was stopped in its tracks while we waited for the new team to get in place and undo what was already in progress." During this period, Burroughs says that "valuable time was lost and some rancor became public."

This dysfunctional relationship almost certainly held the Clark campaign back from reaching its full potential. Many Clark supporters who had been enthusiastic over the summer scaled back their involvement or quit altogether in the fall and winter. These people ranged from an important Hispanic businessman in southern California to a leading environmental activist in Pittsburgh, and even an heiress of the Rockefeller fortune who wanted to put together a large fundraiser for Clark. And many more powerful voices for Clark, like bloggers Matt Stoller and Stirling Newberry, largely went silent. By late October 2003, Lowell Feld became so frustrated with the Clark campaign that he reduced his involvement to keeping the environmentalists and Hispanics websites going, while contributing almost nothing more.

The loss of energy from such people was like "the dog that didn't bark" of the Clark campaign. Who knows how things might have turned out had the pro-Clark netroots kept its energy, motivation, and engagement? Certainly, numerous talented people could have provided tremendous assistance to the Clark campaign if the top-down leadership in Little Rock had been open and respectful, instead of disdainful, of the grassroots.

According to John Hlinko, this was right around the time he came close to quitting the campaign:

> By October, it was pretty clear I was going to have a nice title, but no budget and no authority (literally, I was asked to submit a budget for netroots recruitment, did it, and then never got an answer). In fact, when all this was breaking in the news (about "the draft" being quickly transformed into "the shaft"), I was actually approached about a job in another, competing campaign. Personally, I would've loved to have taken it. But, frankly, I still had a lot of faith in Clark, and kept hoping he would turn things

around. And having been so visible as a draft leader, and the guy who signed the draft e-mails to 50,000 supporters, it was clear that me leaving wouldn't have been just one guy switching jobs, but rather something that could hurt the campaign, and dispirit a lot of supporters. Knowing what I know now, however, I wish I'd taken that job.

Meanwhile, the Clark campaign decided to skip the crucial Iowa caucuses, slated to be held on January 19, 2004. According to Donnie Fowler, "The decision for General Clark not to compete in Iowa typified a disdain for local people ... and a belief that if you live in Washington you know everything that there is to know." Not only that, but "the decision to avoid Iowa was made without talking to anyone in Iowa," including Senator Tom Harkin of Iowa who "thought Clark would finish first or second" in the state. Yet, despite the fact that Tom Harkin understands Iowa like nobody else, the Washington insiders felt that "they knew better." Fowler added that the campaign's decision not to compete in Iowa "was really just an example of a much larger dismissiveness, an arrogance," which was similar to their dismissal of the netroots. Unfortunately, Fowler says, General Clark had never run for political office before, had "no political reference point," and therefore deferred to the people with "exceptionally impressive resumes." That was a big mistake, but an honest one.

On the decision to skip Iowa, John Hlinko notes,

This decision was completely dismissive of the grassroots as well. We had over a thousand draft supporters in Iowa, with some great leaders—one of whom called [the campaign] in tears when he found out about the decision. He wasn't told directly, in fact, he read about it in the *New York Times*.... The sad thing is, had they actually talked to the draft people, had they understood the extent of the support there, I think he might have gone to Iowa, and I have no doubt he would've had a showing that was respectable— at the very least.

The result of skipping the crucial Iowa caucuses was, predictably, disastrous for the Clark campaign. On January 27, just eight days after John Kerry had won Iowa, Clark finished third in New Hampshire behind Kerry and Howard Dean. After winning just one primary—Oklahoma on February 3—Clark announced on February 11 that he was dropping out of the presidential race, one day after he lost the Virginia and Tennessee primaries to Kerry. Could things have worked out differently for Clark if the netroots had been integrated early and effectively with the professional campaign? We'll never know for sure. As John Hlinko notes, "This was a new paradigm altogether." But it certainly would have been interesting to see what could have happened in a rosy alternate history of the 2004 primaries.

In actuality, in the nonalternate history of 2003–2004, the very success of the draft effort proved to be its undoing as soon as Clark officially launched his campaign and brought in the professionals who were dismissive of the draft. Politics is, in part, about momentum and enthusiasm. Unfortunately, the fight between the Clark grassroots and the Clark professionals, combined with an early gaffe by Clark on Iraq and other stumbles for the first-time campaigner, seriously dampened the enthusiasm that had been building for months.

SEARCHING FOR THE SWEET SPOT

One positive outcome stemming from the Clark campaign was that at least some members of each side, both netroots and top down, learned valuable lessons for future campaigns. Jessica Vanden Berg, who managed Wesley Clark's campaign in Oklahoma—the one state Clark won during the primaries—went on to manage Jim Webb's 2006 Senate campaign in Virginia. As we shall see, the Webb campaign took netroots integration to a new level. Yosem Companys points out that numerous grassroots organizers from the Clark campaign ended up "influencing politics in new ways, both from the inside and the outside of the political system." In late 2003 and early 2004, however, the concept of the netroots was brand new, as was the idea that the netroots could be effectively integrated into a campaign for president of the United States.

On the lasting impact of the Clark netroots movement, Debby Burroughs says that "we demonstrated that we could be a force for the first time in modern political history." Burroughs adds that "grassroots activists, many who had never before participated in political volunteerism on this level, were energized and began to see that they could make a difference." No longer did they feel "as though they were on the outside looking in, unable to have a say in choosing their leaders." And that feeling was "an extremely empowering phenomenon that continues in greater force today."

In July 2007, General Clark himself pointed out, "After I left the 2004 presidential race, I urged my supporters to remain focused—to channel their energy into fighting for a better America."[14] A prime example cited by Clark was that "Ben Rahn, who was with us as we launched our campaign in Little Rock ... along with Matt DeBergalis and their great team, created ActBlue."[15] As of September 2007, ActBlue had raised more than $26 million for Democratic candidates and committees in just over three years. That's a significant legacy of the Clark activists, and the netroots more broadly, right there.

Looking ahead, Yosem Companys believes that "future campaign managers will need to find the 'sweet spot' between decentralized organizing online and centralized political campaigning." We agree. In 2003–2004, both Howard Dean and Wesley Clark failed, for a variety of reasons, to find that spot. In 2005, and even more so in 2006, we began to see strong signs that the sweet spot would not remain elusive forever.

Chapter 4

TAKING ON DELAY, INC.

When the Internet-fueled Howard Dean and Wesley Clark campaigns collapsed in early 2004, many observers were quick to write off the impact blogs had on American politics as a flash in the pan, like the "dot com" business boom of the late 1990s. Similarly, when Tom DeLay won the Texas redistricting fight in 2003, some observers assumed that those who opposed him had been permanently brushed aside. Both assumptions would prove to be wrong.

In fact, the netroots organizing of 2003 brought thousands of new activists into the political process. Concern over the Iraq War, combined with the power of online communications, helped keep them involved. For instance, several blogs launched in 2002 and 2003 went on to become much more widely read in 2004 and beyond. In addition, the netroots raised so much money for John Kerry in 2004 that the Democratic nominee came close to matching the incumbent's incredible haul of $360 million. Kerry raised $317 million, an extraordinary sum by any standard. Also, the Dean and Clark Meetups engendered face-to-face relationships that led participants to get involved with other races. People who had never been politically active before the Dean or Clark campaigns turned into serious activists, volunteering for campaigns from the national level down to town council and school board contests. Political neophytes became participants, even pillars, of their party.

HOWARD DEAN CRASHES IN A PERFECT STORM

On December 2, 2003, the first day that candidates could file to appear on the March 9, 2004, Texas Democratic primary ballot, a sizable contingent of reporters was on hand as Glen Maxey and his Dean volunteers handed in more than 20,000 petition signatures for Howard Dean. Most of the other campaigns had opted to pay the $2,500 filing fee, but Maxey had shrewdly focused volunteer efforts on the ballot petition option. Maxey's strategy served several purposes: it gave volunteers a useful task with a clear goal, it built a large contact list of Texans sympathetic to Dean, it sent a message about Dean's broad support, and it provided for some colorful press coverage.

With the Iowa caucuses scheduled for January 19, 2004, Glen Maxey organized hundreds of Texans to travel to that state to canvass for Howard Dean. Supporters of Dean expected their candidate to win; few if any foresaw that their hopes, born during a hot Texas summer, would crash and burn in the snow-covered cornfields of Iowa.

When Austin activist Trei Brundrett arrived at the Des Moines Dean headquarters a few days before the caucus, he recalls that "[t]here were tons of people there, but no one was really in charge." Brundrett describes the scene further:

> There was a whole drama with people fussing about which color hat they got and what kind of badges they were given. There was a whole hierarchy of hats; I got an orange hat and a printed badge. Some people were mad because they didn't get [a hat] at all or they got a hand-drawn badge.

Later, when Brundrett got a look at Kerry headquarters, he noticed that there was little observable excitement, just a bunch of "guys in button-down shirts [with their] heads down at their computer keyboards or on the phone." Kerry staked everything on coming from behind in Iowa, even mortgaging his house to finance the effort. He brought in veteran organizer Michael Whouley, a

A Texas Orange Hat in Iowa, January 2004. Courtesy of Karl Thomas Musselman.

legendary operative who had headed up Bill Clinton's field efforts in 1992. Whouley put together an efficient and lean organization that focused like a laser on one goal—winning the Iowa caucuses.

Whouley's strategy emphasized securing support from the local political leaders who dominate Iowa's unusual caucus format, in which voters meet face to face and publicly declare which candidate they support. Kerry's team capitalized on their candidate's war hero status, recruiting hundreds of Vietnam veterans to participate in the caucuses for the first time. According to Kerry organizer Jim Spencer, another veteran operative brought to Iowa from Massachusetts, Kerry's relative lack of volunteers enabled the campaign to better focus on training the supporters they did have. According to Spencer, "We knew our guys were going to show up and we knew they knew what to do when they got there because we were able to pay a lot of attention to each and every volunteer."

In contrast to the discipline and focus that characterized the Iowa Kerry campaign, Dean supporters found themselves in a chaotic atmosphere filled with the pumped-up volunteers that Dean's insurgent campaign had attracted. As Dean volunteers canvassed registered voters who had attended previous Iowa caucuses, Glen Maxey learned that anyone could participate in them. And, because of Iowa's same-day voter registration laws, they didn't even have to be registered to vote. Maxey aide Rick Cofer calls this the campaign's "ah-ha!" moment: "It meant that all [the canvassers] had to do was find new voters who were for Dean. Instead they were spending all this energy trying to persuade people who had attended the caucuses in the past."

Brundrett remembers attending a big rally a few days before the caucuses at Iowa State University, where rocker Joan Jett and comedian Janeane Garafalo prepped the crowd for Iowa Senator Tom Harkin, who had endorsed Howard Dean on January 10. Brundrett recalls: "There was this older dude there with his teenage son. They were talking and the older man told his son, 'This is why we're going to lose. All these people are just here to see Dean. They're not here to work.'" Brundrett adds, "I could tell [the father] had done campaigns before and I could tell he was disheartened."

On the day of the Iowa caucuses, Dean volunteers were acutely aware that rival campaigns would be watching for any signs of non-Iowans attempting to participate in the election. At the caucus Brundrett attended, the precinct chair had "taken over the stage for Kerry and there were giant round 'Real Deal' Kerry stickers on either side of the stage." According to Brundrett, "The Edwards people had one wall marked off and they were very organized. You could see lots of Dean people, but they were not organized and were just wandering around. One woman carried a homemade 'Dean is right to be mad' sign, and the Dean people gravitated to her. The Kerry people sat on risers right on the stage behind the precinct chair." As Brundrett left the caucus, he observed "a guy, clearly from Massachusetts, going back and forth from the gym to the auditorium and calling in numbers on his cell phone." Brundrett overheard him saying "we're going to win, we've got this wrapped up." And they did. Kerry finished first with 38 percent of the vote, followed by John Edwards at 32 percent, and Howard Dean at 18 percent. The results of the caucuses clearly demonstrate that Kerry's focus on running a disciplined top-down operation trumped the immense but unchanneled enthusiasm of the orange-hat Deaniacs. The failure of Dean's professional operatives in Iowa to effectively organize their army of volunteers actually managed to turn Dean's people-powered advantage into a liability, contributing to the loss of a state that Dean had been widely expected to win.

This was a discouraging result for a candidate who had led in the polls just a few weeks earlier. Brundrett arrived at Dean's "victory" party in time to hear Glen Maxey tell his Texas activists, "We've got a national organization. We'll recover. Gary Hart lost because he didn't have a national organization."

None of the assembled Dean supporters knew that things were about to get much worse. According to those who were at the party, nobody noticed anything unusual about Dean's pep-rally-style speech. The auditorium was packed with raucous activists. But when the cable news networks' video of the event filtered out the background noise and isolated Dean's hoarse voice attempting to fire up the crowd, the candidate came across as someone whose finger you wouldn't want on the nation's nuclear button.

Late that evening in a hotel bar, still unaware of what would come to be known as the "Dean scream," Brundrett and a group of Texas Dean volunteers ran into a clutch of media types, including Chris Matthews, Tucker Carlson, and Paul Begala. When Brundrett happened upon Begala in the restroom, he did not understand what Begala meant when he said, "Your guy really screwed up." But when Brundrett returned to the hotel bar and saw that CNN was replaying Dean's "scream" in an endless loop, he understood. According to Brundrett, "Chris Matthews hadn't mentioned the scream when he was talking to us earlier. But as soon as he saw it playing on CNN he dashed out of the bar. Twenty minutes later we saw him on the TV also running the loop of the scream." Dean never recovered.

Many in the media and the political establishment were quick to conclude that netroots organizing is an inherently flawed model that generates a lot of excitement but doesn't win elections. We could not disagree more. An energized and engaged citizenry is essential to our democracy and is exactly what is needed to counter the cynicism and passivity that have plagued our politics in recent decades. It is incumbent upon our politicians and organizers to learn to channel the energy of the netroots. In contrast to the leadership of the Clark campaign, Joe Trippi and the Dean campaign did recognize the value and potential of the netroots, but they ultimately failed to turn their online advantage into a decisive election advantage. Howard Dean and his advisors are responsible for the failure of his campaign, not his supporters and volunteers.

BEN BARNES DROPS A BOMBSHELL

Returning to December 2003, when the Dean campaign was reaching its apex and the "scream" was still several weeks off, a pair of aspiring filmmakers in Austin, Texas, Todd Phelan and Mike Nicholson, were busy backing John Kerry. Phelan had long admired Kerry as a war hero, as an effective antiwar activist, as a crusading district attorney, as the senator who had led the Iran-Contra and BCCI (Bank of Credit and Commerce International) corruption investigations in the early 1990s, and as the come-from-behind candidate who had fended off a tough challenge from William Weld in the 1996 U.S. Senate election in Massachusetts. Phelan convinced his friend Nicholson to abandon his flirtations with Howard Dean in favor of John Kerry.

Phelan and Nicholson agreed that the nation's political situation was at a crisis point. They decided to put their careers on hold and focus their energies on the 2004 elections. Looking for ways to get involved, the two political neo-phytes discovered Meetup. In 2007, Phelan recalled,

> I had been a political junkie, reading articles but never getting involved. I didn't really know any political people. Nicholson sent me an e-mail about an upcoming Kerry Meetup and we went. I guess it's one of those things where you start looking for ways to get involved and you find what's out there. Everything starts with word of mouth.

Only a dozen or so Kerry supporters attended the first John Kerry Meetup in Austin in December 2003. Phelan and Nicholson noticed that "most of the people there were just socializing." But, Phelan says, "We had organizing skills and we had web skills. Within a month a core group of activists emerged." Soon, Phelan and Nicholson formed their own group, "Austin for Kerry." They put up a website and began promoting the events with T-shirts, bumper stickers, and ads in local papers. When Kerry won Iowa a few weeks later, the two found themselves at the center of a fast-growing organization.

"It went from a dozen people to a hundred showing up for the Meetups in less than six weeks," Phelan recalls. "By this time, we were setting agendas for the meetings with speakers and planned activities. Soon, the local politicos came courting; they quickly realized we were building a constituency and that the new activists we were bringing in could be funneled into local organizing activities." In April, one local politico invited Phelan and Nicholson to an event where Texas political legend Ben Barnes was to speak. At the time, Phe-lan had only a vague idea of who Barnes was, but when Barnes stood up and declared that he "deeply regretted getting a young George W. Bush special treatment and arranging for him to enter the National Guard instead of facing the draft," Phelan pricked up his ears.

Later that evening, when Phelan and Nicholson researched Barnes on the Internet, they realized that the former lieutenant governor and speaker of the

Texas House of Representatives was a highly credible source. The next day, they contacted Barnes and arranged to videotape an interview in his office. To their disappointment, Barnes danced around the topic and avoided the kind of bold declaration he had made at the earlier political meeting. Barnes was cagey, finally agreeing to speak at the next Austin for Kerry Meetup on May 27.

Nate Wilcox had finagled his way onto the speaking roster of that Meetup to promote a project on which he was working. When Wilcox saw the crowd of 300 people and realized that he was speaking on a program with Ben Barnes, it was a heady moment. Barnes was a legend in Wilcox's family and the subject of whispers at family reunions. Wilcox's only famous relative, former Governor Preston Smith, had been brought down in scandal in the early 1970s and the family universally blamed Ben Barnes. Now, Wilcox found himself sharing a stage with the man once anointed by Lyndon Johnson as "the next Democratic president."

In his late 60s, the charismatic Barnes could still electrify a crowd. Barnes's speech was a classic "Texas barn burner," praising the attendees for their patriotism and urging them to help elect John Kerry. As Barnes shared anecdotes from his twenty-year friendship with John Kerry, the crowd roared its approval. And as Barnes capped his speech with a heartfelt apology for helping George W. Bush evade combat in Vietnam, everyone knew that they were in the presence of history. Barnes declared, "I got a young man named George W. Bush into the Texas National Guard. I got a lot of other people in the National Guard because I thought that was what people should do when you're in office, and you help a lot of rich people." Recalling a recent visit to the Vietnam Memorial, Barnes added, "I looked at the names of the people that died in Vietnam, and I became more ashamed of myself than I have ever been, because it was the worst thing I ever did … I'm very sorry about that, and I'm very ashamed."[1]

Fortunately, Nicholson and Phelan had made a last-minute decision to bring their camera equipment to tape Barnes's remarks. In a few months, that decision would reverberate through the national political arena and indirectly lead to the downfall of another Texas legend, Dan Rather. (In September 2004, CBS News was forced to retract a story on President Bush's Texas Air National Guard service after the authenticity of documents used by Rather in his story was called into question.) In the meantime, Nicholson and Phelan posted the video on the Austin for Kerry website and got back to the hard work of organizing activists.

Phelan soon was contacted by Glen Maxey, the Howard Dean organizer who was now heading the coordinated campaign for the Travis County Democratic Party. Through Maxey, Phelan went to work for the local party in July 2004, becoming a full-time political professional only months after first getting involved. The Democratic Party in liberal Austin was well funded and determined to erase the gains local Republicans had made in 2000 and 2002.

Because of the intensity of opposition to Bush in Austin, a torrent of first-time activists was showing up at Kerry Meetups. Phelan and Maxey put them right to work electing local Democratic candidates.

When the votes were counted on November 2, 2004, the local Republican Party would be virtually extinguished in the Austin area, losing seat after seat and watching their most promising young officials driven from office. The local Democratic tidal wave was obvious by October, as Austin for Kerry events routinely drew thousands of people at six locations across the city. Most of the attendees had discovered the Meetups on John Kerry's website or at Meetup online. Soon, many found themselves spending their weekends working for Maxey to get out the vote for Kerry and other Democrats.

PRELUDE TO RATHERGATE

But even as the reinvigorated local Democratic machine headed for a local electoral sweep, John Kerry was getting pounded by a barrage of incoming fire. The Republican smear machine had launched an unfounded but well-funded attack on Kerry's Vietnam War record. The "Swift Boat Veterans for Truth" don't need their story retold here; the very name has become synonymous with destructive, spurious political smear campaigns. Suffice it to say that in Austin, there was a sudden burst of interest in Democratic circles regarding George Bush's Vietnam War records.

Journalist Jim Moore, co-author of the definitive biography of Karl Rove, *Bush's Brain*, found the video of Barnes's speech on the Austin for Kerry website one morning in late August 2004. Moore had pursued Barnes for years in his attempts to confirm the story, but he had come no closer than a sealed deposition Barnes gave in the 1990s. Moore knew immediately that Barnes's forthright statement, "I helped George W. Bush evade the draft," would reverberate nationally. Within hours, he had e-mailed the link to more than 400 journalists and bloggers.

The next day the *Los Angeles Times*, *Salon*, and the *New York Times* all contacted Phelan and Nicholson. But CBS News producer Marla Mapes was by far the most eager for the story. Phelan and Nicholson hustled a Betamax copy of the tape to the local CBS affiliate so that it could be aired as the top story on the Saturday edition of the *CBS Evening News*. Word came that the story would be held, as Ben Barnes had agreed to an interview with *60 Minutes* to air the following Sunday, September 5. (In the end, Barnes's interview aired on *60 Minutes II* with Dan Rather on Wednesday, September 8.)

The netroots pounced on the story. Josh Marshall of Talking Points Memo led the charge, posting dozens of articles on the topic over the next week. For instance, Marshall reported on September 1 that "the Bush folks in Texas have made it clear to [Barnes] that if he spills the beans about the president that they'll do everything in their power to put him out of business in the state."[2]

Marshall added that the "heat" on Barnes had "increased dramatically in recent days."[3] On August 29, Marshall wrote, "not only has Barnes been consistent and his account not been questioned, even Bush himself and his campaign have accepted Barnes's account."[4] Marshall added, "All they have insisted on—though it is *quite* improbable—is that they did not know at the time about his actions and were not involved in any way in requesting it."[5] All in all, the work on this story by Josh Marshall of Talking Points Memo provides an excellent case study in how blogs can focus on a story, amplify it, increase and intensify interest, deconstruct the political spin, and provide additional analysis and research.

Meanwhile, local political operative, veteran media consultant, and former *Houston Chronicle* reporter Glenn Smith had been researching Bush's National Guard record since the Swift Boat attacks on Kerry began. Smith, deeply frustrated by the Kerry campaign's nonresponse to the slanderous attack, put together his own plan to respond to the Swift Boaters. In August 2004, Smith managed to find a retired lieutenant colonel, Robert Mintz, who had served in Bush's Alabama National Guard unit while the future president completed his service requirements. Most interesting, however, was the fact that Mintz could not recall ever having seen Bush on the base. Smith convinced Mintz to appear in a television ad and formed a "Section 527" political advocacy group, Texans for Truth, to put the ads on television. Smith lined up several donors who wanted to help, including MoveOn founder Wes Boyd.

In late August 2004, MoveOn e-mailed about a third of its national members, calling on them to donate money to help air the ads. Within hours, more than $150,000 had poured in, nearly doubling Texans for Truth's war chest. With Barnes scheduled to appear on *60 Minutes II* and Glenn Smith gearing up for a series of television debates with Swift Boat spokesman John O'Neill, momentum seemed to be building for the Democrats' counter to the Swift Boat attacks on John Kerry.

For a brief moment, it appeared that the amateur organizers of Austin for Kerry had helped their candidate strike back against a barrage of slander. Had Ben Barnes's revelation that he had pulled strings to get George Bush into the National Guard in the 1960s been the only story that appeared on *60 Minutes II*, it is possible that the course of the 2004 election would have been changed. Instead, Dan Rather and Mary Mapes chose to combine the Barnes interview with another feature on Bush's National Guard service. The other story featured memos that *60 Minutes II* claimed were written by Bush's commanding officer in the Texas National Guard. The media uproar that resulted when questions were raised about the provenance of the memos completely drowned out Barnes's admissions.

The Austin activists unleashed numerous forces when they released the video of Ben Barnes admitting that he had pulled strings to help George Bush avoid going to Vietnam. And these forces soon spun out of control. A combination of irresponsible reporting on the part of *60 Minutes II*, a ferocious backlash from the right wing, and a national media seemingly incapable of discussing more than one thing at a time made it all for naught.

Todd Phelan recalls, "As a longtime supporter of Kerry—someone who was aware of Kerry's full record as a war hero, an opponent of the war, a crusading prosecutor, the man who shut down BCCI and investigated Iran-Contra, it was heartbreaking to watch them transform him into a flip-flopping terrorist lover." It was equally heartbreaking to watch a potentially election-changing revelation about the character of George W. Bush—in part coming out of the Austin for Kerry group—get mired in the maddening media babble of the television news.

"IN TOUCH LIKE A PRISON GUARD"

Elsewhere in Texas, netroots activists focused their political energies on battling another Texas Republican, Tom DeLay. The conventional political wisdom held that challenging entrenched, well-funded incumbents like DeLay served no purpose. DeLay's district had been redrawn deliberately to be overwhelmingly Republican—more than 70 percent of the electorate in the district had voted Republican in the past. The same changes to the political environment that powered the candidacies of Howard Dean and Wesley Clark in 2003, however, would dramatically change the dynamic in a campaign against Tom DeLay.

In late 2003, Sugar Land environmental attorney Richard Morrison was making plans to run against Tom DeLay. On December 8, an interview with Morrison was published on the Texas blog, Off the Kuff. The blog's founder was Charles Kuffner, who actually is credited as being the first Texas political blogger and therefore known as "The Texas Blogfather." Kuffner was excited, because he had never before been approached by a candidate to do an interview. At that point in the development of the political blogosphere, candidate appearances on blogs were not at all common. But Morrison knew he would have to run a different kind of campaign against Tom DeLay, and reaching out to the blogs appeared to be a smart strategy.

In his blog interview, Morrison expressed his desire to do more than vote against DeLay. Morrison praised Democrat Tim Riley for running against DeLay in 2002, but asserted that Riley "just didn't raise enough money to get his message out." Morrison asserted that the federal budget under DeLay's leadership was a "car wreck." Morrison accused DeLay of having "abandoned the district" on transportation and other issues. People in the Houston area were looking to alternatives like rail, yet "DeLay [was] telling them to keep [their] mouth shut." Instead, Morrison argued, DeLay was interested in a "roads only" alternative that would surely lead to gridlock. Morrison's overarching theme was that DeLay was not connected to his district in a constructive way. Driving home this point, Morrison charged that DeLay was "in touch like a prison guard."[6]

While Morrison was trying to drum up support for his candidacy, Nick Lampson—an incumbent in a district that had been redistricted out of existence by DeLay—also was considering a run. Lampson was a beloved Beaumont educator and a respected congressman. The problem for Richard Morrison was that as Lampson mulled over his option to run, Morrison was severely limited in his ability to raise the money he needed to launch a serious campaign.

A more sinister factor came into play as well. Tom DeLay had long made it clear to the Houston area business community and civic leadership that anyone supporting a Democrat against him would pay a serious price. "The Hammer," as DeLay was nicknamed, was not known for making idle threats. And even if the Democratic establishment didn't take Morrison seriously, it appeared that DeLay did: A local talk-radio DJ had begun reporting that "a local millionaire trial lawyer is going to challenge Tom DeLay and is promising to spend $3 million of his own money to do it."[7] Unfortunately, Morrison was no millionaire.

Morrison was committed to running an open, netroots campaign. In his December 2003 blog interview with Charles Kuffner, Morrison had discussed this strategy, noting that his campaign had set up a website that allowed people to contribute online and enabled them to contact the campaign via e-mail. Morrison said he intended to respond to those e-mails "like a blog." He encouraged "people who have lists" of friends to provide them to his campaign. And he expressed his goal of developing an online presence "much like Howard Dean's."[8]

According to Vince Leibowitz—a Texas journalist, political consultant, and blogger—Morrison "was the first Texas candidate to make effective use of the Internet." Leibowitz was particularly impressed with the Morrison campaign's use of its website and e-mail for fundraising and organizing. In addition, Leibowitz noted, "That was the first campaign in Texas that ever did any real organized and coordinated outreach to blogs and bloggers."

In contrast to Tom DeLay, Morrison declared that his goal was not to be "the most powerful man in Congress," but rather "to go up there and represent the people of my district."[9] Morrison definitely didn't intend to "have all of these outsiders and all of these industry groups say, 'Here. Here's $2,000. We want you to vote this way.'"[10] The Bankston family—Don, Susan, and their son Bryan—were among the first people in the district to support Morrison. Susan Bankston ran a website called Juanita's, the World's Most Dangerous Hair Salon, where she had been lambasting DeLay and the local GOP establishment since 1992. Her site predated blogs, but her snarky attitude and nose for scandal foreshadowed the tone and content of the most successful blogs. Bankston's husband Don, the president of the Fort Bend Democrats, would prove to be a strong ally for Morrison.

CAMPAIGNING ON A SHOESTRING

By spring 2004, Texas district lines for that year's congressional elections were set. Nick Lampson decided to file for a neighboring open district rather than challenge DeLay directly. Lampson's musings about running against DeLay had hampered Morrison's early fundraising efforts, but Lampson nonetheless did Morrison a huge favor by sharing his polling of DeLay's district. That polling clearly indicated that DeLay was not a safe incumbent. Shockingly, nearly half of DeLay's constituents had an unfavorable view of the most powerful man in Congress.

No sooner had Lampson cleared the field than a second Democrat entered the race. The other candidate was a young man in his twenties, Eric Saenz, who had just moved to the area and, other than showing up at a few local Democratic events, had done virtually no campaigning. This was not much of a challenge for Morrison. Morrison's cultivation of the netroots, his aggressive style, and Saenz's lackluster performance gave Morrison a comfortable victory in the March 9 Democratic primary, with 71 percent of the vote. Now Morrison stood toe to toe with Tom DeLay, exactly where he had wanted to be for the past six months.

After the primary, Democratic consultant Jeff Hewitt, already a twelve-year veteran of political campaigns at the ripe old age of thirty-two, devised a budget that would work for Morrison's shoestring campaign. Well-run, traditional campaigns normally spend at least 70 percent of their money on mass communications, mostly television ads and direct mail in the last three weeks before an election. Given his financial constraints, Morrison couldn't run that kind of campaign. With the reluctance of large donors to come on board, the campaign had to raise money from numerous small donors across the country. Securing these donations required an aggressive online campaign involving paid advertising and consultants to write blogs and manage an e-mail campaign. In 2003, Howard Dean had demonstrated that it was possible to use the Internet to build a presidential candidate's war chest in $5, $10, and $15 increments. The question was whether it would work for Morrison at the congressional level.

Hewitt was well aware that he would have to work hard to get Morrison's name out to the Democratic netroots activists and to raise money online. Hewitt set up a budget that could pay Nate Wilcox to devote many hours each week to the online aspect of the campaign, while still putting aside enough money to afford mass communications at the end of the race. The budget also allowed enough room for a campaign manager—Kyle Johnston, fresh from South Carolina where he had worked for the Dean campaign—and a volunteer coordinator—Melissa Taylor, a local Dean activist taking her first political job—to organize things on the ground.

MORRISON, MARKOS, AND THE "MERCENARIES"

Given this netroots-focused strategy, it was crucial for Morrison to grab the attention of Texas and national Democrats who had been energized by the Dean and Clark campaigns and who were now in the habit of making online political contributions. The key to winning over this community was Markos Moulitsas Zúniga, owner of the largest and most influential pro-Democratic website, Daily Kos.

Moulitsas, a diehard political junkie, wanted to focus his energy and coverage on the most competitive congressional races. The match between incumbent Democrat Martin Frost and Republican challenger Pete Sessions in the newly drawn Texas Thirty-Second Congressional District looked like just such a contest. The district had been purposely redrawn to make it impossible for a Democrat to win, but Frost had top-notch fundraising abilities and one of the best operations in Texas Democratic politics. In 2002, Congressman Frost had run against Nancy Pelosi for House minority leader, before throwing his support to her once he realized she was going to win. Now, thanks to Tom DeLay's unprecedented, legally dubious redistricting scheme, Frost was fighting for his political life.

Frost's team was headed by his capable, longtime right-hand man, Matt Angle. Angle was intrigued with the idea of advertising on Democratic blogs after seeing the tremendous fundraising impact those blog ads had created for Howard Dean in 2003 (and also for Ben Chandler's successful special election in Kentucky in February 2004). Getting the Frost campaign to sit down with Moulitsas proved difficult, however. Moulitsas was interested in featuring Frost's race on Daily Kos, but first he wanted to see the campaign's poll numbers. The Frost campaign's response was something to the effect of, "We don't even share those with our staff."

After much discussion, the Frost campaign and Moulitsas gingerly came together. Wilcox, as the Frost campaign's online consultant, decided to pitch a skeptical Moulitsas on Morrison's uphill race. In March 2004, Frost placed ads on Daily Kos. In addition, a time was scheduled for Moulitsas to meet the Frost team and watch a presentation about the campaign's top-line poll numbers. Then, on April 1, four American employees of Blackwater USA, a private firm operating in Fallujah, Iraq, were burned and mutilated by a mob. The charred remains of two of the men were hung from a bridge crossing the Euphrates River. Americans watching this grisly spectacle on their television screens were horrified. At Daily Kos on April 1, Moulitsas commented on the incident as follows:

> Let the people see what war is like. This isn't an Xbox game. There are real repercussions to Bush's folly. That said, I feel nothing over the death of mercenaries. They aren't in Iraq because of orders, or because they are there trying to help the people make Iraq a better place. They are there to wage war for profit. Screw them.[11]

When the phone in his office rang early the next morning, Wilcox wasn't fully awake yet. "Take our damn ads off that damn site," said the familiar but usually friendly voice of Martin Frost's campaign manager. "What? Huh?" Wilcox asked. "We're getting hundreds of e-mails about some comment Moulitsas made. Something about 'screw the people who died in Fallujah.' That's a TV ad, man, that could cost us the race. Confirm he said it and we'll need to pull the ads now." This was followed by a click and a dial tone.

Over a period of months, Wilcox had constructed Frost's website and had convinced the campaign to buy blog ads on Daily Kos. Wilcox had spent the previous weeks acting as a go-between, trying to build a working relationship between the fiery Moulitsas and the cynical but talented operatives who worked for Martin Frost. Now, it all appeared to be crashing down.

Frost pulled his ads immediately. Other advertisers quickly followed suit. Wilcox's other client with an ad on Daily Kos at the time was a challenger from Ohio's Third Congressional District named Jane Mitakides. At first, Mitakides seemed to be holding firm, keeping her ad on Daily Kos in the face of a ferocious campaign organized by the right-wing blogs. Mitakides was even beginning to garner support from Daily Kos readers who were stunned to see how quickly their party leaders had abandoned Moulitsas.

But Mitakides only appeared to be standing resolute. The real story was simply that she couldn't be reached all day Friday, April 2, or over the weekend. On Monday morning, Wilcox finally got her on the phone. All she could say was, "Well I *have* to pull the ad don't I? I'm getting all this terrible e-mail."

Wilcox tried to convince Mitakides that the damage was already done and that by staying on Daily Kos she would become a hero to the burgeoning netroots. Wilcox made the case that if Mitakides stood her ground, she would benefit from a fundraising bonus over the remaining seven months of the campaign. He reminded Mitakides that few of the hundreds of people who had contacted her campaign even lived in her district. But Mitakides pulled her ads, missing her chance to become a netroots hero and ultimately losing her election by a wide margin (62 to 38 percent).

When Wilcox told Richard Morrison about the controversy over Moulitsas's comments on the contractors, Morrison's response was immediate, "Hell, let's put an ad up there. I'm not afraid of Tom DeLay, and I'm certainly not afraid to advertise on Daily Kos." Morrison's blog ad became a huge hit on the site and was the first step in making Morrison a netroots star.

LOYALTY HAS ITS REWARDS

It didn't take long for the budding relationship between the Morrison campaign and Moulitsas to begin paying real dividends. In the last week of April 2004, the Morrison campaign slipped Moulitsas a memo covering the highlights from Nick Lampson's October 2003 poll of the district. Moulitsas ran with it, and the diary he posted on April 28 created the first buzz of excitement around the race:

> I've gotten my hands on some polling data from the district, and it's surprisingly poor for DeLay. His Approval/Disapprovals are 44/48. On the reelect

question, 36 percent would definitely vote for him, 27 percent would consider someone else, and 27 percent would definitely vote for someone else....

The redistricting battle, while a massive victory for DeLay and the GOP,
took a toll on his popularity. And the Earle investigation in Austin—the
one that threatens to indict DeLay—has also garnered him repeated bad
press. And let's not forget the aides who got caught billing Indian tribes $45
million for lobbying.

DeLay is a thug, and it shouldn't be surprising that people in his own
district might be growing tired of him. Those reelect numbers are pretty
brutal. And his money position isn't, to be frank, as overwhelming as might
be expected....

Richard Morrison is the David to the DeLay Goliath. His chances of
winning are slim, but he could be well-positioned to pick up the pieces of a
DeLay implosion. And even if DeLay survives, a little funding could go a
long way toward forcing DeLay to spend time and money on his own race,
rather than other close House races.[12]

Morrison was at his law office meeting with his campaign manager, Kyle Johnston, when Johnston's Palm Treo started going crazy. Johnston had the device
set to buzz anytime the campaign received an online contribution. It began
buzzing, and before Johnston could make his way around the large conference
room table where it sat, the Treo had buzzed so much it actually had fallen on
the floor. Before the day was done, seventy contributions had come in worth
more than $3,000, which was more than the campaign had raised in the entire
month of April.

Compared to the epic sums that Howard Dean had raised online the previous summer, this was small potatoes. But for Richard Morrison's struggling
campaign, it was huge. Wilcox suddenly felt confident that this race against
Tom DeLay would amount to something serious. Wilcox's hunch, that a
national constituency was willing to donate money to a candidate who could
give DeLay a good fight, appeared to be coming true. Over the next three
days, another $10,000 poured in.

For Wilcox, the key challenge would be to come up with a steady stream of
news that could keep the excitement building and the Morrison campaign on
the front pages of Daily Kos and other blogs. One obvious idea was to bring
in Howard Dean. But many Democratic candidates in conservative districts
didn't want Howard Dean campaigning for them because of his image as a liberal firebrand. Wilcox had talked this through many times with Richard Morrison, whose initial inclination was to follow the Chet Edwards model.

Chet Edwards was a conservative Democratic congressman from the Waco
area who typically kept the national Democratic Party at arm's length. Edwards
ran on local issues as well as on his strong personal relationships with friends
and neighbors. One of five incumbent Texas Democrats whose congressional

districts had been redrawn in DeLay's 2003 power grab, Edwards worked hard to distinguish himself from John Kerry, Hillary Clinton, and especially Howard Dean. The other embattled incumbents—Nick Lampson (who had chosen to run in a different district on the other side of Houston rather than challenge Tom DeLay), Martin Frost, Max Sandlin, and Charlie Stenholm—adopted identical tactics. The question was whether Richard Morrison would follow their lead or strike out in a different direction.

CHRIS BELL RINGS UP AN ETHICS COMPLAINT

One of the Democratic congressmen targeted by DeLay, Houston's Chris Bell, had already been beaten in a primary challenge by an African American judge, Al Green, in early March 2004. DeLay's plan succeeded in its short-term goal of getting Bell, a popular figure in Houston with obvious statewide ambitions, out of Congress. But Bell proved to be a resilient adversary. Immediately after his primary defeat, Bell—still a congressman for the remainder of his term—filed a wide-ranging ethics complaint against DeLay with the U.S. House Committee on Standards of Official Conduct (the Ethics Committee). In the works for months, the complaint was extremely well documented and alleged the worst sort of malfeasance by the majority leader: violations of federal bribery statutes, illegal funneling of corporate money into partisan election efforts, improper use of his office to pressure federal agencies to assist in partisan objectives unrelated to DeLay's official duties, and more.

The House Ethics Committee had basically been sidelined by an "ethics truce" between the two parties at the end of Newt Gingrich's reign as House speaker. Gingrich had made aggressive use of ethics complaints to bring down Speaker Jim Wright and other Democratic powerhouses like Dan Rostenkowski. Eventually, Gingrich's own fall would be expedited by ethics complaints filed against him.

The Democrats and Republicans, tired of "mutual assured destruction," had informally and secretly agreed to lodge no more ethics complaints against one another. The principled and courageous Bell was willing to defy this cozy arrangement. Bell assembled his documentation and, along with his staff, found his way to the sleepy, dusty basement office of the House Ethics Committee to make his case. It was a strong one.

MORRISON TAKES A ROCK STAR TURN

After a few months of beating his head against the wall trying to get the help of the Texas Democratic establishment, Morrison won the nomination and his approach evolved. Initially drawn to the Chet Edwards model of distancing himself from the rest of the Democratic Party, Morrison realized that such an approach would not work for his underdog, netroots-oriented campaign. Instead, Morrison decided to take help wherever he could get it, including from perceived liberals like Howard Dean, left-leaning blogs like Daily Kos, and radio shows like *Air America* and the *Ed Schulz Show*—where Morrison became a frequent guest over the course of the summer. The alternative to accepting this help was for Morrison to go quietly into the good night, ignored and unfunded, as numerous other would-be challengers to Tom DeLay had done before. That was not an attractive alternative.

By late May 2004, things were beginning to look up for the Morrison campaign. The rate at which money was coming in from the blogs had actually increased. Endorsements by Howard Dean's Democracy for America and Daily Kos brought immediate windfalls, as did Morrison's numerous *Air America* and *Ed Schulz Show* radio appearances.

Morrison built on his momentum by taking a rock star turn at the Texas State Democratic Convention in June. The convention was held in Houston, close enough to Morrison's home base in Sugar Land for dozens of his volunteers to turn out in their soon-to-be-trademark blue shirts. Everywhere Morrison went at the convention, he was surrounded by a clamoring throng of those blue shirts, and his booth, featuring a basketball goal that conventioneers could take a toss at for a cash contribution, was the hit of the event.

Morrison was the sole candidate to attend the inaugural Texas bloggers' caucus held at the convention. By 2006, such events would be packed with candidates seeking endorsements from the blogs. But in 2004, few candidates even knew what blogs were, and those who did felt they were a potential source of controversy best avoided. The conventional political wisdom after the losses of Howard Dean and Wesley Clark in 2003 was that online support did not translate to votes and, therefore, consorting with bloggers was not worth the risk.

After the blogger conference at the state convention, Greg Wythe of the Texas blog Greg's Opinion offered a prescient take on Morrison and his campaign:

> Morrison is doing well: making himself available is the biggest and best thing for him. His volunteer base is enviable for even the most incumbent Congressman, the quantity of his free publicity does not seem to hurt one iota, and he's well beyond personable. The more people that get to see him in small-crowd settings such as we had, the better.[13]

Unfortunately, Morrison's grassroots popularity never translated into establishment support. Houston Mayor Bill White refused to be photographed with Morrison for fear that DeLay would somehow punish the entire city of Houston. The Texas Democratic Party scheduled Morrison's only speech at the convention early in the morning, and vice-presidential nominee John Edwards greeted Morrison with a blank stare.

The campaign kept working the blogs and hitting the e-mail list to keep the money rolling in, but the momentum slowed over the summer. A CNN crew spent half a day interviewing Morrison and traveling around DeLay's district, but the story never aired.

During the long, hot Texas August, the Morrison team put together its own camera crew and had them spend a day with the candidate. They traveled the district in a black rented Chevy Suburban, taping the candidate talking to the camera. A script was available, but it quickly became apparent that Morrison excelled at speaking off the cuff.

The video was cut down to a sixty-second spot that was released for fundraising. It was then cut again to thirty seconds for cable television. By a stroke of good fortune, the cable advertising zones almost perfectly overlapped the district. The ads would not have the reach of expensive broadcast advertising, but dollars would not be squandered in the massive Houston media market either.

Morrison's first ad presented a likable, earnest candidate struggling through traffic jams on the notorious freeways linking the suburban district to Houston. The ad also depicted Morrison meeting regular folks at restaurants and on the light rail train while saying, "I don't want to be the most powerful man in Washington, D.C., I just want to be the congressman from District Twenty-Two."[14]

PILING ON TOM DELAY

Travis County District Attorney Ronnie Earle and his staff were investigating DeLay's actions in the 2002 Texas elections. Through an eccentricity of Texas law, the district attorney of Travis County, which contains Austin (the state capital), has jurisdiction over any violation of Texas election law. Initially reluctant to pursue a case, Earle and his team had been swayed by the evidence uncovered by Texas clean campaign advocate Fred Lewis (who had brought DeLay's criminal activities to light during the 2002 campaign) and Austin attorney Chris Feldman.

In late September 2004, the Morrison-DeLay race took a dramatic turn when Earle secured indictments against three of DeLay's political associates, his TRMPAC, several corporate donors, and the Texas Association of Business for funneling corporate money into Texas state elections. Texas elections allow unlimited donations from individuals and are overseen by a state ethics commission so lax that it ruled checks could be declared as contributions without listing the amount given. But the few rules that do exist are strictly enforced. For instance, it's a felony to spend corporate donations electioneering for a candidate in a Texas state race. Now, Tom DeLay's PAC was being indicted for doing just that.

The indictments elevated the story of DeLay's corruption from the blogs to the major media. In Houston, the local television news stations began to cover the seamy side of the race, while the *Houston Chronicle* did its best to ignore the growing scandal.

The dam broke on October 1, 2004, when the U.S. House of Representatives Ethics Committee cited DeLay on multiple counts of election fraud, including trading favors for votes. The story made the front pages of the *Washington Post* and the *Houston Chronicle*, received saturation coverage on the local and cable news channels, and sent a shockwave through the race.

Suddenly, it wasn't just a bunch of liberal bloggers accusing DeLay of corruption. It was no longer just one-term Congressman Chris Bell filing an ethics complaint. Now, the Republican-controlled House Ethics Committee had officially "admonished" DeLay for misconduct.

Fred Lewis found himself getting calls from reporters in Washington. Lewis had been pestering reporters locally and nationally for months and had been roundly ignored. Suddenly, the DeLay, Inc. indictments and the House Ethics Committee's ruling had generated a great interest on the part of the Washington press corps as to what exactly had transpired in the Texas 2002 elections.

"There had been a slow, gradual buildup of stories and attention to the scandals, but suddenly there was a burst of interest because of the indictments," Lewis recalls.

> The details were confusing to people, but because we had archived every single article on the 2002 election scandal on the Clean Up Texas Politics website and added a great deal of analysis from a reform perspective, when a reporter would call me or Chris Feldman about the case, we could just refer them to the website. In addition to the reporters using it for background, suddenly we had tens of thousands of people coming to the website in the final months of 2004. Chris and I became go-to people for quotes when the reporters needed to present the reform side of the case.

Suddenly, the DeLay organization understood they were in the midst of a real campaign. DeLay had not faced a serious reelection challenge since 1986. This had freed DeLay to place key staffers and consultants in charge of TRMPAC and ARMPAC (the Americans for a Republican Majority PAC). DeLay even employed his daughter, Danielle Ferro, as his campaign manager. In sum, DeLay was not prepared for a tough race. Still, money was not an obstacle, and the DeLay campaign quickly went on the offensive.

"THE HAMMER" STRIKES BACK

The first thing DeLay did was to hit the airwaves with positive ads. The idea was to counter "The Hammer's" tough guy image. Texas blogger Charles Kuffner wrote at the time on his Off the Kuff blog that he had seen "an amazingly warm and fuzzy ad run by the DeLay campaign ... and not one but two pro-DeLay ads run by the [conservative] Club for Growth." Kuffner asked rhetorically,

> With all of the competitive races out there, with the battleground and the polls largely favoring the Democrats, is anyone going to seriously suggest that someone isn't a little worried about DeLay's re-election chances? It's not like there aren't plenty of other places where the Club for Growth could spend its money.[15]

Nate Wilcox recalls the day the DeLay campaign first took Richard Morrison's challenge seriously. Wilcox was at his desk one October morning when he got a call from a man who identified himself as being with Fannie Mae. "Why do we appear on the client list on your consulting firm's website?" the caller asked. Wilcox explained that he had done work for the real estate lending giant a few years previously while with his previous employer. Wilcox named the executive to whom he had reported. "Oh, I see," the man said, "well can you please do me a favor and remove us from your client list?"

Wilcox realized that someone had found the link to his website on the footer of Richard Morrison's campaign page and had scoured Wilcox's client list. Only one person could produce such a rapid response from the sluggish giant Fannie Mae, and that person was Tom DeLay. Wilcox's months of caution and paranoia about Internet security now seemed pointless—clearly the most powerful man in Congress hadn't been paying attention until he got bad polling numbers. DeLay hadn't even bothered to do professional opposition research on Morrison; instead, DeLay's campaign manager daughter and her local staff had done a last-minute scan of their opponent's website and found material for a few cheap shots.

The one thing that the DeLay people seemed most excited about was a tenuous link between Morrison and the controversial political character, Lyndon Larouche. The Larouche people occupied the fringes of the political spectrum, but they were also passionately anti-DeLay. So, the Morrison campaign had accepted their volunteer help, and one of their events had appeared on Morrison's public campaign calendar. DeLay aggressively hawked the revelation to the press.

"A LEGITIMATE CHANCE TO WIN"

David Donnelly, a longtime advocate of clean elections who previously had helped to revamp election laws in Maine and Arizona, was stunned by the House Ethics Committee findings and had decided to focus on DeLay. "We saw it as an incredible moment to take DeLay—one member of Congress using his position of power to enrich his donors and increase the Republican majority—and make him a symbol of what was wrong in Washington," Donnelly later recalled.

Donnelly's nonprofit, nonpartisan organization, Campaign Money Watch, polled DeLay's district and found that years of pay-to-play politics had taken their toll on DeLay's popularity. Many of DeLay's constituents recognized that they ranked a distant third on DeLay's priority list—after building his own personal power base and establishing a "permanent Republican majority" in Congress.

Campaign Money Watch felt that it could play an important role in election reform by bringing those issues to the attention of DeLay's constituents. Initially, Donnelly approached other progressive organizations, seeking allies and strength in numbers. Other than Howard Dean's Democracy for America, however, nobody believed that taking on DeLay was worth the effort or the risk. And, to avoid even the appearance that Campaign Money Watch was coordinating with a partisan, political campaign, the scrupulous Donnelly broke off contact with Democracy for America as soon as he realized that it had endorsed Morrison.

In mid-October 2004, Donnelly launched a blog, the Daily DeLay, and e-mailed Campaign Money Watch's 18,000 members, all of whom had previously signed one of the group's petitions on money in politics. The members pledged more than $30,000 the first weekend, an enormous sum for a list of that size.

The anti-DeLay campaign proved to be a boon to Campaign Money Watch's membership rolls as well as to its bottom line. The group's national list of supporters grew from 18,000 to more than 30,000 in just three weeks. Encouraged by the strong response as well as by some promising polling the group had done, Campaign Money Watch invested $175,000 during October and November 2004 on television ads aimed at DeLay's constituents.

Activists in DeLay's district were highly receptive when Donnelly reached out to them. According to Donnelly, "After twenty-plus years of being represented by what many called the most corrupt member of Congress, people there were just sick of it. Everyone we contacted was very excited about the district getting interest from a national organization." On October 19, Moulitsas weighed in at Daily Kos: "Remember when we first contributed to this race? Morrison was a nobody. My hope was to simply force DeLay to campaign more in the district, thus keeping him from campaigning and fundraising for other Republicans. Now Morrison is a serious candidate with a legitimate chance to win."[16]

Campaign Money Watch was the only group besides Democracy for America that was willing to invest money in the race against DeLay. For Morrison's campaign, it felt like watching the cavalry ride over the hill. Unfortunately, $165,000 in the huge Houston media market amounted to a pretty small cavalry. It looked even smaller when the conservative Club for Growth began pouring millions of dollars into local media attacking Morrison by name.

Typically, the DeLay organization left nothing to chance. Before long, a man named Thomas Morrison had filed as a Libertarian candidate. In

Houston politics, it is a well-established dirty trick to find a nobody with the same last name as your opponent to file as a candidate. When the Richard Morrison campaign saw the Libertarian's name, it suspected the worst. And when they discovered that the other Morrison was a former employee of former Republican Congressman Dick Armey, they needed no more evidence.

The next surprise was more pleasant. After weeks of refusing to participate in a candidates' debate at the Clear Lake Elementary School scheduled for October 19, DeLay announced thirty minutes before the event that he would attend. For Morrison, an experienced courtroom trial lawyer, this was the moment he'd been waiting for. Morrison supporters packed the room, wearing their trademark blue shirts.

DeLay made a spirited case for his reelection, but Morrison caught him in several contradictions. The crowd clearly backed the challenger. This was a high point for Morrison, who, as *Texas Lawyer* wrote in its October 2004 issue, "finally flushed out DeLay."[17] *Texas Lawyer* added that the majority leader's "mere presence seemed a public acknowledgment that DeLay was in a hard-fought race and perhaps Morrison was someone who needed to be reckoned with."[18]

Austin's Harvey Kronberg, the editor of the Internet insider political tip sheet Quorum Report, credited Morrison with "running a very energetic campaign and not missing any opportunities."[19] Kronberg added that, "anecdotally, I know there are a lot of Republican businessmen in his district who feel DeLay hasn't delivered a lot of bacon to offset the level of discomfort they have with his national profile."[20]

"THE MACHINE NEEDED TO ATTACK"

The admonishment by the House Ethics Committee had generated a lot of bad press for Tom DeLay. The national media began to pick up the story and pursue it even more aggressively than the Houston media ever had. The conservative *Washington Times* wrote a story titled, "DeLay Finds Re-Election Tougher."[21] The results of DeLay's internal polling must have been bad, because his campaign lashed out at Morrison with a sudden angry barrage of television ads and direct mail hit pieces.

According to John Cobarruvias, leader of the Bay Area New Democrats (BAND), an activist group on the eastern side of the district, "It wasn't anything fancy, just 'Liberal, Liberal, Liberal,' which wasn't really accurate at all. Richard Morrison is totally a moderate, not a liberal. But that didn't matter; the machine needed to attack and that's what it came up with."

One DeLay ad was titled "Why?"

Why are Richard Morrison and his liberal friends running a negative campaign against Tom DeLay? To hide his plan to raise your taxes. And Richard

Morrison supports John Kerry's weak and indecisive foreign policy over President Bush's leadership on the war on terror. How liberal is he? He campaigned with Howard Dean and supports radical Michael Moore's campaign to defeat President Bush. Richard Morrison is perfect for John Kerry but not for us. I'm Tom DeLay and I approved this message.[22]

Not exactly subtle, to put it mildly. In response, Morrison went on the local news to discuss DeLay's complaint that he was being assailed by a "left-wing conspiracy." Morrison's best line: "Left-wing conspiracy? He's starting to sound like Hillary Clinton!" The sound of DeLay's veins popping could be heard across the district.

EXCEEDING EXPECTATIONS

But one even bigger surprise was yet to come: on October 21, a Republican precinct chair in DeLay's district, Bev Carter, endorsed Richard Morrison on the pages of the *Fort Bend Star*:

It won't kill you.... Come on, it really won't hurt too much. I promise that parts of your body will not fall off. That's right! You, too, can vote for Democrat Richard Morrison to replace that scoundrel Tom DeLay.[23]

The Morrison campaign hit the blogs and their rapidly growing e-mail list with another solicitation capitalizing on Carter's endorsement. The money poured in during October, including more than $120,000 raised online. In addition, Morrison's incessant phone calls and fundraising events raised a comparable amount.

The sudden influx of cash allowed Morrison to place a response ad during the final game of the 2004 National League championship series featuring the Houston Astros. Reports came back to the campaign that the ad garnered standing ovations in bars across liberal areas of Houston. Unfortunately, not too many bars operated in liberal neighborhoods in Tom DeLay's congressional district. Even worse, DeLay countered Morrison's lone television ad with saturation coverage for the final three weeks of the election, linking Morrison to liberal bogeymen like John Kerry, Hillary Clinton, and Michael Moore.

The week before the November 2, 2004, election—voting occurs early in Texas—Morrison staked out polling locations and talked to people heading into the polls to vote. The first day, Morrison was alone, with no sign of the DeLay campaign. The next day the DeLay team sent a few staffers carrying signs with DeLay's name prominently displayed. That didn't receive such a good reception. Two days later, the staffers changed the signs to read DeLay/Bush. That worked better but not well enough, apparently. By the Thursday before the election, the signs read "Bush/DeLay." The Saturday before the election, the signs had been revised once again, this time to read "Team Bush," with DeLay listed in small print beneath the headline.

The morning of the election, a local television station interviewed Morrison as he shook hands at a polling place. The candidate told them that they were looking at "the next congressman from District Twenty-Two." But that was not to be the case. By 7 P.M., it was clear that DeLay would win easily. The early vote came in heavily for DeLay, and Morrison never caught up. It was a cold, rainy night in the Houston suburbs when Morrison's activist supporters filed sadly home to watch John Kerry lose a presidential race that exit polls had predicted just hours earlier would go his way.

Despite the defeat, Morrison had exceeded expectations. The Twenty-Second District had been drawn to be 70 percent Republican, yet DeLay managed to win only 55 percent of the vote. In a mostly dark election cycle for Democrats, Morrison's loss would be painted as something of a victory. According to Charles Kuffner's postelection analysis, Morrison outpolled John Kerry by seven points across the district. Much of the credit goes to Jeff Hewitt, who devised an innovative cable television advertising plan that made the most of Morrison's limited budget. Morrison campaign staffers Kyle Johnston and Melissa Taylor's effective organizing of Morrison's many local volunteers contributed strongly to the campaign's success. Tom DeLay had been badly wounded, but he would manage to hang on for another year and a half before finally deciding to throw in the towel.

As Jerome Armstrong and Markos Moulitsas Zúniga wrote in their 2006 book *Crashing the Gate: Netroots, Grassroots, and the Rise of People-Powered Politics*, "It wasn't the [Democratic Congressional Campaign Committee] that chose to engage in these races; it was the netroots who took up the fight."[24] The ability of blogs to focus national attention on a long-shot race against the most powerful member of the U.S. Congress changed what would have been a hopeless race into a competitive contest. Richard Morrison's 2004 campaign against Tom DeLay was the most successful of a dozen or so congressional campaigns adopted by the national netroots in that election cycle. The lessons learned in this race and others like it would be applied to the campaigns of 2005 and 2006 with great success. Without Richard Morrison's pioneering effort to run a national netroots campaign in a congressional election—traditionally the largest local race in politics—the later successes of Jon Tester and Jim Webb would have been far less likely.

With regard to Richard Morrison, you might think that a charismatic young candidate—one who had drawn significant votes inside a gerrymandered conservative stronghold and had raised more than $800,000 without the support of traditional Democratic donors—would have been backed eagerly by the Democratic Party establishment against a desperate, damaged Republican opponent. But you would be wrong.

POSTSCRIPT

On November 2, 2004, John Kerry lost the presidential election to George W. Bush by 3 million votes out of 121 million cast. Kerry won nineteen states plus the District of Columbia for 252 electoral votes; Bush won thirty-one states for 286 electoral votes. Many observers attributed Kerry's loss to his campaign's initial decision to ignore the Swift Boat attacks. Finally, when the campaign did respond, it was ineffective—too little, too late. Observers of the bruising race were struck by the stark contrast between the impact of conservative and progressive blogs in the 2004 presidential election. Despite having much larger readerships than the conservative blogs and raising millions more online, it seemed clear that the progressive bloggers had far less impact on the presidential race than did their conservative counterparts.

At two crucial points in the Bush-Kerry contest, right-wing blogs and websites like the Drudge Report had swarmed on John Kerry. First, they had dramatically amplified the charges of the Swift Boat Veterans for Truth. Then, just as Democrats seemed ready to mount an effective counter to those charges—the story on CBS News's *60 Minutes II* that had questioned George W. Bush's Vietnam era service record was crucial—the conservative blogs effectively pushed a counternarrative so quickly that it neutralized the impact of the more serious charges against Bush.

Looking back at that moment in the race, Peter Daou, John Kerry's online outreach coordinator, wondered what had amplified the impact of the relatively low-traffic Republican blogs and diminished that of the far-busier progressive ones. Daou determined that the mainstream media had jumped on right-wing blog stories because Republican spokespeople were swift and unified in repeating them. In contrast, the media had largely ignored stories on progressive blogs in 2004, partly because Democrats, following Bill Clinton's centrist posture, distanced themselves from strong stands made by online progressive activists. And that's no way to win an election in the netroots era.

Chapter 5

WHAT A DIFFERENCE A YEAR MAKES

B y the end of 2004, a pall of near-despair hung over progressives every-where. It wasn't just John Kerry's lost election that had them down. It was the entire past four years, starting with the way George W. Bush became president in 2000, elevated by a Supreme Court that halted Florida's vote recount in a five-to-four decision along partisan lines. As if all that wasn't bad enough, there was also the grim shock of September 11 and the senseless squandering of national unity and global sympathy that followed; tax cuts for people who didn't need them; the Bush administration's assault on the environment, on science, and on reason itself; Vice President Cheney's self-serving, secretive energy task force; and the crude exploitation of the people's grief and fear to hijack the 2002 midterm election.

How could citizens fight this? Certainly, many grassroots movements had been effective in the past—the civil rights and labor movements being prime examples. With the availability of the Internet, however, citizens had more options to express themselves and to organize; they could start a blog, join a politically oriented Yahoo! group, search for information online, and connect with other like-minded people. In short, in the new millennium, citizens could empower themselves in many ways.

Like many others, Lowell Feld had done just that in 2003 and 2004, sup-porting Wesley Clark and then John Kerry. In the aftermath of Kerry's loss, Feld was determined to stay involved in politics. Following the maxim, "think globally, act locally," he decided to do whatever he could to influence Virgin-ia's 2005 governor's race between the Democratic lieutenant governor, Tim Kaine, and the Republican attorney general, Jerry Kilgore. Around New Year's 2005, Feld and his technologically talented friend Eric Grim started a blog called Raising Kaine. The objective was to raise Cain in the sense of stirring things up, but also to raise Tim Kaine to the Virginia governor's mansion in Richmond. Neither of the two Raising Kaine founders had any experience in Virginia politics, which both had largely ignored as they pursued careers in nearby Washington, D.C. For Feld, events in Riyadh or Rabat had held a lot more interest than those in Richmond or Roanoke. This situation would soon change.

RAISING KAINE

Raising Kaine jumped into the Virginia fight aggressively, intending to pre-empt the smash-mouth tactics expected from Republican candidate Jerry Kilgore's notorious media advisor, Scott Howell. In 2002, Howell was the man behind the despicable attack ads that helped send Republican Saxby Chambliss to the U.S. Senate from Georgia. Howell's ads implied that Senator Max Cleland, a triple amputee and a hero of the Vietnam War, was a traitor who had aligned himself with Osama bin Laden and Saddam Hussein for questioning George W. Bush's rush to war in Iraq. The assault on Cleland represented a low point in U.S. politics, and there was ample reason to expect more of the same in Virginia during 2005.

One of the first blog posts on Raising Kaine, "Kilgore's Scumbag Media Advisor," slammed Howell as "one of the nastiest, dirtiest, most vicious men in politics," while expressing impatience at the polite approach that had often kept Democratic candidates on the losing end of knife fights with people like Howell. Instead, Democrats needed to "get ready *right now* to fight back with defenses of Kaine and attacks on Kilgore." And, Raising Kaine noted, "as we've learned from so many Democratic campaigns, we can't count on the 'professionals' to do the job right."[1]

Above all, Raising Kaine introduced a feisty, combative, Democratic group blog onto the Virginia political scene. Previously, the few existing Virginia political blogs had tended to be relatively cordial, collegial affairs. Not that Raising Kaine was against cordiality, but its main purpose was to fight hard for progressive values and for Democratic candidates. Over the past few years, many progressives had grown sick and tired of radical Republicans running—and ruining—the country. They were tired of Democrats who refused to fight back against Republican smear tactics, such as the Swift Boat campaign used to defeat John Kerry. And they were tired of Democratic political professionals who seemed to care more about their commissions than about their candidates.

In early February 2005, Feld attended the state Democratic Party's annual Jefferson-Jackson Day dinner in Richmond along with Sam Penney, a high school student who was one of Raising Kaine's early contributors. The two bloggers introduced themselves to Lieutenant Governor Tim Kaine, who was about to launch his bid for governor of Virginia. Feld told Kaine, "I run the blog Raising Kaine, and our goal is to raise *you* to the governor's mansion!" Whether Kaine thought that was weird, crazy, or naïve is hard to know, but he smiled and took one of the Raising Kaine cards Feld had made for the occasion.

From early 2005 until election day in November, Raising Kaine kept at it, pounding Kilgore and the Republicans while making the case for Tim Kaine and other Democrats. The Raising Kaine bloggers attempted to coordinate with other Virginia Democratic bloggers, although the expression "herding cats" comes to mind in this context (progressive bloggers are an independent, feisty lot). Still, for the most part, the Democratic blogs worked well together, with Waldo Jaquith—one of Virginia's first and best bloggers—leading the way. Jaquith did great work on his eponymous blog, digging into local and state stories more deeply and with more prescience than the corporate media were interested in—or capable of—doing.

From the beginning, the concept was for Raising Kaine to be a full-fledged community blog. The goal was to create a Daily Kos for Virginia, not necessarily in terms of ideology or style, but certainly with regard to Daily Kos's emphasis on building community and helping Democrats win elections.

The Raising Kaine bloggers' strategy was sixfold. First, to rally the fighting spirit of the Democratic base following John Kerry's crushing loss to George W. Bush. Second, to highlight and exacerbate divisions among Republicans wherever possible, portraying them as extremist ideologues when the situation warranted. Third, to nationalize the gubernatorial race as much as possible, tying the Virginia Republican Party to the increasingly unpopular national Republican Party. Fourth, to influence and monitor media coverage of the Kaine-Kilgore race, while providing an information alternative to the woefully inadequate media coverage of Virginia politics. Fifth, to stay disciplined and "on message" as much as possible. And, finally, to define the race on its own terms, keeping the Republicans off balance and never letting an attack on Democratic candidates go unanswered.

On a Saturday morning in July 2005, Feld drove from Arlington, Virginia, to the venerable Greenbrier Hotel in White Sulphur Springs, West Virginia, for the first Kaine-Kilgore debate of the year. The debate would not be on television or radio, so the plan was to "live blog" the event. In the hours leading up to the debate, the entire town of White Sulphur Springs had been plastered in Jerry Kilgore signs. No question, Kilgore had won the sign battle of West Virginia. Fortunately for Tim Kaine and the Democrats, Kilgore was running for governor of Virginia, not *West* Virginia.

The debate was held in an ornate room full of fat-cat lawyers, a smattering of reporters, and a lone "live blogger." During the debate, Kilgore repeated ad nauseum the unintentionally laugh-inducing line, "I trust the people … always have, always will." That line became a running joke among pro-Kaine bloggers during the remainder of the campaign. Another source of humor was the "Jerry the Duck" joke, which centered on Kilgore's desire to "duck" debates and featured Kilgore screeching at Tim Kaine in a high-pitched voice (in reference to an eavesdropping scandal involving Attorney General Kilgore's office), "I have no duty to you, Mister Lieutenant Governor.… You are reckless!"[2]

SUMMER EXCITEMENT IN CINCINNATI

That same July, a special election campaign was gearing up in Ohio's Second Congressional District to replace Representative Rob Portman, a Republican who had been named U.S. special trade representative by President Bush. Portman's district had voted Republican in every election since 1974 and in all but nine contests since 1879. It had voted 64 percent for Bush in 2004. This was, in other words, as solid a Republican district as they come. The special election was scheduled for August 2, 2005.

On June 14, former state representative Jean Schmidt—also president of the Right to Life of Greater Cincinnati—had finished first in a field of eleven Republicans seeking the party's nomination to succeed Portman. The Democratic nominee was Paul Hackett, a Cincinnati attorney and a major in the U.S. Marine Corps Reserve, who had recently returned from a civilian assignment in Iraq for which he had volunteered. The *New York Times* characterized the six-foot-four-inch Hackett as "garrulous, profane, and quick with a barbed retort or mischievous joke."[3] Certainly Hackett, a staunch critic of the Iraq invasion from the get-go, was not the kind of Democrat to pull any punches. At one point during the campaign, for instance, Hackett called President Bush's hypermacho "Bring 'em on" taunt to Iraqi suicide bombers "the most incredibly stupid comment I've ever heard from a U.S. president."[4] When challenged on the statement, Hackett responded, "I said it, I meant it, I stand by it."[5]

Progressive consultant and blogger Tim Tagaris had moved to Canton, Ohio, in May 2005 at the urging of Jerome Armstrong ("the Blogfather") of MyDD, who told Tagaris, "What we're going to do, nobody's ever done before." Tagaris wrote for Grow Ohio, an innovative new blog put together by Armstrong and based on "Scoop," a powerful, open-source software program for community blogging. Grow Ohio was a statewide blog, "allowing people to drill down to the county level to find out what was going on." A map of Ohio enabled readers to click on and read stories from specific counties. The blog was funded by Congressman Sherrod Brown, an ambitious Democrat who represented the Thirteenth Congressional District in northeastern Ohio but was considering a run for governor or possibly U.S. Senate. Representative Brown's top advisor, Dan Lucas, who had worked with Armstrong on previous campaigns, initially conceived the idea and sold the Brown organization on it.

At that point, according to Tagaris, Ohio did not have a large number of local bloggers. One notable exception was Chris Baker, writing at the Ohio 2nd blog, who Tagaris credits with kick-starting the Hackett race and making a strong case that the special election presented a unique opportunity for Democrats in a very red district. Still, because of the upcoming Hackett-Schmidt special election, Sherrod Brown and Dan Lucas recognized that one of the first organizational opportunities was going to be in southwest Ohio.

Brown talked up Hackett's candidacy to Ohio political insiders and sent Lucas to Cincinnati to help the Hackett campaign get organized. Tagaris and Armstrong immediately saw that race as a chance to "test drive" politically oriented Internet communications, and they envisioned an opportunity to provide "a different way to tell the story about a campaign." Tagaris convinced the Brown organization to send him down to Hackett's district. By focusing on the exciting Hackett-Schmidt race, Grow Ohio became the most popular political blog in Ohio. The result would surprise even the most optimistic denizens of the emerging blogosphere.

In his July 13, 2005, blog post, "What a Difference a Day Makes," Tagaris graphically contrasted Paul Hackett and Jean Schmidt.[6] Tagaris described the day in October 2004 when Hackett was airborne in Iraq making the dangerous flight from Fallujah to Ramadi at the same time that Schmidt was being wined and dined by corporate lobbyists in their luxury sky box at a Cincinnati Bengals home game. The piece became a smash hit on MyDD, Daily Kos, and in the blogosphere more generally. According to Tagaris, "donations were flying in" to Paul Hackett's campaign. When the blogs wrote about a Jean Schmidt supporter on talk radio who tried to cast doubt on Hackett's military record, people—still fired up from the previous year's swiftboating of John Kerry—responded with fury and outrage backed up by material support. "Contributions were coming in left and right," Tagaris recalls. When Paul Hackett described George W. Bush as a "son of a bitch" or a "chicken hawk," insults he pointedly refused to retract, he sent Republicans into a tizzy of indignation but electrified opponents of Bush and his war. Even more money poured in.

Tagaris covered the red-hot campaign from Paul Hackett headquarters (located in Batavia, Ohio) for a fascinated national Internet audience. Tagaris used streaming video, still photographs, and colorful text—with a man he described as "the most colorful of candidates"—to "make people feel like they were in Batavia … literally sitting next to me." As Election Day neared, a final call went out on the Internet asking for money for the Hackett campaign. "Within six hours," Tagaris recalls, "we had to tell people to stop contributing because we literally could not spend it all" in the time remaining. "Once when a call went out for volunteers, so many came that the campaign didn't know what to do with them."

That, in a nutshell, demonstrated the power of the Internet to connect people across the nation and to motivate them into action. No traditional media outlet could have produced these results at so little cost.

Most of the feverish activity generated by the netroots on Paul Hackett's behalf continued way below the radar of the official campaign. Tim Tagaris says he got no respect from "the traditional brain trust that came in from D.C." When he came near them at headquarters, "they all went quiet" or made little jokes about him ("Oh, here's the blogger"). Maybe it was because

Tagaris was an outsider and they felt that they were the "real" campaign staff. Maybe it was fear and ignorance of the magic he dabbled in. Whatever it was, "they just didn't get it," Tagaris says. "They had no clue."

Dan Lucas believes that the blogosphere "worked miracles" for the Hackett campaign—raising money from all fifty states—but that the inexperienced Hackett campaign did not make wise use of the money raised online. "The people working the blogosphere did everything they could humanly do. It was the campaign's job to execute plans and use those funds effectively which they did not do," Lucas recalls. Perhaps Hackett's online success came too quickly and easily to fully absorb. Regardless, the Hackett campaign did not invest in the nuts-and-bolts political organizing needed to pull off an upset in such a conservative district.

On August 2, Hackett lost to Schmidt by fewer than 4,000 votes out of 115,000 cast. For a while on election night, it appeared that Hackett would pull off a monumental upset. When is a defeat a victory? Maybe never. Or maybe when the sharply upward trend it reveals is a harbinger of better days to come.

In 2003, the Dean and Clark movements had generated tremendous enthusiasm and had experienced fundraising success online, but their failure at the ballot box led many observers to write off netroots-driven politics as irrelevant. In 2004, the netroots contributed mightily to the Kerry campaign and helped make a number of congressional races—Richard Morrison's, for example—that shouldn't have even been close competitive. But at the end of 2004, the netroots had little tangible success to show for all their hard work and amazing fundraising success. In 2005, Paul Hackett's four-point loss in a bedrock Republican district that had gone nearly 2:1 for George W. Bush just one year earlier hinted at better things to come for Democrats in 2006 and beyond. As Tim Tagaris puts it, this was a "huge victory for the netroots even though we lost." And, Tagaris notes, "after Hackett, a lot of the traditional media recognized that 'if I'm going to do my job properly, I'm going to have to read [the blogs].'"

NOT LARRY SABATO

One notable Virginia blog that began operations during the Kaine-Kilgore election was Not Larry Sabato (NLS), which would later become famous for helping turn George Allen's "macaca moment" into a viral frenzy. The blog's title was an inside joke. The real Larry Sabato was a University of Virginia political science professor known for his eagerness to comment, as well as his knack for getting quoted, as an authority on seemingly every subject. NLS kicked off on April 22, 2005, with blog author Ben Tribbett referring to himself mysteriously as "we" and hoping that "both Democrats and Republicans will find this site to be fair."[7]

What caught people's attention was the incisive, obviously insider information that appeared on the blog. NLS rated House of Delegates races on a scale from "Safe Democratic" to "Safe Republican," and explained why in great detail. People were eager to know who was behind NLS. On June 28, NLS ran a poll entitled "Who Are We?"[8]

Some people speculated that only a team of top political journalists could produce a blog with such accurate information and smart analysis. Only 15 percent guessed that it was only one person, a twenty-five-year-old Fairfax, Virginia, resident and political operative with a photographic memory named Ben Tribbett.

NLS brought to the Virginia blogosphere a unique style that promised "Election Analysis, Predictions ... Gossip and Scandals!" The blog also claimed, on its masthead, to be "99.8 percent accurate so far." On July 12, the *Charlottesville Newsweekly* wrote a feature story on NLS, entitled "Who's Virginia's newest political star? It's Not Larry Sabato."[9] Tribbett was quoted anonymously as hoping that NLS would grow large enough for reporters to quote its content as a counter to comments made by the real Larry Sabato.

In late November, NLS started a "blogroll" of every Virginia blog rated by quality—platinum, gold, and so on. One could not help but be struck by the number and diversity of blogs that had sprung up in Virginia during 2005. No longer was Virginia's political blogosphere the somewhat sleepy, relatively congenial little world that had existed before 2005. For better or for worse, with the launch of the passionately partisan Raising Kaine and the "gossip and scandal" NLS, Virginia's political blogosphere had morphed into an entirely different creature. Waldo Jaquith waxes nostalgic for the "couple of years when the participants were all acting in good faith, when our blogs got a lot less traffic, and when the average IQ was somewhat north of 100." According to Jaquith, before mid-2005, hot-button topics were "simply not discussed." That was certainly no longer the case by the summer and fall of 2005.

"THIS ARRANGEMENT SUITED THE CAMPAIGN"

Among other objectives, Raising Kaine aimed to serve as an amateur "opposition research" shop for Democrats. For instance, on September 2, Nichole Herbig of Richmond wrote a diary examining why Jerry Kilgore was "soft" on enforcement of methamphetamine laws.[10] Herbig wrote, "Not to draw any conclusions here, but isn't it a bit, um, 'interesting' that Jerry Kilgore gets large amounts of money from a man who profits greatly from the trade in Methamphetamines (the manufacture of which relies on an ingredient found in *six* products that his company churns out)? Does Jerry Kilgore care more about John Gregory's profits or a drug epidemic in Virginia?" On September 17, a Raising Kaine column entitled, "Major Kilgore Backer Hires and Exploits Illegal Immigrants," looked into large-scale contributions by pork processor Smithfield Foods to Kilgore and, more generally, Virginia Republicans.[11] These are just two examples of the work that Raising Kaine did in 2005.

Little coordination existed between the pro-Democratic Virginia blogs and the Kaine campaign. Early on, the Raising Kaine bloggers had decided to stay as independent as possible, freeing them to speak their minds and allowing the Kaine campaign to disavow any connection if it so desired. Tim Kaine's netroots coordinator and official campaign blogger, John Rohrbach, says that "this arrangement suited the campaign," because "Raising Kaine could do things the campaign didn't necessarily want to answer for." In addition, Rohrbach understood that most blog traffic went to the independent blogs, like Daily Kos and Raising Kaine, because they were more interesting than the official campaign blog. In Rohrbach's opinion, "what the independent progressive political blogs were saying to them ... was more important than what I was going to say to them."

In other words, there was no need to reinvent the wheel; the pro-Kaine blogs were already doing a great job on their own. And according to Rohrbach, the independent blogs were just about as well informed as the Kaine campaign itself. In fact, Rohrbach notes, "[considering] Waldo Jaquith's institutional knowledge of Virginia politics, there wasn't a whole lot that anyone knew that he didn't." Essentially, according to Rohrbach, a bunch of amateurs blogging in their spare time had the same information a $20 million, statewide campaign did and were equally well informed. It's hard to know quite what to make of that.

AN OFF-OFF YEAR

Lacking both a presidential and congressional election, 2005 was a politically "off-off" year in the United States. Virginia's gubernatorial election was the only major competitive race around. The governor's race in New Jersey was widely considered a lock for the Democrats. It was the special election in Ohio between "Mean Jean" Schmidt and Paul Hackett that consumed the national netroots' attention during July and early August. Still, as hard as the Virginia Democratic bloggers tried, they could not get real traction in the national progressive blogosphere for the Kaine-Kilgore contest.

John Rohrbach says that the Kaine campaign "tried to nationalize the race" but without much success. The Virginia race simply wasn't as dramatic or starkly polarizing as the Schmidt-Hackett battle in Ohio. Also, many progressive bloggers were cool toward Tim Kaine after he had made disparaging remarks about John Kerry's 2004 failure to reveal more about his personal religious convictions. Kaine's comments about Kerry ("I think that John Kerry demonstrated much more comfort talking about windsurfing and hockey than he did talking about his belief"[12]) angered potential supporters in the progressive blogosphere, some of whom saw Kaine as having revived the dreaded Democratic "circular firing squad."

The Kaine campaign's relations with the progressive blogosphere hit another rough patch in late October 2005. At that time, the Kaine campaign pulled its ad from Steve Gilliard's The News Blog, on which Gilliard had depicted Michael Steele, an African American Republican running for lieutenant governor of Maryland, as a minstrel in blackface. In response, Gilliard, an African American himself, wrote a diary entitled, "Tim Kaine Is a Coward."[13] Markos Moulitsas Zúniga at Daily Kos chimed in, writing, "I hate Democrats scared of their shadows," adding that "Virginia's Tim Kaine (or those running his campaign) is one of them."[14]

Fortunately for Tim Kaine, the Kilgore campaign was busy self-destructing at essentially the same time. Kilgore's unscrupulous media advisor, Scott Howell, had produced a television ad claiming that Tim Kaine—a former Roman Catholic missionary—was so opposed to the death penalty that he wouldn't have even allowed Adolf Hitler to be executed. After the ad began appearing on October 11, many Kaine supporters worried that it might work and that Kaine could lose the election. Instead, partly because of a quick and forceful condemnation by prominent Jewish leaders and groups ("demeaning and morally repugnant" were typical of the words used),[15] partly because of the popularity of Governor Mark Warner (who Tim Kaine was aiming to succeed), partly because people liked Tim Kaine and understood his religious views on the death penalty, and partly thanks to the hard work of Virginia bloggers like Waldo Jaquith, the ad completely backfired. After trailing for months, Kaine pulled ahead of Kilgore in the polls and never looked back. On Election Day, Kaine beat Kilgore by a six-point margin (51.7 to 46.0 percent).

WHO *ARE* THESE PEOPLE?

Ben Tribbett reflects that the "conventional wisdom" in 2005 was that "blogs didn't matter." Tribbett adds that, to the extent politicians paid attention to the blogosphere, "they didn't know how to handle it" and were frustrated that they had no control over it. This frustration may have resulted partly from the fact that many of the new bloggers—with exceptions like Ben Tribbett— had not been involved in Virginia politics previously. According to Tribbett, Tim Kaine must have been thinking, "Who *are* these people, what do they want, and why is one of the blogs using my name?" Tribbett also believed that Kaine worried, "What would happen to message discipline if blogs started claiming to speak for Democrats in general, or for the campaign?" Conversely, Tribbett points out, to the extent that the blogs could do things the Kaine campaign couldn't do, Kaine might have been glad that they were around.

One incident late in the Kaine-Kilgore race exemplified what an alert and energized netroots movement can do. On the weekend before the election, voters in northern Virginia started receiving robo-calls, purportedly from the Kaine campaign, that began as follows: "I'm Tim Kaine and I want you to know where I stand on the issues." The calls then spliced together statements Kaine had made on abortion and other issues, twisting them completely out of context in order to make Kaine appear conservative in liberal areas of the state like northern Virginia, and liberal in conservative parts like southwestern Virginia.

As it turns out, the calls were being funded by a PAC called the Honest Leadership for Virginia, a group that had given $3 million to Jerry Kilgore in 2005. After Raising Kaine blasted the PAC, urging people to call and demand that it stop its robo-calls, the group threatened legal action against Raising Kaine writers. One of the PAC's complaints was that its phone number—although listed publicly by the Federal Election Commission (FEC) as required by law—had been published by Raising Kaine. The PAC angrily claimed that the phone was at a private home where children lived. Raising Kaine refused to back down and instead exposed the sham—and possibly illegal—robo-calls to as many people as possible. This may have been the very thing that blunted the impact of the bogus calls and caused them to backfire on Jerry Kilgore.

Although it's hard to quantify, it appears that the netroots, including Raising Kaine, Waldo Jaquith, and NLS, made a significant contribution to Tim Kaine's victory in the 2005 Virginia governor's race. Waldo Jaquith, one of the most knowledgeable people on the subject of Virginia politics, believes that the Kaine-Kilgore race demonstrated that "the media and campaigns could be influenced strongly by bloggers." Jaquith states point blank that "Tim Kaine's netroots supporters made a difference in his gubernatorial race against Kilgore."

Jaquith makes another interesting point, that "the press and candidates alike had only recently discovered political blogs, and the Virginia political blogosphere was small enough, intelligent enough, and interesting enough that these new readers were totally engaged in what they were learning from it." As a result, "they hadn't built up any immunity to blogs," which in turn "gave bloggers enormous sway over the messages picked up by the media, and the ability to knock campaigns back on their heels." In addition, Jaquith believes that the discipline and persistence of the "well-coordinated, agile, and clever" Virginia Democratic blogosphere had an "immediate and obvious" effect on media coverage of the race—and on Kaine's Election Day victory margin.

A few months after his electoral victory, Governor Kaine wrote an article for the Democratic Leadership Council's *Blueprint* magazine, in which he explained "How I Won." Although the article was fairly lengthy, the following were never mentioned: grassroots, netroots, Internet, blogs, blogosphere, or Raising Kaine. Instead, Kaine credited his victory to "three factors: the exceptional popularity of Governor Mark Warner, my predecessor and partner over the past four years; my campaign's understanding of Virginia's changing demographics; and my ability to speak directly to voters and offer them a positive vision for our future."[16] Perhaps this was merely an oversight on Tim Kaine's part, or perhaps it was intentional. Either way, it's striking.

Although 2005 witnessed an important netroots success story in Virginia, that success was not generally acknowledged, at least in public, by Democratic Party officials. The lack of credit given to the netroots may not have been an accident. The fact is that the old model of politics only grudgingly gives credit to the grassroots, let alone to a new breed of netroots activists and bloggers. These sometimes rowdy, unruly Young Turks of progressive politics operate beyond the control and without the sanction of the old guard, and this undoubtedly can be unnerving. In addition, both major American political parties support a generously paid class of professional operatives who create and control campaigns and candidates. It should not be particularly surprising that these operatives would look at a new group of entrants into the process with nervousness, derision, dislike, or even scorn. This is a tension that remains significant and unresolved, even as the old era fades and a new one rises.

Perhaps the significance of the rising netroots takes time to sink in for some people, or perhaps they're just busy. In June 2007, a year and a half after Tim Kaine's victory over Jerry Kilgore, the governor held a warm reception for several Raising Kaine bloggers—Rob, Josh, Eric, and Lowell—at the governor's mansion in Richmond. Kaine praised the bloggers and credited them with helping raise him to the governor's mansion. The reception and the kind words by Governor Kaine were encouraging evidence that at least some enlightened politicians understood the importance of a rising netroots and were coming to terms with it.

FERMENT IN TEXAS

Meanwhile, in Texas, Nate Wilcox continued to work with Fred Lewis's Clean Up Texas Politics and Glenn Smith's MoveOn spin-off, DriveDemocracy. Both groups were busy fighting corruption in the state. Clean Up Texas Politics focused on a bill to eliminate gray areas in the campaign finance laws that had given Tom DeLay's TRMPAC so much latitude for abuse. The group held meetings around the state, using its e-mail list as well as traditional organizing methods such as phone calls, fliers, and newspaper ads to build membership. To sway an undecided legislator, it sent e-mails to activists in the target legislator's district. Generally, a few dozen phone calls from constituents made a sufficient impression on recalcitrant representatives.

Thanks to the strong public support generated for the bill, Lewis persuaded every Democrat and more than thirty Republicans in the Texas House of Representatives to sign on as sponsors of the reform legislation. Despite the support of a large majority of the Texas House, Speaker Tom Craddick kept the bill locked up in committee. Craddick had been the biggest beneficiary of TRMPAC's abusive 2002 endeavors.

The 2005 Texas legislative session saw the emergence of a second wave of Texas bloggers. The first wave had been largely from outside the political process—technophiles and idealistic college students with some exceptions like journalists turned political consultants Glenn Smith and Vince Leibowitz. The new bloggers were coming from within the system. In January 2005, journalist Eileen Smith launched a blog called In the Pink Texas to chronicle the doings of the Texas Legislature. While progressive and unabashed in her political leanings, Smith brought a traditional journalist's perspective to the project. Smith's approach was strikingly more restrained than the strongly partisan advocacy previously seen from Texas bloggers. The Pink Dome blog (the name refers to the Texas pink granite used in the state capitol building), begun by an anonymous former legislative staffer, obviously had a very well-informed network of sources inside the capitol building.

THE TRIANGLE CLOSES ON TOM DELAY

Democratic strategist Peter Daou, John Kerry's online outreach coordinator in the bruising 2004 presidential race, had written about what he called the "Triangle."[17] According to Daou's theory, a news story needed to "close all three sides of the Triangle—press, bloggers and elected officials"—to affect the public debate. A story that closed only one or two sides of this Triangle would have diminished impact. Daou's Triangle had worked extremely well for George W. Bush and the Republicans in 2004, but not nearly as well for John Kerry and the Democrats. In contrast to other Republicans, 2005 would see the Triangle close in on Tom DeLay.

Tom DeLay's public profile was dramatically raised during the 2003 Texas redistricting fight, but his blatant corruption was largely overlooked by the mainstream media at the time. Throughout 2003 and 2004, a network of bloggers in Texas and elsewhere documented numerous stories of DeLay's involvement in legally questionable activities, his seemingly bottomless hunger for campaign contributions, and his penchant for making outrageous pronouncements.

"I *am* the federal government," the *Washington Post* quoted DeLay as telling a waiter who cited "federal regulations" when asking DeLay to put out his cigar in a restaurant on federal property.[18] "It never ceases to amaze me that people are so cynical they want to tie money to issues, money to bills, money to amendments," he responded to questions about contributions to his TRMPAC from Kansas energy firm Westar.[19]

DeLay's willingness to walk close to the edge of truth and legality and way beyond the limits of propriety made him infamous on progressive state blogs like Texas's Off the Kuff and Greg's Opinion, and national blogs like Daily Kos and Talking Points Memo.

Activist groups like David Donnelly's Campaign Money Watch, Clean Up Texas Politics, MoveOn, and the Texas-based Lone Star Project (run by former

Martin Frost chief of staff Matt Angle) monitored DeLay's outrages and reported on numerous investigations into the conglomeration of lobbyists, law firms, PACs, and dubious nonprofit organizations they dubbed "DeLay, Inc." The activists discovered that any e-mail "call to action" to online progressives regarding DeLay got an extremely strong response.

Numerous lawyers were pursuing legal remedies to DeLay's malfeasance. In February 2005, attorney Chris Feldman filed a civil suit against TRMPAC on behalf of Texas Democratic candidates claiming that corporate money had been illegally used against them by DeLay, Inc. Others pursued legal appeals in the Texas redistricting matter. Those appeals resulted in at least two of DeLay's redrawn congressional districts being rejected by Texas courts.

Compared with DeLay and his vast web of allies and underlings, the activist bloggers were minor nuisances. None of them held elected office. None of them had access to major media outlets. Yet the constant attacks by many small opponents ultimately added up. Conservative blogger Glen Reynolds of Instapundit called the anti-DeLay bloggers an "army of Davids" in his book of the same name.[20] Together, their slingshots and rocks took down the giant. An even more apt metaphor might be the swarm of Lilliputians who defeated Gulliver.

The progressive bloggers, activist groups, and lawyers sustained a steady barrage of attacks on DeLay, Inc. throughout 2003 and 2004. Richard Morrison's long-shot congressional campaign against DeLay in 2004 had provided a focus to their efforts. The prospect of mounting a serious electoral challenge to DeLay on his home turf of Sugar Land, Texas, proved compelling to tens of thousands of progressives across Texas and nationally.

The Travis County, Texas, indictments of DeLay's associates and the admonishment by the U.S. House Ethics Committee soon combined with the online outcry against DeLay to close two sides of the Daou Triangle. Bloggers and credible elected officials had both denounced DeLay. The national media—the third leg of the Triangle—had given the story prominent play in the fall of 2004, but upon DeLay's reelection in November, they had largely gone silent on the matter.

Still, Morrison's surprisingly strong showing convinced Democrats in Washington that the corrupt House majority leader was certifiably vulnerable in his home district. Over the winter of 2004–2005, David Donnelly of Campaign Money Watch met with Democrats suddenly interested in helping challenge DeLay. Previously, the same people had advised Campaign Money Watch that it would be wasting its money to take on DeLay. Realizing their mistake, they vowed not to repeat it.

After his defeat by Tom DeLay in November 2004, Richard Morrison quickly announced that he would seek a rematch in 2006. He and his overstressed, underfunded campaign team then took the month of November off. Morrison had ignored his legal practice for almost all of 2004, and with a large family, he needed to get back to earning money.

Democratic power players suddenly determined to mount a serious challenge to DeLay. But their idea of a serious challenge did not include an idealistic young lawyer with a pugnacious style. They did not view Morrison's Internet fundraising success as having resulted from anything special about Morrison or his campaign, Instead, they saw it as resulting from his run against Tom DeLay, who was despised by Democratic activists and therefore tended to fire them up.

Congressional Democrats such as John Conyers of Michigan and Louise Slaughter of New York also jumped into action. From the first day of the 2005 congressional session, they attacked DeLay and fought to expose his corruption. In an innovative move, Representative Slaughter recruited Dean for presidential campaign veteran Karl Fritsch to conduct online outreach—a first for a sitting U.S. Representative. The alliance between the blogs and the chair of the powerful House Judiciary Committee proved powerful.

A CLEARLY EGREGIOUS OUTRAGE

Democrats were not the only ones who moved quickly after the 2004 election. Tom DeLay immediately pushed his colleagues to amend House Ethics Committee rules to allow him to continue to serve as majority leader even if he were to be indicted on felony charges in Texas. The DeLay Rule was adopted in a closed Republican caucus on a voice vote. Only a couple of courageous Republicans, including Connecticut moderate Chris Shays, were willing to say that they had spoken against it. The Texas ethics reform group, Campaigns for People, set up a vote count on its Daily DeLay blog, tracking which Republican representatives voted for the DeLay Rule and which had voted against it. Campaigns for People launched a petition drive and encouraged members who had contacted their own representatives to report back directly on the Daily DeLay blog. "What they found was a lot of hemming and hawing," Donnelly recalls. "Few of the representatives wanted to be on the record. That just fueled the frenzy and got our supporters more excited."

Josh Marshall of Talking Points Memo and David Donnelly both pounced on the ethics vote. Talking Points Memo was then one of the few progressive blogs to be taken seriously by the national press corps, probably because Marshall had been a Washington writer before launching his blog.

Josh Marshall did a brilliant job piquing the interest of local reporters. Even if the national press corps wasn't interested in the story, Marshall gave local reporters a simple question to ask their congressman: "Did you vote for or against the DeLay Rule?" It is quite hard for a congressional office to ignore a direct yes or no question from their local newspaper or television station. When a local paper got an answer and reported it, Marshall would report that news to his national audience, creating a virtuous circle. The local reporters were motivated by the national attention, and this encouraged them to keep pursuing the DeLay affair.

Democratic activists, discouraged after the tough loss in the 2004 election, flocked to the campaign against the DeLay Rule. Tens of thousands of people contacted their representatives and reported back to the blogs. The DeLay Rule was a clearly egregious outrage that generated widespread opposition. Little support existed for the idea of allowing indicted felons to serve in the country's congressional leadership.

In a few weeks, Donnelly and Marshall had persuaded twenty-three Republicans who opposed the ethics rule change to go on the record. "This was a critical number because it meant a majority in Congress opposed the ethics rule change," Donnelly says. "This gave the Democrats a backbone."

When the leaders of the Democratic caucus said they would take the DeLay Rule to the floor for a vote of the entire House of Representatives during the first week of the new session of Congress, DeLay backed down. The rule changes were repealed, and progressive activists around the country celebrated a major victory, one made all the sweeter for coming just a few months after the bitter loss of the presidential election.

DeLay's defeat was more than a simple embarrassment for the man known as "the Hammer." DeLay's power depended on the perception that he could control the U.S. House of Representatives and that any opposition to him was futile. DeLay's sudden vulnerability punctured his mystique and piqued the interest of journalists.

As Donnelly and Marshall continued to draw attention to DeLay's extensive record of gross corruption, other organizations and blogs jumped on the bandwagon. And, critically, so did the national press. From January to March 2005 a flood of powerful investigative journalism examined corruption in the Republican Congress. As stories broke about DeLay and numerous colleagues like California's Randy "Duke" Cunningham and Ohio's Bob Ney, the stories began to feed on themselves. A competitive atmosphere prevailed in the press corps as reporters sought to one-up each other with stories about the corruption. Surely, Republican strategists saw it as a feeding frenzy.

According to Donnelly, "There was a sense that there would be a scalp at the end of this; I think that's what gave reporters the go-ahead to write so many stories on DeLay." Donnelly received frequent calls from reporters asking, "What else do you have on DeLay?" Donnelly laughingly recalls that "they were suddenly thirsting to expose the truth which they had let lie hidden for so long."

In Texas, activist and investigator Fred Lewis experienced the same phenomenon: "After years of not being able to get even local reporters to return my calls, suddenly I'm telling someone from the *Washington Post* to hold on because I'm on the other line with the *New York Times*. It was like a switch flipped." Lewis's website, Clean Up Texas Politics, experienced a boom in readership thanks to the DeLay publicity. The surge in site traffic at the end of 2004 continued during early 2005. Lewis capitalized on the attention, organizing his newly registered supporters to lobby the Texas Legislature for clean election laws.

Meanwhile, the civil case that Chris Feldman was bringing against DeLay's TRMPAC went to trial. Nate Wilcox covered the case for Drive Democracy, MoveOn's Texas branch. Wilcox shared a bench with reporters from every Texas newspaper, as well as several national ones. The evidence laid out at the trial clearly indicated that DeLay's organization had deliberately and knowingly violated Texas election laws. In addition, Delay, Inc. had used the Republican National Committee to launder hundreds of thousands of corporate dollars that were funneled directly to candidates in the 2002 elections. TRMPAC's lawyers could only insist that none of this was illegal, but they were unable to present any evidence disputing the charges.

"It was an amazing period of time," reminisces Donnelly, "DeLay's downfall had its genesis in what [Congressman] Chris Bell did [filing a wide-ranging ethics complaint against DeLay in early 2004], the election results put DeLay on the vulnerable list, then the news frenzy solidified the idea in the public mind that this guy was corrupt."

"I DON'T TRUST THESE D.C. GUYS"

As charges against Tom DeLay piled up, pressure from the Democratic establishment mounted for Richard Morrison not to challenge him again in 2006. Morrison heard that former Congressman Nick Lampson, whose district had been obliterated in the 2003 redistricting, was considering mounting a run. Morrison's campaign team found this news implausible, given that Lampson's 2004 campaign had fared so poorly. Despite spending more than $2 million against a local judge in a district just northeast of DeLay's district, Lampson had received only 44 percent of the vote. Morrison, who had been outspent more than four to one, had performed nearly as well as Lampson, who had outspent his own opponent more than 1.5 to 1. Surely the big Democratic Party players didn't want to reward Lampson for that mediocre performance by putting him up against DeLay?

As it so happened, they did.

Morrison traveled to Washington, where he and Wilcox met with Congressman Rahm Emanuel and his team at the Democratic Congressional Campaign Committee (DCCC). Emanuel made Morrison an interesting offer:

> We want to support the candidate who runs against DeLay next time. We also want to avoid an expensive and divisive primary. What we will do is commission a poll of the district. We'll include you, Lampson and Houston City Councilman Gordon Quan. If you will all three agree that the two who lose the polls will drop out in favor of the candidate that the poll shows to be the strongest, we'll have our candidate.[21]

Morrison was enthusiastic about the offer, but he did not trust Emanuel. Morrison advisor Jeff Hewitt advised him to take the offer, arguing, "We just spent hundreds of thousands of dollars on mail and advertising in the district; you ought to be able to win that poll."

Morrison called Lampson, and the two discussed the situation. Lampson, an exceptionally kind and likable man, had been very supportive of Morrison in 2004—sharing his polling information on the district and even offering to let Morrison stay at his D.C. apartment anytime Morrison was in the capital. Before the call, Morrison had been on the verge of accepting the DCCC's offer. After his talk with Lampson, Morrison decided to decline.

"I don't think Nick's going to run, and I don't trust these D.C. guys," Morrison told Wilcox after he got off the phone with Lampson. It would prove to be a fatal mistake for Morrison's candidacy. Over the next couple of weeks, rumors mounted that Lampson was indeed running. In an attempt to bluff his friend and mentor out of the race, Morrison told the Associated Press that "the streets will run with Democratic blood" if he was challenged for the nomination.[22] Morrison also mounted an aggressive outreach campaign to local and national blogs.

It didn't work. At a dramatic meeting in his father's law office, Morrison confronted Lampson and Gordon Quan, who was also considering the race. Lampson revealed that he had been persuaded to run by a group of Houston area Democratic donors. Morrison learned the next day that his stepmother had been diagnosed with terminal cancer. For more than two years, Morrison had been fighting not only Tom DeLay but also a passive-aggressive Texas Democratic establishment that told him what he wanted to hear but offered no real support. Now that DeLay stood at the brink of electoral defeat, that same establishment decided to push him aside in favor of a candidate from outside the district who had just badly lost a comparable race.

Morrison's father, Richard "Dick" Morrison III, had been his son's strongest supporter, biggest fundraiser, and most trusted political advisor throughout the 2004 run. Now, because of his wife's cancer, Dick Morrison was out of the picture. Richard Morrison knew that he was beaten and withdrew from the race, throwing his strong support to Nick Lampson. Morrison gave Lampson his e-mail list, and proudly and publicly endorsed Lampson's candidacy. Over the course of 2005 and 2006, Morrison would campaign for Lampson at every opportunity. Morrison would also raise money for local party-building and for other Democratic candidates.

TERRI'S LAW

Pressured from all sides, DeLay sought to change the subject. He chose to raise a case in Florida of a brain-dead woman, Terri Schiavo, whose husband Michael wished to take her off life support, but whose parents wished to keep her vegetative body "alive" at all costs. Terri Schiavo had suffered a heart attack in February 1990 and had never recovered. Between 1998 and 2002, Terri's parents (the Schindlers) fought in court over whether their daughter should be taken off of life support. According to Michael Schiavo, his wife had said that she wouldn't want to be "kept alive on a machine" if she had no hope for recovery.[23] Given that she had descended into a persistent vegetative state, this certainly appeared to be the situation. On October 15, 2003, Terri Schiavo's feeding tube was removed.

Until 2003, the Schiavo case had mainly been an issue for the family, the doctors, and the courts. Then, starting in 2003, the Schindlers began to ratchet up publicity, bringing in pro-life activist Randall Terry as their spokesperson. After Terri's feeding tube was removed, however, the politicians swarmed like vultures. One of the first actions was the passage of Terri's Law by the Florida Legislature in late October 2003, followed by Governor Jeb Bush's order to reinsert the feeding tube. More litigation followed, with the Florida Supreme Court in late 2004 striking down Terri's Law as unconstitutional.

In early 2005, the federal government, including Tom DeLay, started to get involved. On March 18, 2005, the Republican-controlled House of Representatives subpoenaed both Michael and Terri Schiavo to testify at a congressional hearing. Tom DeLay—along with Republican Senators Bill Frist of Tennessee and Rick Santorum of Pennsylvania—threatened to hold Florida Sixth Circuit Court Judge George W. Greer, who had ordered Schiavo's feeding tube removed by March 18, in contempt of Congress.

Tom DeLay and the Republican leadership had miscalculated badly. They had expected the Schiavo case to rally their base and to shift the media's focus away from their own corruption. Instead, the tremendous public furor surrounding the case, and the backlash against DeLay's actions, dramatically focused attention on the majority leader. According to a March 23 CBS News poll, 82 percent of Americans said they wanted Congress to stay out of the case. Also, Americans strongly supported removing Terri Schiavo's feeding tube. Suddenly, DeLay was a nightly punch line for David Letterman, Jay Leno, and Jon Stewart.

A NATIONAL EMBARRASSMENT

David Donnelly recalls, "The attention to the Schiavo case caused our blog traffic to go through the roof. DeLay was looking at the case as a way for him to sweep corruption under the rug and formulate a new public persona. He thought the Schiavo case would help him." Instead, Donnelly says, what the public saw was "a Congress out of control, abusing its power on behalf of politics pure and simple in making a clear play to the radical right. It locked DeLay into the public consciousness as someone who was out of touch and abusing his power."

Donnelly helped to illustrate the depth of DeLay's hypocrisy when he found a key passage in a biography of DeLay and brought it to the attention of reporters. As the biography revealed, DeLay in 1988 had personally given the green light to pull the plug on his own brain-damaged, sixty-five-year-old father. The incident highlighted the extent to which DeLay operated under a double standard. In the Schiavo case, DeLay was willing to bring the full power of the U.S. Congress to bear in an attempt to override the wishes of Terri Schiavo's husband—even compelling President Bush to cut short a vacation and fly back to Washington, D.C., to sign legislation Congress had passed on the issue.

On March 15, 2005, the Daily DeLay demanded that DeLay resign from Congress, calling him "a national embarrassment" and announcing that the "Public Campaign Action Fund is launching a new campaign to force Tom DeLay to step down."[24] The blog's e-mail list grew dramatically, as did attention to the case. When corrupt lobbyist Jack Abramoff, a man DeLay had described as his "best friend,"[25] became a celebrity criminal (ultimately pleading guilty to numerous felony counts), the public furor only increased.

On September 28, 2005, Travis County District Attorney Ronnie Earle secured a grand jury indictment against Tom DeLay. The indictment charged TRMPAC with accepting corporate contributions, laundering the money through the Republican National Committee, and directing the cash to select Texas Republican candidates. DeLay likely would have escaped indictment, but he took it upon himself to call a meeting with the Travis County investigators in Austin. At that meeting, with no attorney present, DeLay implicated himself. Earle was quick to react. He sought and gained multiple indictments against DeLay, including one count of criminal conspiracy, a felony punishable by up to two years incarceration. In response, DeLay stepped down as House majority leader. In early January 2006, DeLay further announced that he would not seek to regain his leadership position. It was clear that DeLay's days as a political powerhouse were over.

DeLay hung on into 2006, dragging his party down with him. The "culture of corruption" label that arose to describe DeLay, Inc. was applied to the entire Republican majority, severely damaging the party. Despite all this, DeLay sought and received his party's nomination to run for reelection. On March 6, 2006, DeLay soundly defeated the three brave souls who ran against him, declaring that his victory represented a rejection by district voters of "the politics of personal destruction." But no sooner had DeLay received the nomination than he dropped out of the general election race; on April 3, he announced that he would not run for reelection in November. Most likely, DeLay had looked at the polls indicating that he would lose to a well-funded Nick Lampson. Also, most of the millions that DeLay had raised for his reelection were ultimately spent on his legal defense, yet another instance in which DeLay violated the spirit, if not the letter, of campaign finance laws.

The fall of Tom DeLay from a position of great power to utter disgrace is a powerful story, one that wouldn't have happened without the persistence of citizen activists like Josh Marshall and David Donnelly. In many ways, Marshall, Donnelly, and others like them were following in a proud tradition that had largely fallen out of favor in recent years. In 1973–1974, *Washington Post* reporters Bob Woodward and Carl Bernstein had helped to bring down President Richard Nixon over the Watergate scandal and cover-up. In 2005–2006, netroots activists—in conjunction with congressional Democrats like Louise Slaughter and John Conyers, plus the traditional media once they started paying attention to the story—helped bring down House Majority Leader Tom DeLay.[26] DeLay's disgrace and manifest corruption damaged the Republican Party "brand" and created opportunities for Democrats against even the most entrenched Republican incumbents, such as presumed 2008 presidential front-runner George Allen in Virginia.

Chapter 6

DRAFTING AN AMERICAN HERO

As the Kaine-Kilgore campaign ended, netroots activists in Virginia turned their attention to 2006. Their top priority: Find someone who could stop Senator George Allen, a Bush clone and a leading insider favorite for the 2008 Republican presidential nomination, before he got within range of the White House. The optimal choice was obvious—the wildly popular former Virginia governor, Mark Warner. But Warner had already announced that he wouldn't be running for the Senate in 2006. Instead, it seemed clear that Warner, like George Allen, had his eyes on the White House. Other prominent Virginia Democrats (like former Lieutenant Governor Don Beyer) also had taken their names out of the running or were not available. Which meant that, as of November 2005, the candidate to take on George Allen and have a chance in hell of beating him was basically, well, nobody.

A few Virginia netroots activists believed that Allen was beatable, but the conventional wisdom was the exact opposite. Josh Chernila, the former political director of Democracy for Virginia who later became a leader in the Draft James Webb movement, says that "Virginia's Democratic leadership saw no way to unseat this seemingly popular former governor." Instead, Chernila believes they were ready to give Allen "a free ride to reelection in 2006 and a coronation as the Republican [presidential] nominee in 2008."

WANTED: AN AMERICAN HERO

But at least a few netroots activists were not satisfied with that scenario. For starters, they knew that George Allen had managed to defeat Senator Chuck Robb (weakened by a sex scandal involving a former Miss Virginia) by only 4.6 points in 2000, the same year that George W. Bush had swept the state (53 to 44 percent, against Al Gore). Not exactly a landslide for Allen. Second, they saw that Allen's relatively narrow victory over Robb had come in spite of his having outspent Robb three to one, a situation that could be corrected. Third, polls showed that, since 2000, President Bush's popularity had plummeted in Virginia. As a consequence, Allen would be running against a headwind in 2006 as opposed to the tailwind of 2000. Fourth, they believed that Virginia had changed dramatically since 2000, with the population of politically moderate northern Virginia having boomed and having helped send Democrats Mark Warner and Tim Kaine to the governor's mansion in successive elections. Fifth, they felt that Allen's record—including questionable positions on racial matters—had never been closely scrutinized by the media. Finally, they suspected that 2006 would be different thanks to the active progressive blogosphere that had developed since 2000, as the Virginia netroots had demonstrated in the Kaine-Kilgore race of 2005.

Indeed, since 2000, a vibrant, hard-hitting progressive blogosphere had emerged in Virginia. It had earned its spurs in the Kaine-Kilgore gubernatorial contest of 2005, as well as in numerous local races. Could the Virginia blogs, combined with the other factors mentioned, make up a 4.6-point margin by George Allen? With the right candidate, at least a few Virginia netroots activists were confident that this was possible. But who was that candidate?

On October 30, 2005, as most Virginians focused on the Kaine-Kilgore race, former Reagan administration Navy Secretary James "Jim" Webb gave an interview in the *San Diego Union Tribune*. At the end of the interview, Webb commented—almost as an afterthought—"I have been talking to people about running for the Senate next year against George Allen, as a Democrat from Virginia."[1] Lowell Feld read about Webb's interview on Daily Kos and did what any good blogger would do—he Googled Webb. Feld's online research convinced him that Webb had the potential to become a powerhouse candidate for Virginia: a U.S. Marine Corps veteran who had won the Navy Cross in Vietnam, a "Reagan Democrat" who could appeal to conservative Democrats, a best-selling novelist, and—unlike George Allen, who grew up in California—a man whose Scots-Irish family roots went back generations in Virginia.

As if that weren't good enough, Webb had also spoken out early and powerfully against the invasion of Iraq. In September 2002, Webb had written an opinion piece for the *Washington Post* titled, "Heading for Trouble: Do We Really Want to Occupy Iraq for the Next 30 Years?" The combination of Webb's early, outspoken opposition to the Iraq War and his impressive biography meant that he had the potential to be George Allen's worst nightmare. As netroots activist and blogger Greg Priddy wrote at the time, "James Webb could play a key role if he decides to challenge George Allen for Senate in helping Democrats craft and articulate a better national security strategy and overcome the 'weak on defense' *meme* with the American public."[2] In other words, Run, Webb, Run!

On November 18, 2005, Feld e-mailed Webb, writing that "[I] would be very interested in interviewing you about Virginia politics, and specifically about the possibility that you might take on George Allen in 2006." Three days later, Webb wrote back, saying, "I'm still thinking hard about this, meeting with people from both sides of the aisle whose opinions I respect." And it was no wonder Webb was thinking hard and asking a lot of questions. On December 9, a Rasmussen poll showed Webb—not a candidate but included in the poll because his name was being bandied about—trailing Allen by thirty-one points, 57 to 26 percent.[3] Not exactly an encouraging sign for a Webb candidacy.

FINDING "THE ONE"

On December 20, 2005, Feld wrote an article on Raising Kaine simply titled, "Draft James Webb." After citing Webb's impressive resume, Feld wrote,

> Yes, James Webb used to be a Republican, but now he's a Democrat and several of us here at Raising Kaine believe he'd be a super-strong candidate against George Allen this coming November. Honestly, we feel that of all the names mentioned as potential Democratic Senatorial candidates, James Webb would stand the best chance *by far* of defeating George Allen, or at least of giving him a heck of a run for his money. And, to be blunt, weakening Allen for 2008 is a top priority for "Fighting Democrats" like us; ask yourself, do you want George "let's enjoy kicking their soft teeth down their whining throats" Allen to be your next president? Right, I didn't think so.[4]

The "soft teeth" quote was from a George Allen speech at the 1994 Virginia Republican convention. It was intended to fire up Republicans, and it did at the time, but it also fired up Democrats in the long run to defeat Allen. After reminding readers about Allen's incendiary remarks, Feld concluded,

> That's why we're asking you, if you want James Webb to take on Allen, to click here and tell him how much you want him as your candidate next November. Thanks.[5]

Soon, numerous Virginia Democratic bloggers (and blog readers) were expressing support and interest for a Webb candidacy. Still, nobody knew whether Webb really wanted to run. Equally important, nobody knew what Webb's positions were on many important issues like abortion, the environment, trade, stem cell research, education, health care, or anything else.

On December 22, many of those questions were answered, as Webb sat down with Lowell Feld and two other Virginia Democratic netroots activists— Lee Diamond and Josh Chernila—for an off-the-record discussion. Diamond, in his mid-forties and involved with liberal causes for most of his adult life, had been writing to Webb for several months about Virginia and national politics. Neither Feld nor Diamond knew each other, nor realized what the other was doing. Chernila, who lived in Arlington, was the former political director of Democracy for Virginia and a top blogger in his own right. Chernila knew both Feld and Diamond and brought them together for the meeting with Webb.

The hour the three men spent with Webb left them feeling like they had found "The One" from *The Matrix*. It turned out that Webb was a Jacksonian populist who opposed the antigay marriage amendment on the ballot in Virginia, supported *Roe v. Wade*, and was for "fair trade" as opposed to "free trade." Josh Chernila commented later that although "Jim Webb's early and reasoned opposition to the Iraq War was a powerful incentive for the grassroots, it was really his principled economic policies that were the most compelling reason to support his candidacy." Chernila also pointed out that Webb's "Jacksonian mantra that 'the health of a society should be measured not at its apex, but at its base' was the first cogent message of Democratic populism to have emerged from the Democratic Party since before the Clinton era."

Aside from the policy issues, Webb greatly impressed the three Democratic activists as smart, honest, and down to earth. And Webb truly seemed interested in running for Senate. For his part, however, Webb had two serious misgivings. First, he was concerned about his ability (and desire) to raise the millions of dollars he would need to fight George Allen. Second, he was uncertain how a former Reagan administration official would be received by the Virginia Democratic establishment. This was where the netroots activists decided that they could help, by starting a "draft" to find out how much money and support would be available for a Webb candidacy.

DINNER WITH HARRIS

But first, the bloggers had a bit of business to attend to—that is, a meeting with the Democratic establishment's choice to run against Allen in 2006—a wealthy high-tech lobbyist and longtime Democratic insider named Harris Miller. On December 28, 2005, Chernila and Feld sat down at the MezzaNine Restaurant in Rosslyn, Virginia, for what turned into a three-hour dinner with Miller. Feld was convinced that Webb was the best choice to run against Allen and wanted to move ahead with the draft, but Chernila and others—including a prominent Arlington elected official—urged Feld to at least hear out Miller first.

In the end, the dinner completely backfired on Miller. Chernila and Feld were repelled by Miller's arrogant tone, including his assertions that he was a "genius" and a "visionary." Miller bragged about being all about "hard choices," but in response to a question about rolling back the Bush tax cuts for the top 1 percent, he was only able to stammer that he "wouldn't commit political suicide." So much for hard choices.

As if that weren't bad enough, Miller supported the death penalty so strongly that he asserted he'd "flip the switch" himself. Miller claimed, completely implausibly, that he could compete in southwestern Virginia. He revealed that he had strongly supported the invasion of Iraq in 2003, and he didn't sound as if he had changed his mind since. He patted his wallet and bragged about his wealth. This certainly was not the way to impress two idealistic netroots activists intent on beating George Allen. As Chernila later noted, acidly, "The best that the Democratic party establishment could come up with was a union-busting IT [information technology] lobbyist named Harris Miller who had the charisma of a shoe salesman and political positions ... that would leave the base flaccid and garner absolutely no support in a general election."

A WHIRLWIND OF ACTIVITY

In sum, the dinner with Harris Miller left Chernila and Feld more determined than ever to draft James Webb. Feld called Corey Hernandez, a Democratic activist, contributor to Raising Kaine, and top-notch techie. Feld told Hernandez that if the netroots were going to draft Webb, they needed hundreds if not thousands of online signatures, pledges of money, and other indications of support. And they needed them fast. Webb was heading to Vietnam for about two weeks, and it was important to have something substantial to show him when he got back.

Thus began a whirlwind of activity. On New Year's Day, thanks to Hernandez, Draft James Webb went live. As Greg Priddy wrote on Daily Kos:

> We're a group of Virginia Democrats who are trying to encourage James Webb to run for George Allen's Senate seat in 2006—he's seriously considering it at this point, and is expected to decide before the end of January. The Virginia race doesn't appear to be at the top of the [Democratic Senatorial Campaign Committee's] priority list, so we believe it's critical to demonstrate that we can generate interest, and financial support, from the blogosphere.[6]

The diary received only a few comments, not a particularly auspicious beginning. From that point, however, the situation improved rapidly. On January 7, Feld wrote to Webb's good friend, former U.S. Senator Bob Kerrey of Nebraska, asking for his advice on the draft movement. Kerrey responded right away:

> Thanks for the note and your encouragement of Secretary Webb. I do not know Virginia well enough to speak with your confidence, but I am confident that Jim Webb is needed in the U.S. Senate today. I have been encouraging him to run and will do everything I can to help him if he decides to

go for it. He is a unique and powerful voice which could change the course of our nation's future.

Unfortunately, I cannot advise what you (or I) should do to get him to do this. That's a work assignment for his remarkable heart.

The letter from Senator Kerrey was encouraging, and the Virginia blogosphere was buzzing. Signatures and pledges flowed into Draft James Webb. Lee Diamond and others worked the phones, trying to line up both grassroots and institutional Democratic support for a possible Webb candidacy.

On January 13, the draft team—now including about half a dozen core people—delivered a package to Webb, entitled "Results of Draft Effort." The package provided an analysis of the state of play in the Virginia Democratic Party, including indications that Mark Warner—despite being friends with Harris Miller—wanted the strongest Democrat going against Allen. Intelligence gathered by the draft team (in just two weeks) indicated that Democratic insiders saw Webb as a potentially stronger candidate than Miller, even though Miller had powerful friends in the party. Many Democrats were open to a Webb candidacy, but they had a lot of questions about Webb's stands on the issues. The analysis advised Webb that "it will be very much in your interest to court the Democratic Party" and made suggestions about whom Webb might contact in that regard. It provided an overview of the landscape facing Webb: "We think there is broad support for you to run within the Democratic Party ... once you announce and share your views with people, support for your candidacy will solidify."

The package included information on Harris Miller's campaign, his strengths and his weaknesses. It talked about contacts the draft had made, such as the veterans groups Band of Brothers and VetPac. It recommended that Webb attend the Democratic Party of Virginia's annual Jefferson-Jackson Day dinner, scheduled for February 11 in Richmond. It noted concerns people had with regard to Webb getting in so late, as well as the potential for "opposition research" against him given his voluminous record and writings (Webb himself said that he was an opposition researcher's dream). The memo informed Webb that 340 Virginians (and 563 people total) had signed the draft petition in just ten days, pledging $20,380 to a potential Webb for Senate candidacy. In addition, 145 people had explicitly expressed their intention to volunteer on Webb's campaign, the kernel of what would later become a huge grassroots "ragtag army."

The memo also included comments from the Draft James Webb site, some of which were powerful and moving. "I am proud you served under Reagan," one person wrote, "and can see that the present administration has departed from old-line conservatism.... Thank you for answering the call of duty once more, for Virginia and the nation." Another person wrote, "We desperately need someone to replace George Allen who will do more than merely rubber stamp George Bush's policies. We need a senator who will defend our civil liberties, rights to privacy and restore our reputation in the world community

as one that values human rights." Finally, here's one of the draft team's
favorites:

> I know what a tremendous personal sacrifice it would be to run against George
> Allen. But the U.S. Senate needs a man of your courage and integrity. Our
> beloved country is in great danger. We must take it back from Bush/Allens of
> our time. As a Scots-Irishman from the Shenandoah Valley, I urge you to accept
> the challenge. I am an old guy but am willing to help in any way I can.

On January 18, Feld ran a poll on Daily Kos, asking "Should James Webb
Run for Senate?" The results were astounding, with more than 900 people (98
percent of respondents) saying that they wanted Webb to run. Overwhelmingly, people were excited about the chance that Jim Webb could take on
George Allen and possibly beat him.

The last two weeks of January 2006 were eerily quiet, as the draft group
awaited word from Webb. Nerves began to fray, particularly as people on the
blogs demanded to know what was happening with Webb. On January 21,
Webb wrote to Lee Diamond, "I know many people are anxious and I'm
doing my best to close the loop on this—will be having meetings this weekend
with some key advisers, etc.... I do appreciate all of your energy and effort."
Another week went by with no word. Finally, on January 29, frustrated at still
not having heard from Webb, Feld wrote to Senator Kerrey again. The
response was not encouraging to say the least: "I am sorry to report that I
believe Mr. Webb will not be a candidate."

On January 30, Webb confirmed that he was out of the race, citing "the
reality of fund-raising at this late date," and also "the toll in hours out of every
day that I was advised it would take." Webb's hard-working supporters were
depressed almost beyond consolation, not only for their own efforts, but also
for their state and their nation. For many, the thought of George Allen as
president made them almost physically ill.

Fortunately, Webb's "no go" decision didn't last long. The next day, Webb
wrote to Josh Chernila requesting a meeting. No one had a clue what was up.
What could this mean? On February 3, the core draft group—Chernila, Diamond, and Feld—met with Webb, who was joined by campaign strategist Steve
Jarding. A legend in Democratic campaign circles, Jarding had worked for Bob
Kerrey, John Edwards, and Mark Warner, among others. Jarding announced
that he had come to work for Webb, and the draft group's hopes rose through
the roof. Jim Webb was back in the race. At the February 3 meeting, Feld was
authorized to post the following statement on Raising Kaine:

> As you all know, earlier this week I reported that James Webb had decided
> not to run for U.S. Senate from Virginia this year. This was based on direct
> contact with Webb, and was information that was rock solid at the time.

However, times change. Today, I met with James Webb for three hours, along with my colleagues Josh Chernila and Lee Diamond, and I am authorized to say the following on Webb's behalf: "Webb is definitely not out. Stay tuned for an announcement next week."[7]

By February 6, Draft James Webb had collected more than 1,000 signatures and about $42,000 in pledges for Webb. On February 7, Webb told the *Washington Post* that he intended to be a candidate for the U.S. Senate as a Democrat in 2006. On February 9, Greg Priddy filed Webb's statement of candidacy with the secretary of the Senate. *Roll Call*, an insider Capitol Hill newspaper that covers Congress, published an article speculating that Webb's entry into the race could force Allen to spend millions of dollars in Virginia instead of "coast[ing] to re-election."[8] Still, *Roll Call* maintained that Allen was the "heavy favorite" in the race. Feld wrote at the time that this characterization "wildly overestimates Allen and seriously underestimates Webb."[9]

WHAT A DIFFERENCE A DRAFT MAKES

What impact did the draft have? According to Jim Webb, "Seeing the spontaneous enthusiasm of the 'draft' movement was a very strong motivator for me, particularly as one who had never run for office, and would be running as a Democrat after having served in the Reagan administration." Steve Jarding adds that when Webb started out, he didn't have any money, organization, or connections with the party. Combined with George Allen's incumbent advantages in name recognition and money, Jarding gave Webb only about a 15 percent chance of winning. Reportedly, Webb said "I'll take those odds." Jarding noted, "With the netroots, there was an infrastructure … [the netroots] had some juice, had some experience."

Conaway Haskins, who ran the blog South of the James and who was hired as Senator Webb's deputy state director after the election, observes that "the intersection of pros and amateurs in the Webb effort was unique in Virginia political history." According to Haskins, one reason the Webb campaign relied so heavily on volunteers was that "it lacked financial resources and got started later than what is customary." And Haskins notes that "the authenticity of the Webb movement, the Jacksonian populist element, called for a certain amount of organic, spontaneous social action. Too much integration would have hurt."

Ben Tribbett—who runs one of the top political blogs in Virginia, Not Larry Sabato—contends that the Draft James Webb movement was "noticed by a lot of military people who knew Webb." According to Tribbett, when Webb got "calls from friends, from people he respected [it] really helped to get him into the race."

In January 2006, with the draft well under way, Webb told Steve Jarding that "the netroots guys were pushing him pretty hard to run." According to

Jarding, some people advised him that "the netroots will never work with the establishment" or with a traditional campaign. But Jarding says he decided early on to "embrace the netroots" in a relationship of "mutual respect." According to Jarding, Webb "wanted to run an unconventional campaign" and "the netroots allowed Webb to be a different kind of candidate." Webb hoped to avoid what had happened to Wesley Clark in 2003, when strong netroots activists and their efforts were rejected by the campaign professionals. Ultimately, Jarding considers "what the netroots brought to the table" as "very refreshing, not unlike Jim Webb himself."

The shared strategy of Lowell Feld, Greg Priddy, Josh Chernila, and other Draft James Webb bloggers was to go on Daily Kos, and the pro-Democratic blogs more broadly, talk up Webb's early and vocal opposition to the Iraq War, and make the case that Webb was a true Democrat in the Jacksonian populist mode. Aside from generating support for Webb, the strategy aimed to critique Harris Miller's Democratic credentials. The bloggers would point out that Miller had given money to arch-conservative Republicans like former House Speaker Dennis Hastert and conservative Republican Senator Spencer Abraham of Michigan, had lobbied for the outsourcing of American jobs, and had supported the invasion of Iraq. Given the dramatic contrast between the two candidates, in a relatively short time, Webb's popularity skyrocketed and Miller's plummeted on the progressive blogs.

Also important for Webb's early success were endorsements from Democratic leaders such as former Virginia Delegate Chap Petersen and former Congresswoman Leslie Byrne, both of whom were popular in Fairfax County and Northern Virginia more broadly. According to Steve Jarding, "the netroots didn't necessarily get people like Chap and Leslie [to back Webb], but the netroots gave them a bit more cover [to do so]." In addition, "the netroots may have helped open the door to people like Chap [and to] other electeds with whom we had relationships." More broadly, Jarding believes that "the netroots got Jim really thinking about running," with the money pledged perhaps not amounting to a lot, but providing "another sign that this wasn't unreal."

Webb's deputy campaign manager Adrienne Christian says, point blank, "I don't think Jim would have gotten in without the draft." According to Christian, the bloggers recognized that "we got Mark Warner and Tim Kaine, so why would we not look at another statewide office ... why look at Senate seat any differently than other statewide races?" Indeed, after helping to elect Tim Kaine as governor in 2005 over the heavily favored Jerry Kilgore, Virginia's progressive netroots were feeling empowered. There was no reason for them to think they could not help beat George Allen.

Larry Huynh, an online strategist who worked on both the Clark and Webb campaigns, says that the Webb netroots movement built on what the Clark netroots had accomplished: "There was a precedent from the Clark campaign for 'drafting' someone, drawing them into a race." Netroots activists

Jim Webb and Wesley Clark at Webb for Senate headquarters, Arlington, Virginia, March 29, 2006.

like Feld, who had been heavily involved in the Draft Wesley Clark movement, knew that that such a thing was possible. So, when Lowell Feld, Josh Chernila, and Lee Diamond envisioned a Draft James Webb movement, it wasn't coming from nowhere. Instead, the rapidly developing progressive blogosphere and netroots had a reference point and a track record established during the Clark campaign.

In addition to the netroots, the Webb campaign professionals appeared to understand the value of the netroots better than they might have even a year or two earlier. According to Larry Huynh, "the netroots were definitely better integrated in the Webb campaign than the Clark campaign." Additionally, Jessica Vanden Berg and Steve Jarding were more supportive of the Webb netroots movement "than the professionals in the Clark campaign." In the end, Huynh believes that the Webb campaign had a "more fruitful attitude" toward the netroots (and vice versa) than did the Clark campaign.

NOT JUST "AMATEUR HOUR"

The netroots campaign to draft Webb wasn't just "amateur hour" in Arlington. Lee Diamond, one of the draft's co-founders, attributes its success to "the sophistication of our initial group: technology, where to blog, knowledge of local politics, knowledge of the local grassroots network, and our connections in the blog world and the political world." In Diamond's view, the online efforts meshed with "traditional shoe leather organizing" and this was "synergistic."

From the perspective of the bloggers at Raising Kaine, the synergy worked like this: (1) a Webb event would be scheduled; (2) Raising Kaine would drum up enthusiasm and encourage volunteers to attend; (3) after the event, the netroots would report back, e-mailing photos, videos, and accounts of the event; (4) Raising Kaine bloggers would post the accounts (or the volunteers would post the accounts themselves), letting everyone know instantaneously what had happened. In essence, the Webb volunteers were like a benign version of *Star Trek's* Borg collective, connected via signals beamed across cyberspace, sharing knowledge, and building something much more powerful than any single Webb volunteer could create alone.

Another factor, according to Virginia Democratic blogger Waldo Jaquith, was "a widespread sense among activists ... that Harris Miller had been foisted upon us." Jaquith comments that "we'd never heard of Miller, there was nothing in his biography that indicated he had a shot at winning, and he wasn't a particularly convincing candidate." Worse, in Jaquith's opinion, "it seemed like the party had already decided to lose, and Miller was the guy to do it." Instead of just sitting around and being frustrated, however, citizens took action to change the situation. Josh Chernila says that the Virginia grassroots, feeling "emboldened by Tim Kaine's victory ... saw the opportunity for change and an electoral pathway to victory." All they needed was "the right messenger." Fortunately, the movement found that messenger in Jim Webb.

The nature of the Virginia Democratic blogosphere in 2006 was working in Webb's favor. Waldo Jaquith describes it as "small enough to be cohesive and to collaborate, but large enough to have an impact ... entirely conscious of [its] power, but not yet jaded or weary." In addition, Waldo notes that "the netroots and the grassroots had just begun to intersect, allowing the influence of bloggers to extend offline."

One common misconception was that bloggers were just sitting in front of their computers in their pajamas all day eating nachos. To the contrary, pro-Webb activists were busy both online and offline, working in conjunction with their non-blogging grassroots colleagues. At the same time, blog readership was expanding rapidly. Much of the web traffic came from citizen activists who not only read the blogs, but also followed up what they read with action on the ground. The bloggers themselves were busy staffing phone banks, canvassing, marching, and generally doing everything that non-blogger activists did. The point is this: most bloggers don't just blog, they get out and engage voters, help raise money, organize volunteers, build progressive community, and provide campaigns with capabilities they otherwise might not have or be able to afford.

OFF AND RUNNING—AND STUMBLING

The netroots rallied quickly around the Webb candidacy. By February 10, nearly every Democratic blogger in Virginia had endorsed Webb. In addition, Markos Moulitsas Zúniga wrote on Daily Kos that "Webb is clearly the more attractive candidate and instantly turns Virginia into a competitive Tier 2 contest."[10]

On February 10, the official Webb for Senate website, designed by Corey Hernandez, went live. Webb laid out four major themes for his campaign: (1) "Refocusing America's foreign and defense policies in a way that truly protects our national interests and seeks harmony where they are not threatened"; (2) "Repairing the country's basic infrastructure, which has eroded badly over the past decade, and developing more creative ways to assist disaster-stricken areas such as those in New Orleans and along the Gulf coast"; (3) "Reinstituting notions of true fairness in American society, including issues of race, class, and economic advantage"; and (4) "Restoring the Constitutional role of the Congress as an equal partner, reining in the unbridled power of the presidency."[11] Webb would stick with these themes throughout his campaign.

Webb's netroots activists had a significant presence at the state Jefferson-Jackson Day dinner in Richmond on February 11. The event was attended by about 1,000 people, despite a major snowstorm that was blitzing the east coast. Lowell Feld drove down with Lee Diamond, who stayed in close contact with Steve Jarding by cell phone. Harris Miller was at the event, but Webb was absent, recovering from recent hand surgery. Webb supporters had purchased a table at the dinner and talked up Webb to everyone who would listen. In addition, the Webb campaign had booked the Locust Mountain Boys bluegrass band for predinner entertainment. Lowell Feld and Lee Diamond drove back that evening to Arlington in a blinding snowstorm, feeling pretty good about the event but wishing Jim Webb could have been there (and also trying to keep the car from sliding off the road).

Webb's absence from the dinner created a ripple of discontent in the netroots ranks. At Not Larry Sabato, Ben Tribbett reflected a general feeling that Webb wasn't getting out enough. "Where is James Webb hiding, and why?" he asked.[12] Tribbett scolded Webb for skipping the Jefferson-Jackson dinner, adding that "if Webb isn't going to be serious about this campaign, he has no business being nominated."[13] Throughout the primary campaign, Tribbett's line of criticism became common among both bloggers and grassroots Webb supporters. The tension was the result of having supporters who wanted more of Webb and a candidate who was not particularly enthralled with being a politician. In addition, the Webb campaign seemed reticent to release information about Webb's positions on specific issues. It wasn't until February 23, for example, that Steve Jarding authorized Feld to write that Webb was prochoice.

On March 4, grassroots discontent escalated again at the annual St. Patrick's Day Parade in Old Town Alexandria, Virginia. The day before the

Jim Webb in the St. Patrick's Day Parade in Fredericksburg, Virginia, March 19, 2006. Courtesy of Tuy Le and Brian Vo.

parade, Webb supporters still didn't know whether they would be allowed to march. On parade day, Webb showed up late, missing the preparade volunteers gathering, as well as most of the parade itself. Volunteers were running up and down the parade route trying to find Webb. Others were in tears. After the parade, the volunteers gathered in a back room at Joe Theismann's restaurant in Old Town. Webb sat up front at a private table with Steve Jarding, eating a hamburger, while the Webb volunteers waited in the back, drinking beer and wondering where their hero was. Eventually, Josh Chernila walked up and told Webb that the volunteers would really appreciate a few words from him, and he obliged. In contrast, Harris Miller worked the room of Webb volunteers, shaking everyone's hand despite the fact that he had a bad cold and kept sneezing. First-time candidate Jim Webb's campaign was definitely not off to a smooth start.

Sensing a sagging mood, Feld tried to pump some spirit into the Draft James Webb group on March 6:

> We've got our candidate, James Webb, up and running. This week, Webb will be kicking off his campaign in Richmond, announcing his team, appearing on Colbert, and starting his grand tour of Virginia....
>
> We've got an awesome, amazing, kick-ass talented grassroots team. And *you* are the leaders. When, *not if,* we defeat George Allen this November, *you* will be the ones that deserve tremendous praise, respect, and kudos.

Personally, I am extremely proud of what we've accomplished the past few months, and look forward to what we will accomplish the next eight months. I know that I won't rest until I see George Allen's soft teeth shoved down his whiny throat, and I know you won't either!

We've got a candidate who has the potential to transform the Democratic Party, and in doing so, transform America. People like James Webb don't come along too often, but when they do, we need to make damn sure we don't squander the once-in-a-lifetime opportunity. Hell if I will![14]

The next day, March 7, Webb formally announced his candidacy in Richmond. Two days later, Harris Miller trotted out Lieutenant General Claudia Kennedy, the first woman in the Army to achieve a three-star rank, to attack Webb on his past writings. According to Kennedy, Webb had "made it clear that he doesn't think women are essential in the military."[15] Kennedy was referring to opinions Webb had expressed in 1979 in a *Washingtonian* magazine article entitled, "Women Can't Fight."[16] In that piece, Webb argued that women should not be used in combat roles. Numerous blogs quickly jumped to Webb's defense for expressing a view that was nearly universal at that time. But this issue, repeatedly trumpeted by Webb's opponents, persisted through the primary and until Election Day in November.

On March 14, Raising Kaine posted "A Warnerite's Plea for Neutrality,"[17] which stirred up a fair amount of controversy. The goal was to convince Mark Warner, who had already done a fundraiser for Harris Miller, to do one for Jim Webb as well. The idea came directly from campaign leadership, which was hoping that Warner would honor his pledge to remain neutral in the Miller-Webb race. In the end, Dan Geroe wrote a strongly pro-Warner piece that appealed to Warner's own self-interest. Still, people criticized Geroe and Raising Kaine for supposedly attacking Mark Warner, which had not been the intent of either man. In the end, Warner did a fundraiser for Webb, which helped the campaign a great deal.

Jim Webb worked hard to drum up netroots support for his candidacy. On March 14, Webb participated in the first of his numerous "live blogs" on Daily Kos. Webb posted his thoughts and then stayed for an hour or so to respond to questions from the Daily Kos community. As time went by, Webb began to receive hundreds of comments per diary, the vast majority of them positive and encouraging. In part, this response was the result of hard work by pro-Webb bloggers who promoted their candidate as a progressive and economic populist in the tradition of Teddy Roosevelt and Andrew Jackson. Feld kept an ever-expanding issues list that showed Webb to be far more progressive and economically populist than Miller on nearly everything—the Iraq War, fair trade, stem cell research, net neutrality, and much more. Still, some people viewed Harris Miller as the liberal in the race simply because he had been a longtime Democratic Party operative.

On March 15, the petition drive to get Webb on the ballot in Virginia started cranking up, ultimately providing one of the netroots' finest moments. The task was daunting, to get 10,000 valid signatures across Virginia (400 minimum per congressional district) by April 14. In the end, it was the volunteers who got Webb on the ballot, with the campaign not being forced to spend any money to do so. An amazing volunteer named Mary Detweiler led the way. According to Webb for Senate campaign manager Jessica Vanden Berg, "Without the grassroots, we would not have gotten Webb on the ballot." In contrast, Harris Miller paid people a bounty of $0.75 per signature to get his name on the ballot.[18]

A ST. PATRICK'S DAY MASSACRE

Steve Jarding points to March 17 as marking "a key turning point in which the netroots played a big role." An annual St. Patrick's Day party hosted by Gerry Connolly, Fairfax County Board of Supervisors chair, is known for its turnout of party activists and its straw poll. A major question for the nascent Webb campaign was whether to compete in the poll, particularly given that Connolly backed Harris Miller and that Fairfax was supposed to be Miller Country.

With just a few days until the party, the Webb campaign finally decided to compete, giving the green light to the netroots to get to work. In response, the blogs called for Webb supporters to attend the party, while grassroots activists urged everyone they knew to show up. An extraordinary behind-the-scenes role was played by Chris Ambrose, a forty-something grassroots activist who had been a leader in Wesley Clark's 2003–2004 Virginia campaign. On his own initiative, Ambrose contacted 300 people in Fairfax—including 60 percent of the Fairfax County Democratic Committee—urging those favorable to Webb to attend the party. In addition, Ambrose talked to senior Webb campaign management and to Jim Webb himself, convincing them that they had a chance of winning the straw poll and persuading them to compete.

Andy Hurst, the Democratic nominee for Congress from Virginia's Eleventh District in 2006, arrived at the St. Patrick's Day party at the same time as Jim Webb. According to Hurst, Webb seemed apprehensive at first. Hurst describes what happened next:

> At first, Jim slowed down, reluctant to approach what he thought was a hostile crowd … however, it became apparent that the signs and the crowd were there on his behalf. They were enthusiastic, energetic, and making a visible and compelling presence at the event. I watched Jim's pace quicken, and a small smile start to spread across his face. He strode into a very friendly crowd that had transformed this supposedly hostile venue into "Webb Country."

In the end, Webb won a victory that shocked many people, although not Chris Ambrose. The result of the straw poll was in favor of Webb, 58 to 42 percent, leaving both Harris Miller and Gerry Connolly looking utterly stunned. "If it wasn't for the netroots packing Gerry Connolly's St. Patrick's Day party, Webb might not have won the primary," Steve Jarding believes. Jarding adds that the straw poll victory "was the first concrete moment of victory in the campaign, and it was mainly because of the netroots."

Also on March 17, Feld quit his job with the U.S. Energy Information Administration, where he had worked for seventeen years, to devote all his energies as a volunteer to the Webb campaign. Steve Jarding had asked Feld to help coordinate a "$300,000 in three weeks campaign" online, which Feld could not do as a federal employee under Hatch Act rules. Feld's decision to quit his job was a leap of faith. The campaign was nearly broke—as it had been from the beginning—and had nothing definitive to offer him at the time.

DISCORD AND DISCONTENT

The Webb bloggers kept busy during the primary campaign countering Harris Miller's almost constant attacks on Webb. These attacks fell into four basic categories: (1) Webb wasn't a real Democrat; (2) Webb was a misogynist (he had opposed women in military combat roles); (3) Webb was a racist (he had once called affirmative action "state-sponsored racism"); and (4) Webb was an anti-Semite (one campaign cartoon depicted corporate lobbyist Miller, who is Jewish, with money coming out of his pockets). Several people in the netroots felt that these attacks should have been preempted. Perhaps Jim Webb should have held a press conference soon after his announcement to run so that he could talk about his political evolution on affirmative action, diversity programs, women in combat roles, and other matters. But no such press conference was ever held.

Still, pro-Webb bloggers fought back effectively against Harris Miller's attacks. They marshaled facts to defuse the Miller campaign's hyperbolic charges against Webb. They explained Webb's evolution in thinking and ratcheted up their own attacks against Harris Miller. They started going after George Allen, criticizing his hiring of Jerry Kilgore's dirty tricks ad man Scott Howell and needling him with the slogan, "Jim Webb is George Allen's Worst Nightmare."

Tensions between the Webb netroots and the campaign professionals cropped up, however. Some volunteers expressed the sense that they were the seasoned veterans and the paid staffers were the amateurs. Campaign manager Jessica Vanden Berg responded to the tensions with praise for the volunteers, recognizing that "the petition drive is amazing, our volunteers are in full force and have been doing a beyond kick ass job." Vanden Berg suggested one reason for the tension between the netroots and the professional staff was that "Jim had grassroots before he had staff." Generally, she noted, "it's the other way around and we are trying to catch up in many ways."

Despite Vanden Berg's conciliatory response to the netroots' concerns, the relationship between the professional campaign and the volunteers remained rocky throughout much of the spring. Leading up to the June 13 primary, the situation deteriorated to the point where volunteers controlled half the office space, professionals controlled the other half, and the two rarely interacted. Rumors swirled that, after the primary, there would be wholesale changes starting at the top. In reality, the campaign management was left intact, with no major changes.

Volunteer leader Betty Parrott reflects that "the grassroots was more mature and better educated than the staff." Parrott believes that "we had volunteers that knew far more than … the staff about education, labor, the maritime industry in Virginia, affirmative action," and other issues, but "we couldn't get anyone to utilize these people to prep Jim for appearances before groups." As a result, Parrott feels that Webb "made needless blunders."

Antonia Scatton, the unofficial grassroots communications director during the primary, saw "very little cooperation between the volunteers and the campaign." Scatton sounded a familiar refrain:

> We couldn't get enough materials from the campaign to keep up with the huge numbers of volunteers Jim had in the streets. We had to literally make our own campaign lit[erature]: I wrote it up, got it approved by the campaign, put it up on the website and sent it out so people could copy it. It's just amazing that the volunteers were willing to do this.

Despite such frustrations, grassroots and netroots volunteers generally stayed focused and worked hard for Webb throughout the spring of 2006. Deputy Campaign Manager Adrienne Christian believes that "the volunteers did an unbelievable job," explaining that when things needed to be done, "the grassroots would come out of nowhere." Ultimately, Lee Diamond concludes that "integration did occur" between the professional campaign and the volunteers, and that "the volunteers were crucial to the campaign throughout."

TAKING BACK VIRGINIA

In March and April, Feld had several conversations with Virginia Eighth District Congressman Jim Moran, urging him to rethink his support of Harris Miller. At an anti–Iraq War "peace vigil" in Old Town Alexandria's Market Square on March 19, Feld told Moran that Miller was a big supporter of the Iraq War and expressed surprise that Moran was supporting Miller. Congressman Moran seemed shocked by the information. Feld mentioned Miller's comments about the Bush tax cuts being a "great idea," his flippant "flip the switch myself" remark, and the fact that Miller had donated thousands of dollars to right-wing Republicans like Spencer Abraham and Dennis Hastert.

Moran never officially withdrew his endorsement of Miller. He gave Miller no further assistance, however, and his top staffers began doing everything they could to help Webb. For instance, Moran turned over his extensive mailing lists from the Eighth Congressional District, which is where Webb racked up his victory margin in the June 13 primary. Moran's behind-the-scenes switch from Miller to Webb proved crucial, and it wouldn't have happened without the netroots engaging him and revealing facts about Miller that Moran apparently hadn't known.

The netroots honed the argument against Harris Miller and for Webb down to this, as concisely expressed by blogger Dan Geroe on April 10:

> A vote for Jim Webb is a chance to give everybody a voice. A vote for Jim Webb is a vote to fight social injustice and to give everybody a fair shot. A vote for Jim Webb is a vote to make sure that all Americans have jobs before we start shipping them overseas. A vote for Jim Webb is a vote to include every single American in an attempt to clean up Washington. A vote to end "politics-as-usual." This fall is our chance to remind people what our government should be about: It's not about the spotlight, it's not about the power, and it's not about the favors. It's about doing what's right for those you represent. A vote for Jim Webb is a vote for a better Virginia.[19]

The next day, the AFL-CIO released a memo calling Harris Miller "truly one of the bad guys ... on core issues like trade, immigration, overtime protections and privatization of federal jobs."[20] Also on April 13, Marine reservist Paul Hackett, who had nearly scored a huge upset in a special congressional election in Ohio in 2005, conducted a spirited and highly successful "live blog" for Webb on Daily Kos. Hackett had become wildly popular in the progressive blogosphere for his blunt anti-Bush language and his opposition to the Iraq War. In his live blog for Webb, Hackett saluted Webb as a "role model for me, as well as [for] a generation of young Marine officers who are now running for political office." Hackett dismissed Harris Miller as "a well-heeled special interest machine."[21]

On April 19, Webb supporters descended on the annual Virginia Shad Planking, a unique political festival that had been held annually for decades in Wakefield, located in peanut farm country southeast of Richmond. The festival featured politicians of all stripes working the crowd, who were busy listening to bluegrass music, drinking beer, and eating shad—an oily, bony, salty fish cooked over cedar planks and served with cornbread and potato salad. In a hot election year—and 2006 certainly qualified—the Shad Planking could draw thousands of Virginians. Attendance by serious candidates was all but mandatory and everyone tried to make a good impression. "Sign wars" between campaigns escalated to nearly comical levels.

Corey Hernandez, one of the original draft people who had remained actively involved and who lived relatively close to rural Wakefield, described the scene the morning of the Shad Planking:

> Webb campaign volunteers, including myself, spent last evening/yesterday night putting up signs throughout the Wakefield area and we picked up where we left off early this morning. Volunteers from across the state have shown up to help. Webb has about 10,000 signs, Harris Miller about two or three. Webb has an army of volunteers to walk around with him (the crowd in this conservative part of Virginia—Wakefield, located southeast of Petersburg and Richmond—was overwhelmingly, about 90 percent or so pro-Allen). Miller has the same two or three paid staffers we see at every event; in other words, Miller has *zero* grassroots support. Basically, Miller's support is among people he's scared away from voting for Jim Webb (e.g., African Americans who he deluges with mailings saying Jim Webb was a Reagan official who opposed Affirmative Action).[22]

A telling image from the 2006 Shad Planking was Harris Miller standing around, looking forlorn, with two paid staffers holding Miller signs, surrounded by a sea of Allen and Webb signs and supporters.

Webb began his Operation Take Back Virginia tour on April 26. One goal was to counter criticism from the grassroots and from the Democratic Party people that Webb wasn't visible. Webb was not well known in the state and was perceived suspiciously by some members of the party establishment as having been drafted by a "bunch of bloggers." Why support a Reagan administration official, given how intensely most of those people despised Reagan? Why support someone never before active in Virginia Democratic politics? Why get behind a guy who came out of nowhere and was an unknown, potentially uncontrollable element? Given all these questions, Webb's tour came a bit late. Still, it did promote the candidate around the state in a camouflaged Jeep bearing the slogan, "Take Back Virginia." The Jeep was driven by one of Jim Webb's closest friends since the Vietnam War, a one-armed former Marine named Mac McGarvey.

BE YOUR OWN GENERAL

A dramatic moment in the campaign occurred on May 12, at a party for the volunteers at Webb campaign headquarters, at a time when tensions between the grassroots and the campaign professionals were near their peak. The story, by Josh Chernila, is worth telling in full:

When Webb came in, he looked really tired. But then, when he got in the middle of the crowd and felt the energy, he really brightened. He started talking about how small ground forces had outfought large established armies throughout history. I think he drew the parallel between our efforts and the woodsmen in the Revolution. He said every one of us who takes action in this effort should take up the challenge and work right where we are. He said we shouldn't wait for the campaign or for outside orders, but rather that each of us should lead, each of us should be our own general. Then he thanked us and grabbed a beer. The volunteers were thrilled.

This concept promoted by Webb—"be your own general"—pretty much sums up the concept of a grassroots and netroots campaign. The reference comes from the pivotal Battle of Kings Mountain, North Carolina, during the Revolutionary War, when Colonel Isaac Shelby rallied his band of "over the mountain men" to defeat a better armed British force. "When we encounter the enemy," Shelby told them, "don't wait for the word of command. Let each of you be your own officer, and do the very best you can." And that's just what Webb's "ragtag army" did. The question was, would their best be good enough?

Jim Webb outside the "Take Back Virginia" Jeep by Webb for Senate headquarters, Arlington, Virginia, summer 2006. Mac McGarvey is in the driver's seat. Courtesy of Claude W. Dean.

SEMITES AND ANTI-SEMITES

On May 19, one of the only pro-Miller bloggers in Virginia, an ultraliberal named Alice Marshall, accused Jim Webb of playing "the anti-Semitic card."[23] The Webb campaign had produced a cartoon depicting Harris Miller as a rich corporate lobbyist (which he was) with a cigar in his right hand, money coming out of his coat pocket, and with Miller saying things like "U.S. workers will just have to get used to lower wages ... get those jobs overseas." The flier also called Miller "the anti-Christ of outsourcing," a phrase originally coined by Paul McDougall in *Information Week.*[24]

Josh Chernila, of Jewish heritage himself, responded angrily on Raising Kaine to Alice Marshall's anti-Semitism allegations, calling them "weak, pitiful, and despicable." Chernila reminded readers that 2005 Virginia gubernatorial candidate "Jerry Kilgore used Hitler in his ads, and he lost." Chernila concluded by calling Marshall's charges "the last and least of a string of cowardly moves from Miller."[25]

Virginia's right-wing bloggers chimed in, suddenly finding themselves "outraged" over Webb's supposed anti-Semitism. One conservative blogger, Shaun Kenney, even accused pro-Webb bloggers of "Jew baiting." An irate Josh Chernila slammed back:

This is classic smear politics that originated with Harris Miller's blog-pet, Alice Marshall. That Allen supporters are picking up this Rovian tactic and running with it only proves how deeply afraid the right wing is of a Webb Senate candidacy.... Make no mistake, any vote for Harris Miller is a vote for George Allen, George Bush and the right-wing conservatism that will destroy America if it is allowed to continue unabated.[26]

Soon, many people began asking whether Harris Miller had gone too far, as Jerry Kilgore had done with his infamous Hitler ad against Tim Kaine in 2005. *Washington Post* columnist Marc Fisher weighed in, writing that "the Webb folks deny any anti-Semitism, with good reason: It's a pretty big stretch to find anything anti-Jewish about the Webb flyer."[27] Ben Tribbett later observed, "Miller almost created the Webb momentum by just going so over the top."

Not allowing the phony anti-Semitism issue to distract them, the grassroots and netroots continued working hard for Jim Webb. On May 20, a dozen or so Webb volunteers were at a Democratic school board election in Arlington, reminding hundreds of Democrats to vote for Webb in just three weeks. The campaign didn't seem particularly enthusiastic about working the event, even though it was filled with likely Democratic voters. According to Chris Ambrose, "That was something the campaign didn't want to do," yet there was "no rationale for not doing it." Fortunately, the volunteers didn't need any persuading. Only one Miller staffer was seen at the election, and he left early.

INTO THE STRATOSPHERE

As the Webb-Miller primary wound to its conclusion, former Virginia Governor Mark Warner and his team—which now included Nate Wilcox, recruited by Jerome Armstrong just months earlier—set off for the Yearly Kos convention at the Riviera Hotel in Las Vegas. This was the first-ever national convention of the netroots, and politicians were eager to win them over. Mark Warner, who was considering a run for president, was slated to give the keynote speech, while Warner's Forward Together PAC was footing the bill for the biggest party of the convention. The Riviera hotel's facilities were not adequate for a party of 1,500 people, and the only nearby casinos were the run-down Circus Circus and the silly Stratosphere. A modest party in a basement room at the Circus Circus would cost nearly as much as a major blowout at the Stratosphere, an over-the-top Las Vegas hotel featuring roller coasters on the roof. The Warner camp chose the Stratosphere.

The situation quickly went downhill. Several bloggers (including a few who supported presidential candidates other than Mark Warner) reacted strongly to what they viewed as the decadence of the chocolate fountains and ice sculptures at the party. To the Warner team's dismay, Warner was criticized on the blogosphere for these party embellishments. Even worse, Warner's interview with a group of bloggers following his well-received keynote speech was a disaster. Warner, whose foreign policy positions were still being formulated, came across to the strongly antiwar bloggers at Yearly Kos as conservative, possibly even one of the hated and dreaded "neoconservatives."

Yearly Kos did have its amusing moments. The convention swarmed with reporters, including star *New York Times* columnist Maureen Dowd. One scene suggested an infinite mirror: Maureen Dowd interviewed Markos Moulitsas Zúniga while two local television news crews shot video. Standing outside the circle and furiously scribbling on their notepads were several other reporters, including Ron Brownstein of the *Los Angeles Times*. Surrounding the entire scene, a ring of bloggers sat on the floor with their laptops, blogging away.

JOHN KERRY TO THE RESCUE

On June 12, one day before the primary, Senator John Kerry—the 2004 Democratic presidential nominee—joined Jim Webb at a rally of 300 people outside Webb for Senate headquarters in Arlington, Virginia. The fact that Kerry was there for Webb represented an amazing turn of events, particularly considering the fact that the two men had not shaken hands since the end of the Vietnam War because of their strongly differing views on that subject (Webb supported it, Kerry opposed it). In addition, Webb was aware that the endorsement might anger veterans who felt that Kerry had dishonored their service through his anti–Vietnam war protests and his emotional testimony to the Senate Foreign Relations Committee in 1971. Still, the Kerry endorsement made sense as a sort of Democratic "seal of approval" for the former Reagan Navy secretary running in a Democratic primary.

John Kerry's support for Jim Webb epitomized the unique way the Webb campaign brought top-down political insiders and bottom-up grassroots activists together on the same side. The Webb-Miller race easily could have played out as a contest between grassroots for Webb and establishment for Miller. Instead, the national Democratic establishment, including Senator Chuck Schumer, head of the Democratic Senatorial Campaign Committee, and numerous other national Democrats (including eleven U.S. senators, General Wesley Clark, Max Cleland, and Paul Hackett), rallied to Webb's candidacy. Not one U.S. congressman endorsed Harris Miller. According to Jessica Vanden Berg, the national Democratic endorsements shifted the focus of the campaign to Webb's strong suit, that is, his electability over George Allen (in contrast, the campaign argued that Harris Miller had no chance in the general election). Support for Webb and Miller among Virginia elected officials was about evenly split, although endorsements for Webb increased rapidly as the campaign continued and it became clear that he was likely to win.

At the rally with Webb in Arlington, Senator Kerry noted that, "even when I disagreed with Jim Webb, I respected him greatly" as a person who thinks for himself. Kerry noted pointedly that we need "someone who was born fighting" (a reference to Webb's history of the Scots-Irish in America, *Born Fighting*) and who "will take that fight to the Senate." For his part, Webb movingly pointed out that "John Kerry and I more than thirty-five years ago went to battle in [Vietnam] and came back to a bitterly divided nation." But, Webb said, the Vietnam war and its divisions were over. Webb directly addressed Harris Miller's accusation that Webb opposed diversity. The crowd roared its approval when Webb said, "Let me introduce my wife, *Hong*, and my daughter's longtime boyfriend, *Jose Ramirez*." Then Webb pointed his finger and said, "Mr. Miller, I understand diversity!"[28]

After the rally, several Webb volunteers engaged in a bit of guerilla warfare with Harris Miller. Earlier in the day, Feld had discovered that Miller would be handing out literature at the Pentagon City Metro stop in Arlington from 5 to 7 P.M. Feld immediately decided that Webb supporters wearing Webb shirts and stickers needed to be there as well. Feld recruited half a dozen people to come with him, gathered up as much literature as he could scrounge (there wasn't much left at that point), and headed down to the Metro stop around 4:45 P.M.

When Harris Miller got there with his usual two staffers, his jaw nearly hit the ground as he saw the Webb supporters blanketing the Metro stop. For the next hour or so, until the Webb volunteers' literature ran out, they yelled "Webb for Senate, election tomorrow!" and made sure that everyone who wanted information on Webb received it. The frustrated Miller staffers started pleading with people, "But wait, we're the *other* candidate!" The Webb volunteers handed out hundreds of pieces of literature, with hundreds more people having heard their message, just twelve hours before the election. Mission accomplished.

OUTSPENT THREE TO ONE, WEBB WINS ANYWAY

On primary Election Day, June 13, the grassroots and netroots were in action early, covering polling stations around Virginia with "greeters." Miller greeters were far fewer; as a result, most people received only Webb literature as they walked into their polling place. At the Virginia Centrist blog, Paul Anderson said he suspected that "there are plenty of politicians in both parties who hope Harris Miller pulls this off. For them, a Miller win will signify that bloggers' shrill sense of self-importance is unjustified."[29] If that were the case, plenty of politicians in both parties must have been unhappy that night, as James Webb defeated Harris Miller 53.5 to 46.5 percent, despite having been outspent three to one.

Several factors contributed to Webb's victory. First, Democrats so badly wanted to beat George Allen that they were willing to take a chance on the unknown-but-high-potential Jim Webb as opposed to the known-but-sure-loser Harris Miller. Second, Miller apparently turned people off with his unrelenting negativity toward Webb. Third, Webb gained a huge advantage from his netroots support, both in the streets and on the Internet. Webb had thousands of volunteers—many hundreds of whom were highly active. Miller had

Jim Webb's Democratic primary victory party, Arlington, Virginia, June 13, 2006. Courtesy of Claude W. Dean.

close to zero. The blogs got Webb's message out and successfully countered much of Miller's. The blogs attacked Miller relentlessly, dug up damaging facts, and influenced mainstream media coverage.

According to John Rohrbach, Harris Miller's Internet coordinator, the impact of the pro-Webb netroots was so powerful it was almost impossible to combat. Rohrbach says that the Miller people "were just losing the battle and nothing we [did] seemed to have any impact on it." Rohrbach adds, "We weren't shocked that blogs could have that much impact, just frustrated that we were getting our asses kicked so bad." With regard to Webb's huge advantage in volunteers on the ground, Rohrbach believes that "Webb was dominating the netroots and that helped him dominate the grassroots." Rohrbach concludes that Webb's success resulted from "technology coming together with anger … creating and fueling a candidate like Jim Webb. Harris Miller doesn't tap into that." This is a perfect description of how the netroots works—or doesn't work—for political candidates.

Statewide, Webb defeated Miller by fewer than 11,000 votes out of 155,784 cast. Webb's victory margin came almost completely from two counties in northern Virginia: Arlington (with a Webb margin of 4,477 votes) and Fairfax (with a Webb margin of 8,000 votes), the two counties in which the netroots had the most intensive penetration. That's 12,477 votes in those two counties alone, greater than Webb's overall statewide margin. Other strong Webb locations included Alexandria (Webb margin of 1,344 votes), Prince William (Webb margin of 883 votes), and Loudoun (Webb margin, 1,320 votes)—all in northern Virginia and all areas with heavy progressive blog readership.

Webb fared the worst in southern and southwestern Virginia, areas where people were less wired into the Internet. There, Miller's relentless portrayal of Webb as somehow against affirmative action undoubtedly hurt, and the netroots was unable to respond effectively. For people in those communities, the main contact with the candidates came from television or direct mail, fueled in large part by Miller's three-to-one cash advantage (including $1 million of his own money) over Webb. On balance, however, the battle between Miller's traditional campaign with all its big money and Webb's netroots campaign with its shoestring operation was won by Webb.

After the election, former Virginia Delegate Chap Petersen, who had sought the Democratic nomination for lieutenant governor in 2005, wrote on his blog (Ox Road South), "The Webb campaign was comfortably ahead in Northern Virginia from February due to its grassroots base." Petersen added, pointedly, that northern Virginia "was the home of the 'draft Webb' movement." Petersen noted that Webb volunteers "had [their] 'boots on the ground' at every major event," while online they "filled a void in the media coverage from the mainstream press and got the attention of ordinary voters." And, "due to the high cost of television in the D.C. market," Petersen analyzed, "Miller could not counter-attack except through direct mail, which voters tend to discount." Petersen's conclusion? "Webb's campaign success was from the bottom up."[30]

At Not Larry Sabato, Ben Tribbett echoed what Chap Petersen had written, looking at the numbers and concluding, "Last night was the first major election that bloggers have ever won for a candidate." Tribbett analyzed the numbers and discovered a stark contrast, with Webb winning 63 percent of the vote in northern Virginia, but only 47 percent in the rest of the state. According to Tribbett, "I don't see how anyone can look at these numbers and not give us credit for this victory."[31]

In the *Washington Post,* columnist Marc Fisher concurred with regard to "the increasing influence of political bloggers in races with low turnouts." Quoting Webb senior strategist Dave "Mudcat" Saunders, Fisher wrote that there was "no question about it, the bloggers were driving this."[32]

Perhaps unsurprisingly, others in the mainstream media largely missed that point. In the *Washington Post,* Michael Shear and Robert Barnes asserted that the netroots movement that "helped woo Webb into the race" really amounted to no more than "a lot of chatter between a small number of young computer geeks."[33] That last phrase was incorrect on nearly every count. For starters, the number of Webb's netroots supporters was certainly not small; in the month leading up to the June 13 primary, Raising Kaine and Not Larry Sabato combined received more than 100,000 visits, more than the 83,298 votes Webb won in the election. Second, the average age of the early draft leaders was over forty, not exactly "young." Finally, many of the Webb citizen activists knew little about computers; many had never blogged previously and most did not have any particular knowledge of computers. For instance, Josh Chernila was technologically savvy, but that had nothing to do with his decision to help draft James Webb. That decision came from reading up on Webb and Miller, meeting with both of them in person, and using his political judgment to determine who had the best shot at beating George Allen in November.

Despite their mischaracterization of the netroots, Shear and Barnes did recognize the "emergence of a new kind of campaign structure that Webb can tap in his race against Allen."[34] In the end, that's what helped propel Webb to victory over George Allen.

THE DAY AFTER

Josh Chernila reported that it was "very quiet" at Webb campaign headquarters the day after the Democratic primary. According to Chernila, "People were happy they'd won, but held no great belief Webb would win" against George Allen. In contrast, Chernila said that he was "childlike in [his] optimism," but that the campaign people "were just happy they still had jobs for a couple more months."

Could the Webb campaign have won the primary without the netroots? Jim Webb says that "there are so many dynamics in play in an election campaign," but that "it would not have been possible to get the word out regarding the campaign, particularly during the primary, without this [netroots] support." The question, as of June 14, 2006, was whether Webb's netroots magic had been a fluke. Or, was it something that could be repeated in the fight against a seemingly invincible George Allen?

Chapter 7

WIN ONE, LOSE ONE

Jim Webb was not the only example of the "netroots rising" during 2006. In addition to Virginia, great netroots stories were emerging from all around the country, in states like Connecticut (Ned Lamont), Montana (Jon Tester), Pennsylvania (Joe Sestak, Patrick Murphy), New York (Eric Massa), California (Jerry McNerney), and many others. Here we present just two of those stories.

JON TESTER: THE NETROOTS BACKS A WINNER

Unlike in Virginia for Jim Webb, there was no netroots draft effort for Montana's Senate President Jon Tester. Still, Montana bloggers like Matt Singer, founder of the blog Left in the West, were active in helping persuade Jon Tester to enter the U.S. Senate race in 2006. The Montana Democratic Party establishment had not settled on one candidate as they had in Virginia with Harris Miller; instead, some supported State Auditor John Morrison while others supported Tester. In contrast, Singer says that a small number of national political consultants—from the Democratic Senatorial Campaign Committee (DSCC), primarily—attempted to "clear the field" for Morrison, a moderate-to-conservative, insider politician with a "heck of a Rolodex" and gobs of money. In other words, Morrison was a good choice if your main concern was traditional fundraising capabilities, but he certainly was not the typical populist, progressive, authentic candidate with great netroots appeal.

A strong progressive at heart, Jon Tester was a leader in the Montana State Legislature who was well respected on both sides of the aisle. Tester's background resembled that of Democratic Governor Brian Schweitzer, who in the last election had far outpaced typical Democratic performance in rural areas of the state. Tester was a farmer who grew organic wheat and barley on land his grandparents homesteaded a century ago, while Morrison was a lawyer from Helena whose primary argument for his own candidacy was that he was the most "electable."

Singer points out that, in previous elections, Morrison ran against two far-right-wing Republicans, outspent them, and still had not won in "the blowouts that could be expected under the circumstances." Morrison's claim to electability thus looked a bit shaky on closer examination.

As in Virginia, the Montana and national bloggers were drawn to the candidate seen as more progressive and more authentic, while still having a good chance of winning. In contrast, according to Matt Singer, the DSCC people "didn't seem very enthused about Tester," although they became more favorably inclined as the primary got closer. Early on, however, "it was all about money so people were more for Morrison."

The main question for Jon Tester was whether he could compete financially with Morrison, who was already in the race and was known as a tenacious fund-raiser. Tester was starting from scratch, but he received early and enthusiastic netroots support. Singer particularly credits Markos Moulitsas Zúniga of Daily Kos with being "behind Tester from Day One." Other bloggers soon followed.

In August 2005, Matt Gross, who was Howard Dean's former Internet strategist, and Matt Singer were contracted by the Tester campaign to work on blog outreach. From August through December, they focused mostly on list building, because people were not yet interested in the 2006 Senate race. Online fundraising started picking up, with about 60 percent of donations coming from Montana and 40 percent coming from out of state. At the end of 2005, Singer left the campaign staff but continued to support Tester through his blog.

Poll numbers as of early 2006 showed that either Democrat—Morrison or Tester—could be competitive with Conrad Burns, who had first been elected in 1988 and reelected twice since. In 2000, Burns had barely managed (by four points) to defeat Democratic challenger Brian Schweitzer, despite outspending Schweitzer by a two-to-one margin—an indication of potential vulnerability. In addition, like all national Republicans, Burns was being weighed down by the "culture of corruption" in Washington, as well as by the increasingly unpopular Iraq War. For his part, Tester pledged to run an ethical office if he was elected, and to fight to bring U.S. troops home from Iraq.

By March, more money started flowing into the Tester campaign and the polls showed Tester doing better. Then, a big story hit about Morrison cutting a deal with the husband of a woman with whom he had had an affair. Singer says that "the blogs did a [great job] of making sure that story really stayed [alive]." Given that only around 100,000 Democrats were likely to vote in the primary, with perhaps a 10,000-vote victory margin, the blogs' ability to keep a damaging story about Morrison alive—and to communicate it to opinion leaders—was significant. For instance, the U.S. attorney for Montana under President Clinton told Singer that she had switched her allegiance to Tester because of what she had read about Morrison on Left in the West.

In addition, Singer notes that blog readers "are the sort of people who are likely to be volunteers for campaigns," and in the closing weeks of the Tester-Morrison primary campaign, that's exactly what they did—they began cold-calling identified Democratic voters and asking them to support Tester. On the first night of calling, Singer recalls that it was "about one-to-one Tester/ Morrison." But after that, "the numbers just kept getting better." By the end, Singer recalls, "It was unlike anything I've ever seen in an election ... we had entire call sheets with fifty names on them and not a single Morrison sup- porter on them."

According to Singer, "What happened in the primary was a perfect storm in some ways: a pump primed by the netroots, a scandal hitting the opponent, a largely undecided electorate, no opposing field effort, top-notch paid media, and just enough money to keep staff employed and ads on the air." In addi- tion, Singer points to the work of Dan Kully, who produced Jon Tester's tele- vision ads—including the clever "Creating a Buzz" ad, which depicts people getting Jon Tester's flat-top haircut. That ad was highly popular, and Kully later won a Pollie Award from the American Association of Political Consul- tants for its creation.

A week before the primary, although Morrison had outspent Tester three to one, polls showed a tight race, with one poll indicating a dead heat. Singer recalls, "Volunteers all over the state mobilized—organizing their own lit drops and phone banks from Flathead County in northwestern Montana to the flat cities of the Eastern plains." Phone banks were run entirely by volun- teers. In contrast, Morrison's campaign had few volunteers and little excite- ment. On election night, June 6, the Tester folks were expecting to lose Yellowstone County, but instead they won it by nine percentage points. Out of fifty-six Montana counties, Tester won forty-eight. Overall, Tester won the Montana Democratic primary by more than twenty-five percentage points, 61 to 35 percent.

The general election contest pitted Tester against Conrad Burns, the three- term incumbent Republican. In 2000, Burns had been reelected by a narrow margin, and the Democrats had taken over the Montana State Legislature in 2004. In part because of his ties to the Jack Abramoff corruption scandal, Burns had high disapproval ratings and was considered one of the most vulnerable incumbent Republican senators of the 2006 election cycle. Despite this vulnerability, Burns had won the Republican primary on June 6, 2006, over state legislator Bob Keenan by more than a three-to-one margin.

Jon Tester entered the general election against Senator Burns with a definite shot at winning, but to do that he needed help against the far-better-funded incumbent (and in a state that George W. Bush had carried by twenty-five points in 2000 and twenty points in 2004). One innovative tactic employed by the Montana Democratic Party was to have a staffer follow Burns every- where, filming him and posting the results on YouTube. In addition to the Democratic Party's activities, the state and national blogs raised money for Tester and shaped perceptions of Burns. Perhaps most significant, the blogs played up the infamous early August incident in which Burns insulted a team of firefighters, who had traveled 2,000 miles from Augusta County, Virginia, to battle forest fires in Montana, as doing a "piss-poor job." The *Newport News Daily Press* described the scene this way:

> After days spent in the heat and flames of the Billings fires, the Augusta fire-fighters were finally on their way home, ... waiting to board their flight to Virginia. That's when the senator showed up.... Burns stormed up to the Virginia crew and cussed them. "See that guy over there? ... He hasn't done a [expletive deleted] thing.... You probably paid that guy $10,000 to sit around."[1]

In addition, blogs pushed the story that Burns was tied to felon-lobbyist Jack Abramoff, specifically Burns's actions in securing a $3 million appropriation earmarked for an Indian tribe in Michigan that employed Abramoff as its lobbyist. Overall, Matt Singer says, the state and national blogs "kept beating the drum, fact checking, trying to influence the media." And sometimes it worked.

At the end of August, the *Missoula Independent* reported on the impact of Montana's online activists, stating that they were "changing the balance of power in Democratic politics." The story quoted Tester as calling the blogs "critically important to this campaign." Tester added, "They've brought more people into the political process, and I have nothing but high praise for what they've been able to do and what they've given me." The article continued:

> It's hard to gauge just how many people the blogs have brought into the political process—none of the major blogs maintain reliable records of visitor volume—but it's clear that they've brought donors to Tester's campaign, and the man from Big Sandy has plenty of reasons to be thankful.
>
> Support for Tester on national blogs like MyDD, Daily Kos, and Swing State Project has inspired some 2,400 donors from around the country to give upward of $114,000 to his campaign so far. And much of Tester's national popularity has to do with the early Internet grassroots—or "netroots"—support his campaign received from Montana bloggers. Rallying behind Tester's primary defeat of Democratic Party favorite and early big-money front-runner John Morrison, the Montana blogosphere is energized....
>
> For their part, Montana's bloggers believe Tester is in a position to become the next poster boy of their liberal Internet activism. Take Conrad Burns's Abramoff-induced vulnerability, add to that his inability to keep his embarrassing antics out of the headlines, then mix in the fact that Montana is a cheap date when it comes to political advertising, and what you end up with is a decent possibility that netroots activism—and the dollars it generates—could help topple an entrenched three-term Republican.
>
> The bloggers themselves downplay their importance to Montana politics. They might just be modest, or they might not realize how far their voices travel. After all, they say, their blogs get only a few hundred hits a day, and

that's hardly enough voters to elect any candidate, even in a sparsely populated state like Montana.²

Throughout the general election campaign, Matt Singer worked to push stories about the Tester-Burns race on the national blogs, while Tester himself live blogged several times (June 7, June 27, August 15, and September 7) on Daily Kos. Tester also was popular on the popular social networking site, Facebook, and raised more than $340,000 through ActBlue, the online center for netroots fundraising.

On election night, Tester defeated Burns by less than one percentage point, 50.4 percent to 49.6 percent, despite being outspent $9.2 million to $5.6 million. Many factors led to Tester's victory, the blogs being only one of them. Still, the netroots had encouraged Tester to get into the race, had helped him defeat John Morrison in the Democratic primary, and also had played an important role in the general election (largely by beating the drum on anti-Burns stories). Not bad for a handful of unpaid citizen activists!

NED LAMONT: WINNING THE BATTLE, LOSING THE WAR

In December 2005, progressive activists inside and outside of Connecticut were looking for a candidate to challenge Democrat Joe Lieberman, who was running for his fourth term in the U.S. Senate. Although Lieberman had been Al Gore's running mate just five years earlier, by late 2005, the progressive netroots had concluded that the senator had gone over to the dark side—supporting the war in Iraq, literally kissing up to George W. Bush, parroting White House talking points on Fox News, and losing touch with citizens of the Nutmeg State.

But who would challenge Lieberman for the party's nomination? Names prominently mentioned were former Connecticut governor and U.S. Senator Lowell Weicker; John Orman, the 1984 Democratic nominee for Congress from Connecticut's Fourth District; and state Attorney General Richard Blumenthal. Largely because of blogosphere buzz, progressive activists coalesced around a relative unknown, a Greenwich selectman and telecom multimillionaire named Ned Lamont.

Aldon Hynes, who served as Ned Lamont's technology director, believes that Lowell Weicker "planted a bug in Ned's ear" about running for the U.S. Senate. By the end of 2005, Lamont was talking to various people about this possibility, and word got out to the blogs. Hynes says that this "pushed things along a little bit faster than some of the people trying to put together Ned's campaign originally were hoping for."

One key netroots activist was Keith Crane, a member of the Branford, Connecticut, Democratic town committee. One day after Lieberman voted to confirm Alberto Gonzales as attorney general, Crane started the website, DumpJoe, as well as an affiliated Dump Joe movement. As *The Nation*

Blogger Beau Anderson ("Spazeboy") standing next to the Lieberman-Bush "The Kiss" float in Connecticut, summer 2006. Courtesy of Beau Anderson.

magazine pointed out at the time, Crane "built the [Dump Joe] organization ... using connections and skills he gained participating in meet-ups for the Howard Dean presidential campaign."[3] Dean had encouraged his supporters to get involved with their local Democratic Party organizations—and many did, including Keith Crane. According to Aldon Hynes, "If you were a Dean supporter in 2003, you were a Lamont supporter" in 2006. One netroots movement thus begat another.

Hartford Courant reporter Mark Pazdiokos later commented:

> [A] key moment in [the Lamont-Lieberman] campaign was really last fall, after Congressman John Murtha, a conservative Democrat, got up and called for the withdrawal of U.S. troops. Twelve days later, Senator Lieberman had an op-ed piece in the *Wall Street Journal*, and the headline was, "The Troops Must Stay." That infuriated Democrats here, and that really fueled the movement that led Ned Lamont to jump into the race. It was really about that time that Ned Lamont got together with Tom Swann, who became his campaign manager. He's a grassroots organizer in Connecticut, and it quickly went from there.[4]

Tim Tagaris, who served as Lamont's Internet director, says that in early 2006, Matt Stoller of the popular Democratic blog MyDD "came up to Connecticut to meet with Lamont [and] wrote about the experience." Tagaris says that he ultimately hooked up with Lamont because of Stoller, who knew Tom Swann. The three netroots activists—Tagaris, Stoller, and Swann—would all come to play crucial roles in Ned Lamont's campaign. In early 2006, the bloggers started to build a "buzz" around Lamont as a possible winning candidate against Lieberman.

In March, Lamont announced his candidacy for U.S. Senate against Joe Lieberman. From that point on, it was a netroots campaign through and through. As with Jim Webb's campaign in Virginia, Lamont relied on volunteers for everything from gathering petitions to get on the ballot to blogging and raising money. According to Tim Tagaris, the Lamont campaign didn't even have to hire a research department. It was getting all the information it needed from the netroots, and it was getting it for free.

The bloggers kept busy both locally and nationally. Tagaris counts Matt Stoller (MyDD and later Open Left), Markos Moulitsas Zúniga (Daily Kos), Duncan Black (Eschaton), and Jane Hamsher (FireDogLake) among "the loudest voices nationally." In mid-May, the Lamont campaign even produced a television commercial starring Moulitsas. Tagaris gives great credit to the strong netroots support for Lamont nationally, but says that "the best work was really done locally"—running the field campaign, doing press outreach," and much more. According to Tagaris, "Mark Pazdiokos of the *Hartford Courant* read the Lamont Blog before he read his own newspaper every morning."

Tagaris recalls that the Lamont Blog was "by far and away the best source of information about the Lamont campaign," but it wasn't just that one blog. "What was great about these local sites is that they came together and formed a great machine in which the whole was greater than the sum of its parts," he explains. The Lamont Blog provided "a steady diet of Lamont information." Connecticut Bob "would go out and do the ambush videos, [capturing] great original video content." A blogger who went by the name Spazeboy (but whose actual name is Beau Anderson) "would pull together the best clips onto one page [of] Ned Lamont resource[s] so you had video from all types of shows, radio, Air America, etc." Another blogger with the screen name CTBlogger "would show up at all these events across the state, videotape them and get them on the site that night." And a guy named "Scarce"—Tagaris doesn't even know his real name—"would find a way to put up any clip of Ned Lamont." Besides blogging, the netroots helped so much with fundraising they were called the campaign's "finance department."

Maura Keaney, who wrote at My Left Nutmeg—a high-quality Connecticut community blog with an amusing name—had been a prominent Virginia blogger and executive director of Democracy for Virginia before moving to Connecticut to care for her ailing parents. In mid-July, Keaney had an encounter with Joe Lieberman at the Tigin Irish Pub in Stamford. Lieberman was there to receive the endorsement of the Irish-American Democrats of Connecticut. After his speech, Lieberman waded into the crowd to shake hands. When he got to Keaney, she mentioned her father, and Senator Lieberman said (erroneously, according to Keaney) "I think I know him well." Keaney confronted Lieberman:

> My dad was a very loyal Democrat until he died. You mentioned how Irish American Democrats are great supporters because they're not fair-weather friends, and I totally agree. So why are you being a fair-weather Democrat, saying you'll only respect the results of the Democratic primary if you win?[5]

Keaney recalls, "All of a sudden I found myself with a bunch of microphones in my face," while Senator Lieberman "looked slightly stunned." Keaney quickly pledged to support whoever won the Democratic primary, challenging Senator Lieberman to do the same. Instead, Lieberman replied, "Well, let's make sure I win in August!" Keaney was "mobbed by reporters asking how to spell my name."[6] When video of the confrontation appeared on YouTube, it was a big hit.

As it turns out, this was not Maura Keaney's first brush with television cameras. In March 2005, she had appeared on ABC's *Nightline* after blogging about a bill sponsored by Republican Virginia Delegate John Cosgrove that would have punished women who failed to report a miscarriage with up to twelve months in jail and a $2,500 fine. Keaney's story was picked up by newspapers and television stations around Virginia, causing a strong reaction, and forcing Cosgrove to withdraw the bill. This incident illustrates once again how even just one engaged, informed citizen activist can influence the political process in America.

Another great netroots moment came in Hartford on July 3, 2006, when Joe Lieberman announced that he would run as an independent if he lost the Democratic primary. As Lieberman held his press conference, bloggers were messaging each other all over the country. Lieberman commented, "I will stay a Democrat, whether I am the Democratic Party's nominee or a petitioning Democratic candidate on the November ballot," then tried to duck out of the press conference.[7] Jane Hamsher quickly got video of Lieberman's remarks out to the blogs with the headline, "Lieberman Cuts and Runs from His Own Press Conference." Tagaris calls that "definitely a turning point" in the primary campaign.

Aldon Hynes says that the Lamont netroots formed a "passionate army, some of them particularly creative." Among other things, the Lamont netroots came up with "The Kiss" button, which depicted an infamous embrace between George W. Bush and Joe Lieberman in the U.S. Capitol immediately after Bush's January 2005 State of the Union address. According to Hynes, "The volunteers made [the kiss buttons] themselves" and "paid out of pocket ... It was completely grassroots." One activist, Jeff Talbot, constructed a giant paper-maché float of "The Kiss" and drove it everywhere Lieberman went. It was great theater and highly effective politics.

In contrast to Lamont and his thousands of eager volunteers, Lieberman relied on paid staffers, even hiring "paid volunteers," a bold oxymoron if ever there was one. It's particularly poignant when one considers that Ned Lamont was the megamillionaire, and Joe Lieberman certainly was not. By all rights, it should have been Lieberman relying on volunteers and Lamont paying for staffers, but it was the opposite. And the Lamont volunteers didn't help just Lamont, but also other Democratic candidates in Connecticut.

Nearing the primary, the limitations of netroots campaigning circa 2006 appear to have been exposed. According to Tagaris, the Lamont team worked hard, but they had numerous people who "had never worked for a political campaign before, much less a political campaign that was *the* focus of the national media." In contrast, Tagaris says that the veteran Lieberman campaign—which employed people like national political operative Dan Gerstein and others with presidential-level experience—"destroyed us in the traditional media." For instance, Tagaris points to Lieberman's "closing argument" speech just before the Democratic primary as garnering coverage by "everyone in the state." In addition, there was "Joe's tomorrow tour," also covered heavily by the Connecticut media.

The Lamont campaign and their blogger allies fought back. For instance, the netroots helped to get Democratic politicians and candidates on record saying that they would support the winner of the Connecticut primary. Then, Tagaris says, "the next thing you know, the press started asking the question on their own." On the national level, "people like Markos and Jane began to get national figures" to say "we will support the winner of the primary." Tagaris recalls,

This was such an effective part of the way we used the Internet in this campaign, that on primary night, candidates couldn't send us their $5,000 checks fast enough, and their press releases were flying out faster than their $5,000 checks. People couldn't wait. John Edwards was like, "Hey, we were the first to call Ned Lamont, I sent him the first $5,000 check."

On August 8, Ned Lamont narrowly defeated Joe Lieberman in the Connecticut Democratic primary, 52 to 48 percent. At Daily Kos, Markos Moulitsas Zúniga declared Lamont's win a victory for "people-powered politics." Moulitsas continued,

What tonight showed is that democracy *can* work. That even the most powerful, entrenched forces can be dislodged by people-power. That the combined mights of the Democratic and Conservative establishments couldn't hold the gates against the barbarian intruders.[8]

At Raising Kaine, Lowell Feld wrote that "2006 politically has so far been the year of Jim Webb, Jon Tester, and Ned Lamont."[9] Yet instead of dropping out, Senator Lieberman announced that he would run in the general election as an "independent Democrat." And, amazingly, after all that netroots energy and Lamont's primary victory, Lieberman would go on to win in November. So what happened?

According to Tim Tagaris, the first mistake was that the Lamont campaign had "maybe a little too much faith that others would try to force Lieberman to leave the race." Tagaris insists that the campaign kept working hard, that "it's not like we took our feet totally off the gas." Although Lamont went away for a few days of vacation on Cape Cod, "while he was [there] he did one of the Sunday talk shows, radio interviews, press calls." Ultimately, however, Tagaris says, "We were hoping Lieberman would drop out"—but he didn't. Tagaris adds that, after the primary, Lieberman ran a "total disinformation campaign" regarding his position on the Iraq War, repeating over and over, "No one wants to end this war more than I do." Of course, that was absurd; just about everyone else who called themselves a Democrat wanted to end the war more than Joe Lieberman. But many Connecticut voters ended up accepting Lieberman's deceptive line on that issue.

Tagaris recalls, "From the media perspective, the story was over, Lieberman had lost." Lamont-Lieberman moved from center stage and became one of hundreds of races. Then, a week after the Connecticut primary, George Allen's "macaca" moment happened and national attention shifted heavily toward Virginia. Nonetheless, Tagaris believes that the Lamont campaign attracted plenty of national netroots attention all through the general election and insists that "the local netroots never stopped." But in this odd three-way race, in which Republicans de facto abandoned their candidate (state representative Alan R. Schlesinger) and supported Lieberman, netroots support alone could not provide the margin of victory. The final election results on November 7 were 49.7 percent for Lieberman, 39.7 percent for Lamont, and 9.6 percent for Schlesinger. In early September 2007, a poll commissioned by Daily Kos indicated that, if the Senate race were held again, Ned Lamont would defeat Joe Lieberman 48 to 40 percent.

Despite the unfortunate final election results, the Lamont campaign had utilized the netroots in several innovative ways that can serve as lessons learned for future progressive efforts, of which there will be many. Matt Browner-Hamlin, an activist blogger who assisted Tim Tagaris with Lamont's netroots efforts, says that "what the Lamont campaign did was historic and should be celebrated." Browner-Hamlin believes that Joe Lieberman "was exposed as a fraud" and that the netroots overall did a tremendous job.

According to Tagaris,

> In the primary we created a culture in which the things that were happening on the blogs were news. We would release our commercials through blogs first before we released them on our own website. We would put out stuff

you'd normally give the press to blogs first, before it was even out in a press release. We created a culture where the traditional media had to pay attention to the blogs if they were going to cover the race effectively. In the general election, we created a culture in which e-mails were important and created earned media ... building the narrative, using the Internet to build the narrative of party united behind Ned Lamont.

What Tim Tagaris describes above perfectly exemplifies how the netroots is changing political campaigns and empowering citizen activists. In Connecticut in 2006, the blogs and the mainstream media developed a working relationship, providing a major asset to the Lamont campaign, without which Lamont almost certainly would not have gotten as far as he did.

Chapter 8

COMBAT BOOTS VS. COWBOY BOOTS

B
attered by a bruising primary challenge, nearly broke, and facing a George Allen campaign with $7.5 million cash on hand, the Jim Webb for Senate campaign steeled itself for the upcoming general election against an entrenched Republican incumbent. One of Webb's first tasks was to unite the state Democratic Party after what had been, by almost any standard, a bitter primary. On June 16, a conciliatory Harris Miller said, "Jim Webb is going to be a great United States senator and I'm going to do everything I can to help him get there."[1] Miller's rhetoric, however, was not matched by concrete action; Miller went on vacation and was barely heard from again.

Six days after Webb's primary victory, Draft James Webb co-founder Josh Chernila wrote an e-mail identifying several major challenges Webb needed to overcome, including the following: (1) lack of money (party leaders believed "Webb lacks the discipline to raise the money"), (2) residual bitterness from the primary (Miller endorsers and supporters expected Webb to make "a big show of welcoming them to his campaign"), (3) a sense of abandonment by volunteers and committee chairs ("especially south of Charlottesville and in Richmond"), and (4) a severe shortage of campaign materials ("for the coming rush of festivals and events between now and Labor Day").

STAGGERING INTO THE GENERAL ELECTION

Chernila's evaluation—a candidate who hated raising money, a divided Democratic Party, and a frustrated volunteer base—did not augur well for victory in November. To make matters worse, Webb lacked the full support of the blogging community. Chernila wrote that "there's definitely some resentment [among bloggers] that they aren't appreciated, acknowledged, etc." One such disgruntled blogger complained:

I sure would like to know whether or not blogs are being thrown to the curb because (1) it's the best strategy for incorporating the mainstream

[Democrats] or (2) because of jealousy and resentment on the part of the campaign staff ... Do you think I am being over sensitive? Just that I feel that I really worked my ass off and received a couple of mass e-mails. For me, a phone call, a note, a personalized e-mail would have been nice.... Have I done something offensive? What?

It was clear that this blogger wasn't alone in feeling unappreciated. To integrate grassroots and netroots elements more smoothly into the campaign, draft leader Corey Hernandez proposed a "campaign volunteer Internet portal" that would "give volunteers some ownership in the campaign," using tools like "an interactive events calendar," allowing volunteers "to recommend events ... the campaign should attend," business cards for the volunteers, "coordinated opposition research efforts," and more. Few of Hernandez's suggestions were ever implemented. A volunteer portal was created, but it never got much use. Perhaps this was due to top-down resistance, or perhaps it was simply an indication that integrating the netroots within a professional campaign is easier said than done.

Good news arrived on June 22, when a Zogby Poll indicated that George Allen had slipped below 50 percent, dangerous territory for an incumbent. Some attributed the incumbent's decline in the polls to the victory days earlier of Jim Webb, an attractive, credible Democratic alternative with sterling national security credentials to his name. Then, on June 26, Markos Moulitsas Zúniga of Daily Kos announced his support for Jim Webb with his front-page post, "VA-Sen: let's help Jim Webb get elected." Perhaps most important, Moulitsas added Webb to the netroots ActBlue page maintained by MyDD, Swing State Project, and Daily Kos. Eventually, the Webb campaign took in nearly $200,000 via that page, which allows the netroots to give to the candidate or candidates of their choice. Kos singled out "the kick-ass, aggressive, and effective Virginia netroots: Fresh off their help in getting Tim Kaine elected governor, blogs such as Raising Kaine, Not Larry Sabato, and VA Progressive have helped build buzz and activism for Jim Webb."[2]

PROBLEMS, PROBLEMS

Despite such positive signs, discontent continued to grow among key Webb volunteers. On June 29, Josh Chernila wrote in an e-mail that "our troops are demoralized and feeling ostracized," and that "every one of the volunteers I speak with feels completely ignored and underappreciated by this campaign." Mary Detweiler, who had almost single-handedly gotten Jim Webb on the primary ballot and was beloved by just about everybody in Webb's ragtag army, was extremely frustrated and on the verge of quitting. On July 2, Detweiler wrote a long memo to senior strategist Steve Jarding and campaign manager Jessica Vanden Berg highlighting problems with the Webb campaign as she saw them.

Detweiler's main complaint was a near-total lack of "communication from campaign staff to volunteers who have taken on leadership roles." According to Detweiler, that gap resulted in uninformed volunteers, whose presence and potential were unappreciated by the professional staff. In addition, Detweiler cited problems like insufficient phones for phone banking, lack of a shared volunteer database system, and no follow-through on projects. Willing volunteers with unique and valuable expertise went unused. The troops were willing to "be their own generals" in the field, but they needed to understand the campaign's strategy and objectives to be optimally effective. Detweiler concluded that to "compensate for the vast financial resources of Webb's opponent" and win the election, "we must work hard [and] in a far more efficient and effective manner than we can under the current campaign leadership." Essentially, Detweiler was calling for a significant shift in campaign leadership.

A day or so later, Detweiler met with Jessica Vanden Berg and relations between the "top down" and "bottom up" appeared to improve somewhat. Most important, Detweiler didn't quit the campaign, but rather she kept working tenaciously through the summer and fall, helping to build the ragtag Webb army to a potent force of more than 8,000 people.

Several of the campaign professionals had mixed feelings about the volunteers. Steve D'Amico of the campaign's research department commented that volunteers can't do what professional political consultants can do "because they don't detach themselves from how much they love their candidate." In D'Amico's opinion, such emotional attachment "often blinds [the volunteers'] objectivity when it comes to strategy suggestions." In contrast, D'Amico asserted that campaign professionals "can leave their emotions at the door" and "suck it up" if their advice is rejected, a difference that "creates a natural tension" between the two. Whether natural or not, Lowell Feld and Nate Wilcox had observed such tensions and lack of understanding between professionals and volunteers on numerous campaigns.

CALL IN THE NETROOTS!

On July 6, after several conversations and e-mails about turning things around, Feld met with Jessica Vanden Berg and Steve Jarding, and they offered him a job as Jim Webb's netroots coordinator. Simultaneously, Josh Chernila was offered a job as volunteer coordinator. For better or for worse, the Webb campaign had decided to officially bring in the netroots in a serious way.

Jarding viewed the hiring of the two bloggers as "the institutionalization of the netroots into a modern campaign." He and Vanden Berg were aiming to shore up a novice candidate who was reticent about asking strangers for money and highly protective of his independence, a quality that politicians routinely compromise in the quest to get elected. Jarding wanted to raise $1 million online by Election Day and needed the netroots to do so. That was Feld's first assignment.

Jarding's hiring decision wasn't greeted warmly by everyone in the Democratic establishment. According to Jarding, it became "a source of angst and dissension for some party people who saw the netroots taking credit for Webb's victory" in the Democratic primary. Several of them even "denied that the netroots had anything to do with it." Jarding surmises that "they were jealous because the netroots were getting a lot of buzz and publicity." After all was said and done, Jarding believes he "made the right choice" in sticking with the netroots and not "cut[ting] the cord." By Election Day, the campaign took in $4.2 million over the Internet out of about $8.4 million total raised.

Feld's announcement to the blogosphere of his new netroots coordinator job created controversy. He had decided, in the interest of full disclosure, to put a disclaimer on all his future posts at Raising Kaine. He had not been asked to do so by the campaign; they seemed completely unconcerned. The disclaimer read, "The views expressed by Lowell Feld are his own and do not necessarily represent official positions of the Webb for Senate campaign."[3] One persistent critic argued that "you can't have it both ways," that "you are either an independent blogger who we can trust to tell it how it is ... or you are a paid consultant to the campaign who will be viewed as nothing more than a propagandist."[4]

Feld disagreed, as did almost everybody else who commented at Raising Kaine. Still, in spite of its belligerent tone and black-or-white worldview, the comment on Raising Kaine raised a valid question regarding the relationship between bloggers and campaigns. Ben Tribbett of Not Larry Sabato later observed that "Raising Kaine could have lost Webb the general election if the press had picked up everything [the blog] had said and reported it as a Webb staffer writing it." Tribbett added that "on any other campaign ever, if you're out there making public statements, you're held accountable." For instance, John Edwards's early 2007 hiring of two liberal feminists to blog for his presidential campaign blew up in the candidate's face. As luck (or full disclosure) would have it, that never became a major problem for the Webb campaign.

This question isn't going away; bloggers increasingly and routinely join political campaigns or are paid money to blog "independently." Disclosure—in this case, letting people know where you're coming from—seems to be the key, although it does not solve all problems or answer all questions. For instance, if bloggers' credibility stems in large part from their perceived independence, can they be effective as paid campaign staffers? The court of public opinion has not yet reached a verdict on that issue; perhaps each case will be judged on its individual merits.

Feld received a small budget, which he used to run ads for Webb on blogs like Daily Kos. He felt that the campaign should have run more blog ads, especially because they seemed to bring in significantly more money than they cost. More crucially, the netroots and volunteer coordinators should have been integrated more fully into the campaign at senior staff levels. Instead, the netroots coordinator job was placed in the finance department of the campaign, as opposed to the research, communications, or field shops. In reality, the blogosphere cuts across all those areas, and a netroots coordinator ideally belongs in all of them. Although he involved himself with volunteers, research, and communications, his general feeling was that the netroots coordinator role was viewed primarily as a potential source of income for the campaign.

Aside from blog ads, one of Feld's first priorities was to line up surrogates to "live blog" in support of Jim Webb. On July 21, popular netroots personality Paul Hackett—the U.S. Marine who had nearly defeated Republican Jean Schmidt for Congress in 2005, bluntly criticizing President Bush in the process—live blogged on Daily Kos with a diary simply titled, "Why I Support Jim Webb." The event was highly successful, with Hackett extolling Webb as having "more integrity than almost anyone else I know." Hackett, who had studied Webb's career and held him in high regard as a military man, declared that Webb "cannot be bought" and "in fact ... hates the current system of big money donors, lobbyists, and special interest influence on our elected officials." Hackett urged Daily Kos readers to "support Jim Webb just as you supported me in my campaign against Jean Schmidt" in 2005.[5] Throughout the campaign, surrogate bloggers like Paul Hackett served as important "third-party validators" for Jim Webb, vouching for his credentials as a strong Democrat and as a serious candidate for U.S. Senate.

Another priority for Feld was to report on Webb-related events. On July 22, he drove four hours with Webb campaign staffer Jason Korta (a twenty-three-year-old "Fonzi" look-alike) to the first Webb-Allen debate, held at The Homestead resort in Virginia's beautiful Allegheny Mountains. The debate wasn't being televised and was being held on a Saturday morning far from major Virginia population centers. Thus, the blogs offered the best opportunity for detailed coverage—which, trailing in the polls, the Webb campaign badly needed. Waiting in the campaign's "war room" before the debate, Jim Webb was full of nervous energy, and it was hard to blame him. This was a heavily Republican, pro-Allen crowd, and it was Webb's first debate of the campaign.

At the debate, Feld focused on typing as fast as possible as the two candidates spoke. Later, he was able to analyze that both candidates "did fine in terms of stage presence," but that "Allen seemed a bit nervous and off his game at the beginning." Allen had asked Webb about a relatively obscure Virginia port project known as "Craney Island." Webb had never heard of it, nor had most people in the audience. Feld wrote:

Look, [the Craney Island project] might very well be an important issue for Hampton Roads, but there's only one reason George Allen brought it up today: to engage in debate "gotcha" with Jim Webb. Obviously, Webb can't know everything, but he's learning fast. Far more important, in my view, is

Allen's unfamiliarity with the nominee to be Federal Reserve Chairman, with the GI Bill of Rights, or with what's going on in the Senate while he's sitting there bored out of his mind.[6]

The Craney Island question, and Webb's unfamiliarity with the issue, received a great deal of press coverage. But, because almost nobody in the general public had ever heard of Craney Island either, it wasn't much of a gaffe. Still, the question highlighted the fact that Webb had been focused most of his career on national security and foreign policy matters, not on the intricacies of Virginia politics. That's what the Allen campaign was trying to bring out by asking about Craney Island. The message was that George Allen was the "real" Virginian, even though he had grown up in southern California. In contrast, Allen attempted to depict Jim Webb—who had lived in Virginia for most of his adult life and whose family went back generations in the state—as an interloper. In the end, Allen's strategy of pretending to be the "real Virginian" (and a Confederate cowboy to boot) backfired in ways his campaign could never have imagined.

An important part of Feld's job was to keep in touch with other Democratic bloggers and identify their concerns. One issue on the minds of top bloggers like Matt Stoller of MyDD was "net neutrality," that is, the concept that the Internet should remain an open marketplace of ideas and speech, not restricted in any way, and with no discrimination against web content because of its content, source, or ownership. Feld felt that the Webb campaign should issue a strong statement in support of net neutrality, both on its own merits and also as an area of interest to Democratic bloggers like Stoller. Indeed, Webb's July 28 statement in support of net neutrality gained him positive publicity in the Democratic blogosphere. Matt Stoller, in particular, highlighted Webb's statement, which helped to cement the image of Jim Webb as a strong netroots candidate.

Despite positive signs like this, the Webb campaign remained in the doldrums both in terms of money and polling. On July 30, a Mason-Dixon poll showed Allen with a sixteen-point lead over Webb, 48 to 32 percent. Internal polling conducted by the Benenson Strategy Group indicated a smaller, but still significant, eight-point lead for Allen in July. On the positive side, Allen was still polling below 50 percent, indicating potential vulnerability. The Webb campaign, however, had yet to take advantage of that potential.

Through the long Virginia summer, Webb volunteers kept busy. For instance, Todd Smyth—one of the toughest fighters in Webb's volunteers corps—wrote on August 6 that he was "hoping to have about 2,000 Jim Webb, 'Vote Democratic' fans in the audience when George Allen gets up to speak" at the Old Fiddler's Convention (the "Woodstock" of bluegrass) in Galax, Virginia, on the border with North Carolina. Webb was not going to be able to make it, so Smyth helped organize a road trip of Webb supporters to be there on Webb's behalf.

Another successful grassroots initiative came from Susan Mariner, one of the best Webb volunteers of the entire campaign. Her clever invention—some would say stroke of genius—was the "Webb Wagons." On August 7, Mariner took a red Roadmaster steel-bed children's wagon, decorated it with Webb stickers, and filled it with Webb goodies. That weekend, Virginia Beach was holding a large event, the Princess Anne Park Arts and Crafts Festival. No political "tabling, was allowed, which prevented Allen's campaign from showing up and campaigning. Fortunately, it didn't stop the Webb volunteers led by Susan Mariner. As Mariner wrote on Raising Kaine, "Allen's camp didn't show at this major event," but Webb volunteers "spread the word about Jim to thousands of people at the event this weekend, distributing smiles, literature, bumper stickers [which] we put into our newly constructed 'Webb Wagons.'"[7]

The wagons were a big hit and highly effective; they functioned as mobile tabling units and "generated a lot of attention for Webb from folks of all ages." Mariner added, "There's something magical about a wagon, isn't there?"[8] Well, yes, and there's something magical about passionate, committed citizen-activists equipped with Webb Wagons and other homemade products of their creativity and enthusiasm. People respond to this kind of enthusiasm in ways they never would to a traditional mailing or the 500th airing of a television ad about Candidate X. A Webb Wagon is far more memorable.

The Webb Wagons were also important in boosting morale among Webb volunteers. On August 8, Mariner wrote to Feld, that "there are huge numbers of people who are extremely motivated by the bottom up concept," which is exactly "what the Webb Wagon represents." Mariner added, "A 'Webb Wagoneer' is the epitome of the grassroots taking on a powerful, monied, Republican machine." It says to the volunteers, "You can make a difference. It's not ALL about money. You are important, and you have power. Hit the road, and together we'll take Allen down."

Fortunately, the Allen-Webb race was not all about money. If it had been, Webb probably would have lost, given Allen's huge cash edge for most of the campaign. "People power"—epitomized by Mary Detweiler, Susan Mariner, Todd Smyth, Jan-Lars Mueller, Marc Greidinger, Dave Leichtman, C.W. Dean, Peter Churchill, Annabel Park, Eric Byler, Barbara Kreykenbohm, Cassie Arnold, Ken Kukovich, Tom Counts, and thousands of others—ultimately defeated George Allen. But as of early August 2006, victory was still just a dream; there was a lot of work yet to be done to make the dream a reality.

On August 8, Ned Lamont narrowly won (52 to 48 percent) the Connecticut Democratic primary. Many in the Virginia netroots had been rooting for a crushing Lamont victory, both on its own merits and also to grab more of the blogosphere's energy and attention for Webb. The thinking was that if Lamont had won big and if Lieberman had then dropped out of the race, the story would have ended and attention would have shifted to Webb. In contrast, a narrow Lamont victory just might keep Connecticut at the top of the blogosphere's attention through Election Day. Instead, to a large extent, Lamont faded from the radar screen after his primary victory. Then, a few days after the Connecticut primary, an encounter between George Allen and an Indian American college student with a video camera changed history. Netroots attention increasingly shifted to Virginia.

WHAT THE HECK IS A "MACACA"?

The "macaca" story has been told many times, but misconceptions persist. The foremost misconception is that after George Allen's blatant display of racism, he simply melted down like the wicked witch in the *Wizard of Oz*. The reality is that the Webb campaign had been working to expose the real George Allen for months, starting in February 2006 with the slogan, "Jim Webb Is George Allen's Worst Nightmare." Under the guidance of senior strategist Steve Jarding, the Webb campaign had been laboring long and hard to undo the affable image Allen had built over the years. With that strategy in mind, many Webb campaign press releases began with a variant of, "You *think* you know George Allen...." In addition, irreverent bloggers and the campaign attempted to rattle Allen by taunting his staff and him with nicknames like "Dick Wad(hams)" for Allen's campaign manager and "Felix" for Allen himself, referring to the candidate's middle name. Little did the Webb campaign know that "Felix" actually was the name of George Allen's maternal grandfather, a Jew from Tunisia, where "macaca" (derived from a genus of short-tailed monkey) is a common racial epithet.

One undercurrent about George Allen that had never been fully explored despite Allen's tenure as Virginia governor and U.S. senator was his questionable past with regard to racial issues. Mainstream media reporters didn't seem much inclined to dig into Allen's past, including his odd fascination with Confederate flags (one had hung in his living room), despite the fact that his family had no connection to either side of the Civil War. The media had allowed Allen to get away with his "aw shucks," amiable cowboy routine for many years. Allen's dark side—nooses hanging in his office, racial epithets, ties to racist organizations—had never been exposed to the light of day. In August 2006, that began to change.

On Friday, August 11, Allen appeared at a campaign rally at The Breaks Interstate Park in southwest Virginia. A young Webb summer intern, S. R. Sidarth, had been sent to track Allen (follow him around and videotape him, just as the Allen campaign was doing to Webb) during his southwestern Virginia campaign swing. After the election, Sidarth told his story in the *Washington Post* in an article entitled, "I Am Macaca." Sidarth related that "in Breaks Interstate Park, located on the Kentucky border, Allen acknowledged my presence for the first time in one of his stump speeches." But it wasn't a friendly, "hey, how's it going?" acknowledgment. Instead, Sidarth—an American citizen of Indian heritage who had lived in Virginia all his life—relates that he was "singled out at a GOP … picnic, identified as 'macaca or whatever his name is'—despite the fact that Allen knew my name, as we had been traveling the same route for five days." This was followed by Allen's infamous comment, "Welcome to America and the real world of Virginia."[9]

Allen's sneering comment was nasty and even frightening, but Sidarth kept his cool and got it all on videotape. After the event, Sidarth immediately called the Webb campaign and told them what had happened. Joe Stanley, a video editing expert who was working for the Webb campaign, says that on Saturday, he "was called by [Webb staffers] Kevin Druff and Jon Paul Lupo about some tracker video" shot by S. R. Sidarth. Stanley, who lives in the Roanoke area, was informed that "Sidarth would be traveling back north that evening and it would be easy for me to meet up with him and take the tapes."[10]

Sidarth met Stanley on Saturday evening "at about 10 P.M. in the Target parking lot in Roanoke." Stanley recalls that Sidarth "gave me seven DV [digital video] tapes and advised me to watch tape six first." Sidarth said that George Allen had pointed at him and called him "macaca." Like most Americans, Joe Stanley had never heard that word previously, but he could see that Sidarth "was clearly bothered," not only by the racial epithet but because "it was a U.S. senator who was responsible for the name calling." Sidarth said that he hoped there was something on one of those tapes that the campaign could use. With that, Sidarth "got back in his car and drove off."[11]

Early Sunday morning, Stanley went to the office and watched tape six. Stanley says that he "went through about forty-five [minutes] of the sixty-minute tape and thought perhaps [Sidarth] was mistaken." Then, suddenly, "the screen blinked and there was [a] clear change of venue. The senator was addressing folks under a picnic shelter. He turned, pointed to the camera, and said"—

> My friends, we're gonna run this campaign on positive, constructive ideas, and it's important that we motivate and inspire people for something. This fellow here over here with the yellow shirt, macaca or whatever his name is, he's with my opponent he's following us around everywhere. And it's just great, we're going to places all over Virginia and he's having it on film and it's great to have you here and you show it to your [sic] opponent because he's never been there and probably will never come.… His [sic] opponent right now is actually with a bunch of Hollywood movie moguls. We care about fact not fiction. So let's give a welcome to macaca here; welcome to America and the real world of Virginia.[12]

Stanley was stunned by "Allen's effort to bully and humiliate Sidarth." Allen's words ushered in a new era in American politics. In Stanley's opinion, "with that finger pointing to the camera, we saw in our U.S. senator a character flaw that we had never seen on display in such a manner." After reviewing the video several times, Stanley called Webb campaign manager Jessica Vanden Berg and told her "It's bad, very bad." Vanden Berg asked Stanley to send her the video as soon as possible. Stanley transferred the video onto his personal YouTube account, "mak[ing] the clip private until we wanted to release it."[13]

In the middle of processing the video, his phone rang. It was Ben Tribbett, saying "he had heard there was a tape." Stanley laughed, and Tribbett replied, "There is [a tape], I knew it!" According to Stanley, Tribbett "asked to see the tape and I told him no, that I couldn't." Stanley continues: "Thus began a day of wrangling back and forth with Tribbett over the tape. While he continued his negotiations with the campaign, I loaded the video and sent the link to Jessica. Within a couple of hours, Tribbett broke the story to the world without the video."[14] The large-font headline on Not Larry Sabato read:

MAJOR SENATE RACE SHAKEUP
  "George Allen steps in it. Video coming …
  "What George Allen just did, sent a chill down my spine. Video coming …
  "Developing …"[15]

Jessica Vanden Berg says that she "watched [the video] and watched it," but "didn't know what we had." Vanden Berg also says that she doesn't know how Ben Tribbett found out about it. Vanden Berg thought that "there [was] no way [Tribbett] was going to get it first," but instead she intended to release the video initially through the mainstream media and then through the blogs. Vanden Berg, however, says that "on Sunday, Tribbett put the story up [with the title] 'Video coming soon.'" After that, Vanden Berg says the campaign leadership "all sat down, tried to figure out how to deal with it." Pretty quickly, the campaign team realized that they "had something because of the way [Allen] looked at [Sidarth]."

On Monday morning, the campaign sent the "macaca" video to *Washington Post* reporter Tim Craig, a young man who had not been on the Virginia beat for long. The campaign thought Craig might have an open mind about the video and be able to determine whether it was a story. According to Vanden Berg, "We decided to try to get the mainstream media to bite on it, write about it, put a framework around it." Interestingly, Vanden Berg says that "at first, Tim [Craig] wasn't sure if it was news." Craig confirms this, adding that neither he nor his colleague Michael Shear made the ultimate decision whether to publish the story. Neither reporter was sure it was a story, and kicked the decision to their editor, who made the call to run with it.

Craig notes that the angle the campaign was pushing was not the word "macaca" per se. Instead, it was the "welcome to the real world of Virginia" comment made by Senator Allen to a young, Indian American man. Vanden Berg believes that resistance to seeing this exchange as a story may have stemmed from the feeling that it was "just who Allen [was]" and the belief that "everybody knew that George Allen had this in him, but nobody cared." By Monday afternoon, however, the *Post* had decided that if nothing else, having a video of George Allen making these comments was news. According to Vanden Berg, "next thing you know, Tim Craig and Michael Shear wrote about it on [WashingtonPost.com], we put it up on YouTube, then everybody had it."

Ben Tribbett, a central player in the explosion of the "macaca" scandal, has a somewhat different take on how it all played out. According to Tribbett, he had been told about—and ultimately shown—the video on Sunday. The campaign denies this, but obviously Tribbett knew enough about the video to write about it extensively on Sunday and Monday morning. Tribbett says that when he first saw the video, he thought, "oh my God, it's huge." That's in stark contrast with the *Washington Post* reporters, who weren't sure whether it was news. At a minimum, Tribbett believed that Allen's "inside the Beltway" comment, implying that people who lived there weren't "real Virginians," was offensive, "a clear derogatory reference to where minorities live."

Throughout Sunday and into Monday, Tribbett built a buzz on his blog. Hundreds of comments poured in, even without the actual video. The Webb campaign was determined to break the story in the *Washington Post*, not on the blogs. In fact, the only reason Feld was aware of the story was from reading Not Larry Sabato. By Monday morning, Tribbett was getting frustrated that Vanden Berg wouldn't negotiate with him. Tribbett says, "I could hear her in the background when I was on the phone with [research director] Jon Paul [Lupo]—'put him off, fifteen minutes.'" In fairness, the campaign apparently wasn't sure what Tribbett had exactly and was trying to push the story out via the *Washington Post* for maximum impact. It was a tense few hours at Webb campaign headquarters.

On Monday, Tribbett posted an update describing what was on the "macaca" video. Tribbett spoke with Tim Craig, who said that they were uploading the video to the *Washington Post* website. As soon as it was up, Tribbett linked to the video, helping to fuel the frenzy—10,000 views within the first hour, thousands of visits per hour on Not Larry Sabato, television coverage, the whole works.

At Webb headquarters, Steve D'Amico of the research department (which shared the same room with the press department) had gotten the go-ahead from management and was busy sending out instant messages (IMs) of the "macaca" video link "to everyone in politics we knew." According to D'Amico, "AOL Instant Messenger is the best kept secret in politics." D'Amico points out that "press secretaries talk to reporters with [IM]" in real time, and that IM "was one of the many, many ways 'macaca' took off."

Meanwhile, Ben Tribbett was busy working the phones to the Republican bloggers he knew, trying to find one (or more) who would condemn Allen's comments. Within hours, Tribbett hit paydirt, as Vince from Too Conservative wrote that he was "outraged" by Allen's behavior. On Monday night, another Republican blog named Bearing Drift chimed in, opining that "this is not the Republican Party." Tribbett also contacted Republican blogger (and later, Republican Party of Virginia communications director) Shaun Kenney. According to Tribbett, "Kenney has political ambitions, so I told him, 'this is not the future of Virginia, you might want to get out ahead of this story.'" The next day, Kenney condemned Allen's remarks. Within a few days, Tribbett says, "It was completely out of my hands." Still, Tribbett continued "linking to everyone talking about it" on the blogs, in newspaper editorials, on television, and elsewhere.

Tribbett makes the interesting point that had the Webb campaign had its way, the video "would have come out on the *Washington Post* and YouTube, but it would have taken a lot longer" to gather momentum. Tribbett argues that "the way Jessica [Vanden Berg] wanted to do it, I don't think it would have become a frenzy, it would never have gone as viral [and] Webb would have lost." Joe Stanley agrees that without Tribbett building it into a frenzy, "I firmly believe [the story] wouldn't have been as big." Tribbett and others believe that had the Webb campaign managed to control the "macaca" video better, it wouldn't have had as large an impact as it did. This points to a larger truth—that trying to control an authentic, dramatic story in the age of the blogs and YouTube is next to impossible. It might even be counterproductive in the end. Thus, ironically, the Webb campaign's inability to completely control the "macaca" story release probably helped it in the end. Netroots politics works in mysterious ways.

The "macaca" video ultimately received more than 600,000 views on YouTube, not to mention heavy media exposure on television and elsewhere. But it didn't immediately result in Jim Webb taking the lead in the polls. Jessica Vanden Berg believes that the "macaca" story "generated [a great deal of] media attention, started poking holes in what George Allen was about." In spite of "macaca," the polls and money didn't change much right away. For instance, an internal campaign poll several weeks after the "macaca" incident showed George Allen leading Jim Webb by six points, down only slightly from an eight-point Allen lead in late June. A steady erosion in Allen's "favorability" ratings was apparent, however. Pete Brodnitz, the Webb campaign's pollster, offers an interesting, somewhat counterintuitive perspective on the significance of the "macaca" incident:

> [T]he data never showed [macaca] to be the major issue in the race. Allen was vulnerable before that ever came up because he was weak in northern Virginia and positioned as a status quo candidate in a change election (and he dug that hole deeper because for most of the race he was more focused on the GOP presidential primary than on the Webb challenge). The main impact of [macaca] was that it got potential donors and members of the press thinking that Allen might be vulnerable and it brought attention to

the race. When voters subsequently saw [Webb] take on Allen on *Meet the Press*, things took off because people outside of the campaign began to believe that Webb could take him on. Inside the campaign that was already clear—our main challenge was raising money to show voters that they had an alternative to Allen and after *Meet the Press* money started to come in (largely over the Internet).

In early September, the Webb campaign spent $100,000—a small amount of money in the expensive northern Virginia market—for a television ad featuring President Ronald Reagan extolling then Navy Secretary Webb for his "gallantry." According to Vanden Berg, although the Reagan ad was strong, she was concerned that "the [Democratic] netroots would turn on us because of [our using] Ronald Reagan." In the end, Vanden Berg believes that the Reagan ad "received so much [earned] media attention, we probably got $500,000 worth out of it." After that, Vanden Berg believes that people really started getting interested in the Webb-Allen race. Then, "we went on *Meet the Press*; Webb "did a great job against George Allen on that show," and within twenty-four hours, the Webb campaign raised around $150,000 online. Vanden Berg calls that "the money turning point."

Through all this, the Allen campaign and the pro-Allen Virginia blogs attempted, but were unable, to change the narrative. On August 15, an obviously frustrated blogger on Virginia Virtucon dismissed "macaca" and cluelessly wondered, "Why is the Webb campaign wasting money sending a staffer around to videotape George Allen on the stump when they don't have and never will have enough money to buy any real advertising to show any of it on?"[16] The comment by Virginia Virtucon demonstrates the relative lack of thoughtfulness and sophistication that characterized pro-Allen bloggers active in the campaign. Jon Henke, a Republican who blogged at QandO and was hired by the panic-stricken, post-"macaca" Allen campaign as their netroots coordinator, felt that the problem with the Allen campaign not having a "blog/netroots strategy prior to September of '06" is that "they missed the opportunity to develop a pro-Allen netroots movement." As a result, "they missed the events occurring in the Leftosphere, the developing narrative, which would have tipped them to the coming storm and how to deal with it."

As to the "macaca" issue itself, the Allen campaign stumbled through a series of bizarre, half-baked excuses for what Allen had said, ranging from "He meant to say Mohawk" to "No, he really meant to call Sidarth 'caca.'" Needless to say, none of these excuses had any effect except to make matters even worse for George Allen. According to Ben Tribbett, "every time Allen came up with an excuse, Raising Kaine just skewered him." As a result, "Allen kept having to pull back his explanation" and the controversy dragged on and on.

Jon Henke doesn't believe that the Allen campaign thought the "macaca" incident "would be as big as it was." Also, they "were genuinely surprised that people thought it was somehow racial in nature." Henke hypothesizes that their surprise stemmed from the fact that "the 'racism' angle played up by Democrats was very much at odds with the man they knew," so "they were surprised that people believed that." And, Henke adds, "since the 'macaca' interpretation was consistent with the narrative that the Leftosphere had worked to develop over a long period, it was easier for the Leftosphere to frame it as they did."

"Macaca" certainly hurt George Allen, but it did not by itself do him in (as Pete Brodnitz notes above). Instead, Allen's demise was the result of an almost continual series of laughable mistakes and truly bizarre behavior by the candidate, his staff, and his supporters in the blogosphere.

Why did the Allen campaign "misunderestimate" (as George W. Bush might say) the progressive netroots so badly? Jon Henke's impression is "that the early failure of the Leftosphere to win races, combined with the over-the-top rhetoric had made the establishment believe that the Leftosphere was more of a 'far left fringe' that was (a) generally incapable of turning out voters, and (b) making the [Democratic] Party look bad." Henke believes that "the first assumption is correct"—the blogosphere doesn't really get out the vote. Henke points out, however, "that's not its function." As far as the "far left fringe" making the Democratic Party look bad, Henke says that this "was probably incorrect, because the vast majority of the public didn't know/care about the overheated rhetoric that sometimes occurred/occurs in the sphere." The Allen people, Henke concludes, "failed to understand ... that blogs are very effective at framing things for the influentials, and that's where they lost track of progress being made in the Leftosphere."

The first indication of a "macaca" effect in the polls came on August 21, with SurveyUSA pegging the race at Allen, 48 percent, Webb, 45 percent. According to SurveyUSA, "Since an identical SurveyUSA poll released June 28, 2006 ... Allen's lead has shrunk from 19 points to 3 points."[17]

On August 22, the Hotline blog reported, "Senator George Allen's campaign is seeking a conservative blog maven who can blunt future attacks and help rally conservatives in the state and elsewhere behind Allen's campaign." The Hotline reported that "Chris LaCivita, Allen's longtime strategist, and other Allen aides believe that the campaign has so far failed to appreciate the generative role that bloggers can play—and the consequences that pertain when the GOP netroots aren't mobilized on behalf of candidates." The Hotline concluded that "Virginia Republican bloggers have yet to rally behind Allen with the same intensity that the liberal netroots has circled James Webb."[18]

Jon Henke was hired in late August to rally the Virginia Republican bloggers behind Allen and to shape the narrative in Allen's favor. It was much too little much too late, however. Henke recalls, "The Allen campaign had only done minimal outreach to the blogosphere and had never really integrated blogs into its messaging, communications and strategy before late August." In the final months, Henke feels, Allen's campaign and supporters "were much more aware of the problems and better capable of addressing them within the same medium." But "by that point, the narrative was set and we were forced to play defense until the end."

Why couldn't the Allen campaign turn things around? Henke's theory is that "virtually all Republicans were surprised at the effectiveness of the Democrats' Internet media machine." Henke suspects that "a few years of apparent impotence had lulled them into the belief that the LeftRoots movement was just the 'fringe crazies.'" But, Henke says, they were wrong. The idea that the "LeftRoots" is just a bunch of lunatics and fanatics "misses the real power and influence of the liberal blogs ... which is much more about narrative development and messaging to the influentials than about fundraising and [getting out the vote]." Unlike the rest of the Allen camp, Henke apparently understood what the progressive, pro-Webb netroots had been up to all those months.

Henke recalls that "George Allen had a small cadre of supportive bloggers, but there was not a 'grassroots/netroots movement.'" Henke points to the fact that the Allen campaign "didn't do anything to develop a movement in advance, and by the time the importance of the new media became apparent— mid-to-late August—the only option left was to hire somebody to engage bloggers and spread the campaign message within the new media." This is when Henke came in, but it was way too late.

Virginia Democratic blogger Waldo Jaquith comments that "the smarter Republicans became quieter as the summer wore on, as they were marginalized by louder, harsher conservatives." Jaquith believes that "there was a sense of embarrassment among Republicans, an understanding that Allen's loudest supporters were behaving even more poorly than some Webb supporters had during the primary." As a result, the right-wing bloggers' "largely monolithic, at times lockstep support structure became stripped down, never turning into a marketplace of ideas but losing the benefit of uniformity." In the end, Jaquith concludes, "The lesson of the Webb-Allen race was that the netroots could become the grassroots and actually make things happen."

VOLUNTEERS TO THE RESCUE

In the closing months of the campaign, volunteers for Webb swarmed in from across the country. Activist Annabel Park and filmmaker Eric Byler, both Asian American, came from Los Angeles to help out for a couple weeks on the campaign. The next thing they knew, they were totally involved (and falling in love, but that's another story), contributing far more than they ever imagined they would. Annabel Park first heard about the "macaca" incident on the television news, "not through the blogs." After that, she looked for more information, coming across a blog called Raising Kaine. Before that, she hadn't even realized that there was a progressive community in Virginia. Eric Byler says that he saw the "macaca" video on YouTube, and that it "brought me back to my youth in Virginia, dealing with racists like [George Allen] pointing me out as the one person who looked different in the crowd, and getting people to laugh and ridicule in exactly the same way."

Both Park and Byler assumed that Webb would lose to George Allen. Still, Byler says, he wanted to "make sure that even if we lost, that people of color in Virginia answered that 'macaca' comment, that we stood up and gave a counterargument to the idea that the real Virginia is for whites only."

Coming to Webb campaign headquarters in Arlington for the first time, Park found it "shocking, in a good way, how much it was driven by volunteers." She was "surprised how young the staff was," and felt "really at home" and welcomed by "volunteers like Mary [Detweiler] and Barbara [Kreykenbohm]." According to Jessica Vanden Berg, this controlled chaos was in large part by design, given that "we were an insurgent campaign" and "needed to grab everything we could." In fact, Vanden Berg argues, "We would have never won if we hadn't done it that way (e.g., netroots swarming all over campaign HQ, students coming down from Yale Law School, Eric Byler filming things)."

Park and Byler quickly rose to become Webb volunteer superstars. Park believes, correctly, that her biggest accomplishments were in "creating a vision for how we could all work together and in coming up with a message for [what came to be known as] 'Real Virginians for Webb.'" According to Park, the idea of Real Virginians for Webb came to her while working on writing better talking points to summarize Webb's positions. She kept wondering, "what would be a meaningful slogan to deal with the diversity issue?" Finally, "It just came to me ... from Allen's 'welcome to the real world of Virginia'" comment in the "macaca" video. Park had found her mission. Having planned to stay only ten days, she decided to stay through the election. After selling Real Virginians for Webb to Field Director Larry Byrne (husband of former Congresswoman Leslie Byrne) and deciding to keep it as grassroots as possible (not directly under the campaign) Park came up with three values: "respect, opportunity, fairness" that defined Real Virginians for Webb. She and Byler began raising money through their networks of friends and colleagues, mainly Asian Americans in California.

Under the banner of Real Virginians for Webb, Park and other volunteers did a great deal of effective work. They filmed videos of "real Virginians"— young, old, white, black, Latino, Asian—that they posted on YouTube. They printed up Real Virginians for Webb t-shirts. They worked tirelessly to rally the Korean American community in northern Virginia for Webb. Eric Byler asserts that without the Real Virginians for Webb ethnic outreach, "we wouldn't have won" the election." Annabel Park credits Josh Chernila with letting volunteers work outside the traditional campaign "box." In Park's view, Chernila gave volunteers "a sense of empowerment, made people feel like he was really listening, that our ideas were valuable." The volunteers did the rest.

Another volunteer success story was Sportsmen for Webb, which encouraged attendance at gun shows, where Democratic candidates are not often well represented. This group was led by volunteers like Todd Smyth, Jim Kirkman, and Marc Greidinger. Instead of giving up on traditionally pro-Republican gun enthusiasts, people like Greidinger manned Webb booths at gun shows, sometimes dressed in a donkey costume. Greidinger and colleagues would take photos that could be disseminated via the blogs and Yahoo! groups.

In addition, Greidinger would go onto pro-Allen, pro-gun blogs like Spank That Donkey and engage people online. The impact of these efforts is hard to quantify with any degree of certainty. Nonetheless, in Greidinger's view, "If you get in touch with people who are strong activists on single issues, convince them that your candidate isn't that bad," you might be able to change "a couple hundred votes." In a tight race, a couple hundred votes here, a couple hundred votes there can make all the difference. Most significant was the fact that Democrats were actually engaging a traditionally solid Republican voting bloc. In the past, most Democratic campaigns had ceded these voters to the Republicans. Fortunately, the Webb campaign had people like Marc Greidinger, who were tenacious and would not accept that a group as large as the Virginia gun enthusiasts should simply be abandoned.

In the Korean American community, according to Annabel Park, "Allen was hugely popular ... because he's considered a friend, had supported Korean American Day." But in the end, Park estimates that "something like 50,000 Asians voted ... around 65 percent for Webb, maybe as high as 75 percent." Park says the turnaround began at the Annandale Korean American Day celebration in late September. At that event, Park perceived deep emotions that could be tapped to help send Jim Webb to the U.S. Senate. According to Park, "[I] talked to one man, seventy years old, and handed him a flyer in Korean." The man "pointed at the George Allen-Tom Davis table and said 'those people are all liars and thieves, we've got to stop them.' ... He was so enraged that he was shaking." At that moment, Park understood the importance of the election. Korean Americans might not openly defy the powers that be, but "they were sick to death of Republicans lying to them."

Eric Byler says that before he and Park started working on outreach, "What we were looking at was an absolute shutout. George Allen would have taken the entire Korean American community if Annabel hadn't come to town." What changed, in his view, was "Annabel marching in there and saying there *is* a fight here; there *is* a contest." After that, "people stood up and said we can do something."

Byler recalls that the Annandale Korean American Day event was "plastered with Allen-Davis signs, but not a single Jim Webb sign" when they got there.

The Republicans had "balloons, booths, elephant shaped fans, volunteers." By showing up at the fair, Byler says, "Instead of it being ten to zero for Allen, we won seven to three, because ten people showed up for Webb." The volunteers did it all themselves: "We made the flyers [in English and Korean], photocopied them in the Webb for Senate office." Thinking fast, they even "grabbed a corner table that would have cost $2,000, but somebody didn't show up." They stayed all day, making lots of converts for Jim Webb. Truly, as Woody Allen says, "90 percent of success in life is just showing up." But in this case, the Webb volunteers—led by Annabel Park and Eric Byler—did a great deal more than just show up.

Annabel Park agrees that, if she hadn't organized her outreach effort, "the Korean community would have been totally ignored, so people would either have voted for Allen or not voted at all." Instead, Park contacted Korean newspapers and radio stations, finding reporters "very interested" and excited by her activities. Once Park put out the word, she says, "it spread like wildfire." That's a microcosm of how netroots activism works: two citizens hear about "macaca," check YouTube and blogs like Raising Kaine, and put their lives on hold to help defeat George Allen and take back the U.S. Senate.

Eric Byler contends that Asian Americans saw the Allen-Webb election as a "race where our honor was at stake, where our place in the society was at stake." He notes that "Asian Americans are very much connected into the web, probably more than any other demographic." George Allen's racist language against an Asian American, combined with the availability of the Internet, prompted fellow Asian Americans to take action. According to Byler, "We never had that kind of unity before."

The democratization of technology—cheaper, easier, more accessible—is a key part of what makes the netroots effective. Ten or twenty years ago, if someone wanted to get out their message, it was difficult and expensive, requiring sophisticated technical skills that few people possessed. When Eric Byler was first breaking into cinema, he recalls that "it was very difficult for filmmakers who wanted to tell stories about marginalized communities." Most people could not afford the $200,000 or whatever amount it took. So, "the people who told their stories were either those who had stories that were easily marketable or had rich uncles." But "technological breakthroughs at the end of the 1990s and into the early 2000s made a movie like *Charlotte Sometimes* possible."

Byler recalls that he made *Charlotte Sometimes*, a complex and haunting "Asian American anti-romance," for $23,000 on digital video. In addition, Byler points to *Charlotte Sometimes* as evidence that "technology has democratized the art form of narrative film, feature film." Once that technology became accessible and affordable enough, it allowed Byler and others to reach a mass audience after having been "muted up until that point." The same can be said for the grassroots and the netroots. If someone like Lowell Feld, Josh

Chernila, or Eric Byler had wanted to effect political change by themselves in the 1980s or even the 1990s, they could have canvassed and stuffed envelopes but not much more than that. In 2005 and 2006, however, the technology to be far more effective was there—and they used it.

The impact of technological change is not necessarily predictable, nor is it inherently good or bad. For Eric Byler, the democratization of filmmaking "allows the audience to choose what is news" and makes it "harder to concentrate power in the hands of a few." This crucially important point applies to the power of the netroots as well. Byler believes that although the Internet is still in its infancy (he compares bloggers to "fleas hoping to leap on the back of the behemoth mammals—the mainstream media"), it nonetheless has the power to connect people and to magnify the power of previously marginalized individuals and communities. In the case of Eric Byler, it helped to lead him from his home in Los Angeles to a transformative and empowering experience on the Webb campaign. It empowered him to "give voice to people directly" with his movies and videos. And it led him to help create Real Virginians for Webb. Multiply this story by several tens of thousands, and you start to get a feel for the potential power of the netroots.

THE "RACIST" RUCKUS

On August 29, *The Nation* published a story on George Allen's ties to the blatantly racist CCC (Council of Conservative Citizens). On Raising Kaine, Feld asked, "Is anybody out there still seriously arguing that George Allen isn't an outright racist?"[19] The right-wing blogosphere, predictably, attacked the messengers—*The Nation* magazine and Feld. Did Feld go too far in asking that question? Suffice it to say that nobody on the Webb campaign ever reprimanded Feld for writing what he wrote or threatened to fire him. Moreover, the CCC story helped promote the public image of Allen as a closet racist.

Feld even received acknowledgment from the pro-Republican National Review Online:

> Lowell Feld, Webb's netroots guy, has done a great job keeping the "macaca" story alive. If anything, this line of attack on Allen will intensify. The story, however, is as much to build momentum with fundraising as it is to sway voter opinion. For example, authors Stephen King and John Grisham will be headlining a fundraiser for Webb in the coming weeks. One reason why the DSCC [Democratic Senatorial Campaign Committee] was holding back funds to Webb was that it didn't see the Webb campaign as able to compete financially against Allen. Now that Webb seems to be raising a little bit of money on his own, the DSCC is coming in with some support. The amount of support from the DSCC, however, remains to be seen. Webb needs to keep raising cash on his own, and since the "George Allen is a

racist" storyline is working for Webb as a fundraising tool, the story will be kept alive as much as possible.[20]

Feld tried to crystallize many of the things that the campaign had been saying by quoting Allen, who commented, "You can tell a lot about people by the folks they stand with."[21] Feld listed some of the people Allen stood with, including the oil industry, lobbyist-felon Jack Abramoff, the CCC, George W. Bush, and the "morning after" contraceptive maker Barr Laboratories (social conservatives considered the pill to be a form of abortion). Feld's article was a textbook example of how bloggers attempt to influence the media narrative. By doing extensive research and pulling the threads together into a coherent storyline, Feld was attempting to hand overworked reporters their stories on a silver platter. At a minimum, his strategy was to plant a seed in reporters' minds and hope that it would bear fruit sometime later.

On September 3, the right-wing blog, Virginia Virtucon, asked "When will Jim Webb do the Honorable Thing?" and fire Feld for making "outrageous comments."[22] The blogger, Jim Riley, was angry that Feld had more or less called George Allen an "outright racist." Feld e-mailed Jessica Vanden Berg and Steve Jarding to inquire, half jokingly, whether or not he should start packing his bags. Jarding's e-mail response was one word: "No." In person, Jarding told Feld to "wear the right-wingers' attacks as a badge of honor."

A few days later, Riley continued his assault, claiming that the Raising Kaine PAC was in violation of federal elections law for Feld's "dual role as both a paid staffer of the Webb campaign and a leader of Raising Kaine PAC."[23] In reality, Raising Kaine wasn't violating anything, except for George Allen's carefully crafted phony persona. Raising Kaine's PAC treasurer, attorney Brian Patton, explained why in a post entitled, "Riley and Logic 101":

> The initial flaw in Mr. Riley's defamatory post is that the committee must first make an expenditure before any analysis as to limits and reporting of such expenditures are applicable. As stated above, Raising Kaine has never donated a penny to Jim Webb, nor has it spent any funds in Webb's behalf. Any accusation to the contrary is without merit and false.
>
> The secondary defect in Mr. Riley's defamatory statement is that a Virginia committee cannot donate to or spend any funds on behalf of a federal candidate. To the contrary, any state committee, including one only registered in Virginia, can donate directly to or spend on behalf of a federal candidate up to $1,000.00 per calendar year. Although Raising Kaine has not exercised this right yet, the option to do so remains available to the committee.
>
> Raising Kaine, therefore, is not in violation of federal election law despite Mr. Riley's frivolous accusations. We eagerly await an apology from him.[24]

Needless to say, Raising Kaine never received an apology. On the other hand, Riley's harassment on that subject stopped.

THE *WASHINGTON POST* WEIGHS IN

On September 18, the lead story in the *Washington Post* focused on the role of "paid bloggers" in the Webb-Allen race. According to the *Post*, "Lowell's Virginia site ... has been at the center of blogging influence and of controversy."[25] The *Post* continued:

> In recent posts, Feld has referred to Republicans as "rightwing crazies" and has changed the name of Allen's campaign manager, Dick Wadhams, to a locker room epithet.
>
> Recently, Feld wrote about a picture that shows Allen standing next to a group of white men who allegedly belonged to a white supremacist group.
>
> "Finally! I mean, seriously, how long does it take the supposedly 'mainstream media' to pick up on evidence that a man who wants to be President is a racist?" Feld wrote.
>
> Asked whether she believes Allen is racist, Webb spokeswoman Kristian Denny Todd said: "I don't know. You'll have to ask George Allen." Told about Feld's post, she added, "Well, you know, Lowell doesn't speak for the campaign."
>
> Feld's online statements—and the Webb campaign's attempts to distance itself—have outraged conservatives who accuse Webb of illegally using the Raising Kaine site and its bloggers as a vehicle for election-year messages without officially reporting it as a 2006 campaign expense.
>
> [Commonwealth Conservative blogger Chad] Dotson accused Feld and other liberal bloggers of making "huge misrepresentations" on their sites and said the Webb campaign should be held accountable.
>
> "His campaign has been so inept that if he didn't have left-wing bloggers screaming at the top of their lungs, he wouldn't have a campaign," Dotson said.[26]

None of these conservatives ever proved that there were "huge misrepresentations" on the pro-Webb sites, or that we were violating any laws. That they were upset, however, is no surprise—their candidate was in the midst of melting down, in part due to the relentless pressure from the Virginia and national progressive netroots, as well as their own inability to counter that pressure. Kristian Denny Todd's comment that Feld wasn't speaking for the Webb campaign was amusing, given that Feld was writing numerous times a day as well as speaking to reporters. Should Feld have used the word "racist"? In hindsight, it was probably not necessary from a tactical point of view. On the other hand, there was mounting evidence that it was all too true, and the right-wing reaction supported the belief that the racism angle had touched a raw nerve.

The *Washington Post* concluded that Federal Election Commission rules "appear to give bloggers such as Feld and Henke virtually unlimited freedom," similar to the way "newspapers and television programs are free to comment without fear of government regulation." But, the *Post* wrote, "Feld and Henke are testing the federal laws by claiming to be members of a campaign staff one moment and independent campaign bloggers the next." The *Post* observed that "campaigns such as the ones in Virginia are changing the way bloggers are perceived." The newspaper quoted Feld explaining that "blogging is evolving ... to become more like professionals, like journalists and other campaign people."[27]

Looking back on all this, Henke reflected that "it was very clear that the Left/Webb/DNC [Democratic National Committee] people were busy building a 'racism' narrative against Allen and if the Allen camp didn't address it soon, it would be too late when they had it built." Henke added, "It was a bit depressing to see [the Allen campaign] ignore what seemed so apparent to somebody who paid attention to the blogosphere, understood how the progressive infrastructure worked and how it saw narrative development/framing/etc."

In other words, had the pro-Allen blogs spent more time and effort doing research and formulating coherent arguments instead of worrying about the progressive blogs, they might have been more effective. Jon Henke admits that the pro-Allen blogs "were, er, inexpert." That appears to be diplomatic language for "the pro-Allen blogs not only didn't help Allen, they might have even hurt him" by being so shrill. In contrast, Henke believes that "the Webb netroots team did a very good job selling Jim Webb as an electable candidate with a real chance of winning." One of the Webb netroots' most impressive achievements, in Henke's opinion, was "rallying the national netroots around his campaign," which in turn "did a great deal to enhance [Webb's] stature in the media and with potential donors." In addition, Henke feels that "the Left-Roots was also very successful at surrogating the Webb campaign and DNC oppo[sition] research to the media."

"MAKING ASPERSIONS"

On September 18, one day after they had debated on *Meet the Press*—one of the highlights of which was the iconic, under-the-table photo of Jim Webb's combat boots (worn in honor of his Marine son Jimmy, who was being shipped off for duty in Iraq) next to George Allen's cowboy boots—Webb and Allen met again, this time in front of around 600 people crowded into a ballroom at the Hilton McLean Tysons Corner. This match-up was sponsored by the Fairfax County Chamber of Commerce and moderated by ABC News's George Stephanopoulos.

Although the debate ostensibly focused on domestic issues like the economy, stem cell research, and health care, the big news story stemmed from a question by WUSA (Channel 9) reporter Peggy Fox regarding Allen's Jewish heritage:

> You've been quoted as saying your mother's not Jewish, but it had been reported her father, your grandfather Felix, whom you were given your middle name for, was Jewish. Could you please tell us whether your forbearers include Jews, and if so, at which point Jewish identity might have ended?[28]

Allen's angry, almost violent response overshadowed almost everything else said that day and made headlines around the country. *Washington Post* reporter Dana Milbank described the scene well:

> Allen recoiled as if he had been struck. His supporters in the audience booed and hissed. "To be getting into what religion my mother is, I don't think is relevant," Allen said, furiously. "Why is that relevant—my religion, Jim's religion or the religious beliefs of anyone out there?"
>
> "Honesty, that's all," questioner Fox answered, looking a bit frightened.[29]

Feld, sitting in the Webb "war room" at the debate, watched incredulously as Allen continued:

> Oh, that's just all? That's just all? ... let's ask questions about issues that really matter to people here, in Virginia, such as how we're going to bring this country together, make us more secure ... preserve our foundational values, and one of those values is freedom of religion and not making aspersions about people because of their religious beliefs.[30]

Following the debate, Feld shared his impressions of Allen's reaction to Fox's question:

> So here's the takeaway message out of all this: George Allen has a nasty, sadistic, vicious, violent streak that flares up all too frequently. Over and over again, George Allen has shown himself to be a bully towards women, towards minorities, towards men who wear bicycle helmets, and now towards a female reporter who dares ask him about *his own heritage!*
>
> Perhaps George Allen could take a lesson from Wesley Clark, a man who is *proud* of his Jewish heritage and not afraid—or ashamed—to talk about it? Or perhaps George Allen should, after he is defeated on November 7, start the long process of self discovery and personal reflection originally invented by Sigmund Freud?[31]

According to Ben Tribbett, "The initial reaction was anger at Peggy Fox for asking the question [but] the story turned within a few hours from Peggy Fox to George Allen's inappropriate answer." In Tribbett's view, the reason the storyline shifted was "absolutely the blogs." This threw the Allen campaign on the defensive again, and as Tribbett observes, "once you get into that part of the campaign where you're on the defensive, it's very hard to dig out."

On September 24, following the "making aspersions" remarks—including a bizarre remark by Allen after the debate that he might be part Jewish, but he "still had a ham sandwich for lunch"[32]—the conservative *Weekly Standard* lowered the boom on George Allen. The magazine's cover photo depicted the senator with a monkey on his back, with the headline, "George Allen Monkeys Around: Forget the Presidential Campaign—Can He Still Win His Senate Race?"[33]

After a lengthy, blow-by-blow, highly unflattering description of the "macaca" incident, the *Weekly Standard* concluded that although Allen wasn't actually a racist, he was an "oaf" who was "at odds with Virginia's future." A lengthy analysis followed about how Virginia was rapidly turning Democratic "blue." The article lambasted Allen for his response to the Jewish heritage question. It ridiculed him for having "clumsily joked to the *Richmond Times-Dispatch* that his mother's Judaism [was] 'just an interesting nuance to my background'" and that she "made great pork chops" to boot. The article called Allen "a sort of bumbling phony, confused about his identity and his message."[34]

Needless to say, that's some seriously bad press for a Republican candidate coming from a leading conservative magazine. And most of it stemmed from stories either begun or amplified by progressive blogs.

Finally, money started rolling into the Webb campaign. After raising about $290,000 online in August, the campaign took in another $200,000 online from September 1 to September 17. In the two weeks after the *Meet the Press* debate, the campaign hauled in $1.1 million online, followed by $1.5 million over the Internet in October. Jim Webb believes that this was "the true turning point in the general [election] campaign."

In addition to online fundraising, the Webb campaign held a unique event at the Paramount Theater in Charlottesville on Sunday evening, September 24. Best-selling authors Stephen King (*Misery, The Shining, The Shawshank Redemption*) and John Grisham (*A Time to Kill, The Pelican Brief, The Brethren*) were joined by fellow author Jim Webb (*Fields of Fire, A Sense of Honor, Born Fighting: How the Scots-Irish Shaped America*), Virginia Governor Tim Kaine, and about 1,000 people in the audience. Each author read from his latest book (*The Innocent Man* by Grisham, *Lisey's Story* by King, and *Born Fighting* by Webb). Governor Kaine served as master of ceremonies, joking about Senator Allen: "I don't know if you've noticed, but one of Senator Allen's main points of attack on Jim Webb is that he writes *books*. . . . You know the campaign is going pretty negative when they attack somebody for writing *books*. Didn't Jefferson . . . I think Jefferson may have written a book."[35] In addition, Stephen King commented that "George Allen would not succeed as a fiction writer, because he can't seem to stick to his story."[36]

The Charlottesville event also marked the first showing of the "Leadership We Can Trust" video, which featured several of the men who had fought in Vietnam with Jim Webb. One of the most emotional moments came when Mac McGarvey, who had lost his arm while serving under platoon commander Webb, said, "If he is elected, they will see honesty like they have not seen honesty in a long time. Jim Webb cannot be bought. Lobbyists cannot influence him. If he doesn't believe it, it won't happen."[37] Powerful.

A different type of powerful statement came on September 30, when Dr. Ken Shelton, a former teammate of George Allen's on the University of Virginia football team, accused Allen in an "open letter" of being a racist. Among other things, Shelton said that Allen had "used the N word often, except in the presence of blacks." Perhaps this was the worst:

> After a successful deer-hunting trip on family land of Billy Lanahan near Bumpass, VA, George asked our hunting companion [Lanahan] where the local blacks lived. George placed a severed deer head in their large mailbox. This occurred not long after the film the *Godfather* was released featuring an intimidation scene with a severed horse's head.[38]

Attempting to change the subject from deer heads and racism accusations, the Allen campaign purchased two minutes of television time across Virginia for October 2. Many observers expected Allen to try to clear the air. Instead, Allen lashed out bitterly at "baseless personal attacks," as if all the people who had made statements about Allen's shameful past behavior were liars.[39] On October 5, a *USA Today* poll showed the Webb-Allen race in a statistical dead heat.

On October 9, Feld was at the public broadcasting studios of Community Idea Stations in Chesterfield County to live blog the last of four Webb-Allen debates. One memorable moment in the debate, which was moderated by Russ Mitchell of CBS and sponsored by the League of Women Voters, was when Webb exacted payback for George Allen's Craney Island question at the July 22 Homestead debate, with his own question to Allen about the disputed, uninhabited Senkaku Islands located in the East China Sea between Japan and China. Allen's response was a blank stare.

After weeks of growing anxiety and frustration, the DSCC finally jumped into the Webb-Allen race on October 10, with an initial ad buy of $1 million in support of Webb. Not surprisingly, the first DSCC ad highlighted Allen's "macaca" moment. George Allen was not going to escape that one—no way, no how.

ATTACKING THE NETROOTS, AND JIM WEBB'S WRITINGS

On October 16, with internal polls now showing the race a dead heat (47 percent to 47 percent), an apparently desperate George Allen campaign lashed out at its tormentors, the netroots. The Allen campaign demanded that the

Webb campaign return "Over $130,000 in Tainted Money" from a "Liberal Blog That Gloats about Contractors Mutilated in Iraq."[40] The $130,000 referred to money raised for Webb on the joint netroots ActBlue fundraising page led by Daily Kos, the most popular Democratic blog. The reference to "contractors mutilated in Iraq" reminded people about a controversial comment that Markos Moulitsas Zúniga had written in early 2004, criticizing the use of paid contractors by the U.S. military in Iraq. Kos had later apologized for the harsh tone of his words. Why on earth was the Allen campaign bringing this up now? Obviously they were concerned about the massive influx of financial and volunteer support Jim Webb was generating from the netroots. And, just as obviously, the Allen campaign's attack didn't work; money continued to flow into Webb's campaign from readers of Daily Kos and other progressive blogs. Ultimately, the Webb campaign raised nearly $900,000 via ActBlue, including $200,000 from the netroots page run by Daily Kos, Swing State Project, and MyDD.

In fact, the Webb for Senate campaign was one of the most successful 2006 Democratic campaigns in terms of its ability to raise money over the Internet. That success had to have gotten under George Allen's skin. The Allen campaign's attack on the progressive blogosphere seems to have been an attempt to tie Webb to the most outrageous statements of his online supporters. That could have been an effective strategy, except for one problem—that is, the rabid right-wing bloggers who supported Allen. This "glass house factor" may have explained why the Allen campaign quickly abandoned this line of attack.

On October 18, the *Washington Post* endorsed Jim Webb over George Allen. Most major Virginia newspapers did the same. Do such endorsements matter, and if so, how much do they matter relative to the netroots, grassroots, television ads, debates, and personal voter contact? Future analysts will best determine which factors are most crucial in deciding the outcome of today's political races. No matter what, it's certainly more pleasant to receive newspaper endorsements than to watch them go to your opponent.

One of the Webb-Allen race's weirdest moments came on October 26, when a panicked Allen campaign and its allies began attacking Jim Webb's highly praised, award-winning, best-selling fiction writing for its supposed inclusion of pedophilia and other sex acts. One right-wing Virginia blog, Mason Conservative, opined, "I don't care if its fiction or not, what kind of mind thinks this stuff up? This guy wants to be a U.S. senator? This is perverted stuff in these 'novels,' something out of Stanley Kubrick's imagination."[41]

There were numerous problems with the Allen campaign's line of attack against Jim Webb's fiction writing: (1) Webb's war novels are based on actual events he witnessed in the field; (2) Webb's great Vietnam War novel, *Fields of Fire*, is part of the U.S. Marine Corps's Professional Reading Program; (3) the right-wing Free Republic blog recommends *Fields of Fire*, as well as "anything written by James Webb," on its Military History and Strategy Reading List;

and (4) the attack was reminiscent of Jerry Kilgore's infamous "Hitler ad" in his 2005 governor's race against Tim Kaine, and that attack backfired badly.

Perhaps most important, the attacks on Webb's writings angered him greatly, leading to one of his best moments in the entire campaign. In Annandale at a Get Out the Vote rally on October 28, Webb cut loose and laid into Allen, his voice dripping with utter contempt:

> I've lived in the real world and I've reported the real world in my writings. I started working when I was twelve years old. I fought in a brutal war and I saw its ugliness while George Allen was hanging out at a dude ranch. I got shot at again covering the Marines in Beirut in 1983 as a journalist. I went on operations in Afghanistan, not as a pampered government official coming in for his dog-and-pony show briefings, but as a correspondent walking on combat patrols and sleeping on the ground. And I was reporting from the slums of Bangkok when George Allen was schlepping around in his limo.... I have written about what I have seen, and that is the duty of a writer, to help people understand the world around us, with all of its beauty and all of its flaws. Now, maybe George Allen doesn't understand that since I'm told he doesn't read books ... I've *written* more books than George Allen has *read*.[42]

For good measure, Webb slammed Allen as having "nothing to report" after six years in the Senate. Webb concluded by charging that, although the Allen campaign people certainly bore some of the blame for their gutter tactics, "the fish rots from the head down!"[43]

A "RELENTLESS EMBARRASSMENT"

According to Jon Henke, George Allen's netroots coordinator,

> That entire [attack on Webb's fiction writing] episode was a relentless embarrassment. I don't know if you noticed at the time, but I never criticized Webb for writing what he did. I had zero problem with it, and thought it should have been a total non-issue. What I *did* write was that (a) it's not "unfair" to reproduce work Webb has published and cited as part of his resume as a politician, and (b) a lot of Democrats previously argued that such sex-fiction was bad.

Needless to say, the attacks on Jim Webb's writings didn't work. Instead, they may have backfired, as polls on October 30 indicated leads for Webb of four to five points.

Another strange event came at the end of October, when Allen staffers tackled Mike Stark, an Iraq War veteran and liberal activist with no ties to the Webb campaign. Television news programs showed a tussle in which Allen's bodyguards swarmed on Stark, threw him onto the ground, and then picked him up and marched him out of earshot of Allen, at whom Stark had been yelling questions. This event received a significant amount of press coverage and made the Webb people nervous, fearing it would throw them off message and become an unwanted distraction in the campaign's closing days. In the end, it didn't seem to make much difference one way or the other.

Meanwhile, on November 1, Eric Byler released a Real Virginians for Webb video starring Tuy Le and Wasim Entabi, two devoted volunteers with Jim Webb's campaign. Tuy Le, a native of South Vietnam, spoke emotionally about the time "I was twelve or thirteen years old when the Communists burned my house.... Jim was the leader of the company protecting the village from the Communists."[44] It was a powerful video, produced by the netroots, that received more than 3,000 views in just a few days on YouTube.

In the closing weeks of the campaign, large numbers of dedicated volunteers streamed into the Webb for Senate headquarters. One group came from Yale Law School to help with voter protection. Another group, led by a volunteer named Julia Duncan, focused on an intense and well-organized Women for Webb effort. The fact that so many people were inspired and moved to action by the Webb for Senate campaign says much about the tremendous appeal that a strong, netroots, populist-fueled political campaign can have in America today. Perhaps the Webb campaign was unique. Time will tell, but it's hard to see any reason why that should be the case.

Election Day, November 7, 2006: At the start, many Webb supporters were cautiously optimistic but nervous. It would come down to turnout, and the weather was looking nasty over much of Virginia. Webb volunteers swarmed over the state, made last-minute calls, drove people to the polls, and urged their fellow citizens to come out and vote. As the day wore on, the weather got worse, and nervousness increased. Returns started coming in and Allen took an early lead. Nervousness turned into high anxiety. As the night wore on, Allen maintained a slim edge. Early Wednesday morning, late results came in from Richmond and other strongly Democratic areas, plus absentee ballots from Fairfax County and elsewhere. Webb took the lead for the first time. The explosion of joy at the Webb victory party in Tysons Corner was deafening as CNN flashed the news. If you have a chance, watch it on YouTube. It's awesome.

After briefly considering calling for a recount, George Allen conceded two days later, having lost his Senate seat by 9,329 votes to a guy who had never run for anything in his life, and who had been drafted by a bunch of netroots activists in January 2006. With that, the Republicans lost control of the U.S. Senate by one seat. How sweet it was.

HOW DID WEBB WIN?

Virginia grassroots political operative Chris Ambrose says that Webb won because of a number of factors: (1) the candidate—"we wouldn't have won without Webb"; (2) the "macaca" incident; (3) the netroots effort; and (4) "the traditional Democratic Party infrastructure." In addition, Ambrose believes that "Steve Jarding did some great strategy, good tone setting, hit back hard and brutally." But Ambrose still believes that "the Webb campaign did not really do their job." The last point is highly debatable; the Webb campaign did many things very well, including research, communications, work in the "field," and fundraising. Perhaps Ambrose's frustration comes from a feeling that a great deal of potential wasn't realized, that Webb's victory could have been much bigger than it was.

Ben Tribbett believes "100 percent" that the netroots changed the outcome of the primary and general election. George Allen's netroots man, Jon Henke, concurs: "Without the netroots, Webb would not have won" and "may not even have been close." Finally, Webb's pollster, Pete Brodnitz, says that the blogs "clearly ... had a big role in pushing stories like macaca, and if not for the Internet fundraising the race would not have been winnable."

Why were the pro-Webb netroots so much more effective than their pro-Allen counterparts? According to Henke, it's simple: "the Democrats 'got' the netroots in 2006, while Republicans did not get it at all." Even in 2007, Henke believes that "Republicans are just now at the same place Democrats were in late 2002/early 2003: they know this whole 'new media' thing is important and they know they should try to figure it out, but it's still a bit of a mystery to most of them."

Former blogger Conaway Haskins, later named Senator Webb's deputy state director, concurs with Henke. Haskins says that "the pro-Webb blogosphere was amazingly effective ... as weapons in the Democratic arsenal," while the "pro-Allen blogosphere was mostly ineffectual because they mindlessly regurgitated campaign and GOP talking points." According to Haskins, the pro-Webb bloggers "outfoxed their GOP counterparts." Haskins believes that the pro-Allen bloggers' attacks on Jim Webb (as a "pedophile" and the like) were "clear examples" that "they just couldn't get it together." Finally, Haskins notes that "the Webb bloggers led the mainstream media to water on several important stories," with the whole "macaca" incident being "emblematic of that."

Webb's deputy campaign manager, Adrienne Christian, says that "the grassroots is what really made the campaign for Jim Webb." Christian recalls traveling with Jim Webb and the reception they would receive. They would show up somewhere, not knowing what would happen, and be met by a crowd of excited supporters. In Christian's opinion, "That was because of the grassroots.... They never let us down." Christian says that "we would arrive [at an event] and we would say there were going to be fifty people there, then there'd be 300." This was important for an increasingly exhausted Jim Webb, who "fed off of the energy" and the "excitement" of seeing all those enthusiastic supporters coming out to cheer him on. According to Christian, "To see young, old, black, white … was exciting and powerful." Webb's supporters "made magic happen." Christian continues,

> If I had to rate the grassroots on producing in the state of Virginia at events from northern Virginia all the way down to southern Virginia, on a scale of one to five they were always a five. In some areas, they were a 5.6. The grassroots, given the chance, they came alive. When they became inspired—coming together, meeting like-minded people [through the] netroots and the blogs—that was an unbelievable thing.

On January 24, 2007, Jim Webb remarked, "The netroots have been a tremendous help to my campaign and a huge inspiration to me personally." Webb added, "I am where I am in large part because of their support."[45] In a June 2007 interview for this book, Webb commented, "My campaign was truly a bottom-up endeavor." Webb elaborated that his campaign "relied very heavily on volunteers, word of mouth, and netroots/grassroots in order to build support." In particular, Webb cited "the quick-response reactions to character assassination and the misrepresentation of my views, both of which were emblematic features of the Karl Rove campaign formula."

Echoing that sentiment, Senator Chuck Schumer (head of the DSCC) wrote in his book, *Positively American*, "It seemed somehow appropriate that as a new majority dawned for Senate Democrats, two candidates [Webb and Tester] who had been propelled by the growing 'netroots' (Democratic-leaning bloggers), had made the difference in the end." Schumer added that the netroots represent "a new and hugely significant advantage for Democrats," in part by "help[ing] identify and encourage viable candidates, like Jim Webb and Jon Tester, in the early stages of their races." Beyond that, Schumer cited the netroots' "success with fundraising and field organizing," and declared, "[i]n many close elections, their contribution made the difference."[46]

Without a doubt, the netroots helped to win the U.S. Senate race for Jim Webb in 2006. The only question was whether this victory was a fluke, a "perfect storm" of forces that would never be repeated, or the consequence of "macaca" (and other Allen gaffes) rather than the result of the successful efforts of bloggers. We believe that "macaca" was a classic "forced error" (as in tennis). Had the Draft James Webb movement and a Webb for Senate candidacy not been spurred on by the netroots movement, George Allen would have spent 2006 in Iowa, New Hampshire, and South Carolina running for president. And if that had been the case, it is highly unlikely that Allen would ever have been in The Breaks, Virginia, to make his "macaca" gaffe in the first place.

Chapter 9

WHAT'S NEXT FOR THE NETROOTS?

We wrestled with what to say in this chapter, in part because the two of us, like many thousands of other progressive activists across the country, have been feeling a disconnect with the national political process. After working hard to bring down the corrupt Republican majorities in Congress and succeeding beyond most reasonable expectations, Democratic activists like us are frustrated. Of course, we realize that in our system of government, it takes sixty votes in the U.S. Senate to get much done, and two-thirds majorities in both Houses of Congress are needed to override a presidential veto. Still, as social networking guru and former Dean activist Jon Lebkowsky, co-editor of the book *Extreme Democracy*, argues, many netroots activists can't help but feel that "If we were really empowered in a big way, you would think we'd be leaving Iraq, rather than 'surging.'"[1]

As opposed to 2003, when opposition to the Iraq invasion galvanized the Democratic base and created an irresistibly dramatic narrative with clear battle lines—party establishment vs. insurgent campaigns, bloggers vs. the media, online small donors vs. $2,000 check writers—the overarching political narrative of 2007 appeared to be the inability of the Democratic leadership in Congress to find an effective way to rein in the widely unpopular Bush administration on Iraq and many other areas. As a result, most progressive activists felt frustrated and angry in 2007. At a time when many in the netroots, including moderates like Josh Marshall of Talking Points Memo, were calling openly for the impeachment of George W. Bush, the Democratic Party's congressional leadership continued to insist that it was focused on more important matters.

The classic example of Democratic capitulation to Bush came right before the August 2007 recess, when Congress passed a far-reaching bill extending and expanding warrantless wiretapping on American citizens. The measure had been demanded by the Bush administration, then railroaded through the halfhearted objections of Democrats, who feared being labeled weak on defending America—particularly if a terrorist attack occurred while they were on break. Congressional Democrats seemed like homeowners busy redecorating while a pack of burglars backed up a moving van to the garage and loaded up.

Wesley Clark's first presidential campaign manager, Donnie Fowler, has argued that the netroots is like a "wild, raging river" that can be harnessed to the Democrats' advantage. Fowler believes the alternative is to dam up the river, leading to an outcome that is "even worse than letting the river run wild." And we fear that the failure of the Democratic congressional leadership to find a compelling and effective way to oppose the excesses of the Bush administration has done just that. Following their impressive—and heady—victories of 2006, the netroots activists and bloggers entered 2007 looking to work with the Democratic leadership in Congress. They expected to play a key role in mustering public support for the antiwar initiatives, which they anticipated coming from the new Democratic congressional majorities they had just helped elect. Instead, they felt frustrated and stymied at every turn.

The failure of the congressional leadership to create a compelling narrative of opposition to a president with a 29 percent approval rating in the polls acted like Donnie Fowler's theoretical dam. The unchanneled energy of the netroots turned against the Democratic establishment and threatened to damage the very causes in which they believed. In September 2007, MoveOn published an advertisement in the *New York Times* that mocked the name of General David Petraeus, calling him "Betray Us" for his report on the Iraq "surge." The reaction to MoveOn's ad was passionate on all sides, with Republicans condemning it, progressive bloggers defending it, and congressional Democrats once again getting caught between a rock and a hard place. In the end, the MoveOn ad handed Republicans another opportunity to distract people's attention from the disaster of Iraq and return to the perceived excesses of the antiwar left. Ultimately, the Senate voted seventy-two to twenty-five (including twenty-two Democrats) to condemn the ad.

Even worse, the MoveOn brouhaha threatened to reopen a severe schism in the Democratic Party between its antiwar grassroots origins and its cautious political establishment dating back to the late 1960s and the Vietnam era. MoveOn itself enjoyed a surge in donations from its members, but its polarizing rhetoric was unlikely to have brought many other Americans over to its cause, or to have hastened the day when the United States withdraws from Iraq.

Did anyone win in all this? It's hard to see.

WHERE WE ARE AND WHERE WE'RE GOING

Many of the first-time activists of 2003 and 2004 are now established political players. In addition, many incumbents owe their election success to the netroots and to their use of new methods and technologies. Yet controversy persists about whether and how well leading presidential candidates are adapting to this online world.

Democratic presidential campaigns in 2007 enjoyed record online fundraising and site visitors, exceeding those of the Howard Dean and Wesley Clark
campaigns at their highest points. Despite these successes, however, none of
the campaigns came even close to matching the excitement that surrounded
the 2003 Dean and Clark movements. Instead, Democrats appeared to be
playing it safe, calculating every move and utterance, and acting confident that
their party's eventual nominee would win the White House in 2008. In addition, Democratic presidential campaigns showed no sign of truly embracing
the netroots movement, or, for that matter, of running people-powered campaigns. Rather, the people running Democratic presidential campaigns seemed
happy to achieve a mere semblance of such openness—that is, as long as the
money was coming in to fund ads and other traditional activities. For their
part, rank-and-file activists were feeling demoralized and frustrated at the
party's failure to change the course of politics on Iraq, global warming, warrantless wiretapping, and much more.

The eye-popping online success of Barack Obama in the first half of
2007—surpassing Howard Dean's total number of campaign donors by the
end of the third quarter and registering hundreds of thousands of "friends" on
the social networking site Facebook—seemed to indicate that the netroots
movement continued to grow rapidly. Jerome Armstrong told the *Washington
Post*, "What we're seeing here is Obama's broad, wide, mainstream appeal, and
he's bringing in new people ... people who aren't necessarily political junkies
who follow the blogs."[2] But Armstrong also pointed out on his blog, MyDD,
that the Dean and Obama campaigns "are drastically different in origina-
tion."[3] Whereas "Dean depended on the [I]nternet and small donors, Obama
got 70 percent of his [first quarter] money from $1,000 and up donors."[4]

The question raised by Zack Exley—founder and president of the New
Organizing Institute and an advisor to Howard Dean in 2003—in February
2007 remained: "Will Obama put on the makeup?"[5] Exley concluded that
campaigns still don't fully comprehend the netroots phenomenon, just as
Richard Nixon didn't comprehend the new medium of television in his 1960
debate with John F. Kennedy. Exley noted that Nixon "refused to wear
makeup to improve his appearance on TV, fearing embarrassment in the
press." As a result, "Even though [Nixon's] performance was comparable to
Kennedy's, he lost the debate in the voters' minds because he just looked
awful." All because Nixon wouldn't put on the makeup.[6]

Donnie Fowler was puzzled by the Obama phenomenon as well: "He's got
this massive movement of small donors, but it's not being reflected in the
national polls." Fowler continued, "This is one of the few grassroots things
I've experienced in twenty years that I just am baffled by." Perhaps Fowler was
baffled because Obama wasn't running a true netroots campaign. Certainly,
Obama managed to capitalize on the dramatically increased reach of the Internet to attract new donors and recruit volunteers. But, because his campaign

was being run in a traditional top-down manner, it lacked the explosive implications of Dean and Clark's online revolution of 2003.

Meanwhile, Hillary Clinton led the Democratic pack throughout most
of 2007, despite the fact that she was definitely not the netroots candidate
regardless of whatever other positives she possessed. Who were the netroots
activists excited about? Al Gore, but he wasn't running. Wesley Clark, but he
wasn't running either (in September 2007, Clark endorsed Hillary Clinton).
John Edwards and Barack Obama to an extent, but response paled in compar-
ison to the Clark and Dean excitement of 2003. As Open Left blogger Matt
Stoller wrote on September 8, 2007:

> The people that backed Dean and Clark in 2004, and then Kerry, have not
> unified behind any one candidate in the primary. Some support is behind
> John Edwards, and some is behind Barack Obama, but some of it has either
> dissolved into apathy or into lower ticket races. For progressives, the lack of
> leverage in the presidential race is disheartening.[7]

Despite the disillusionment and frustration with campaign politics, numerous
political campaign insiders and netroots activists who we interviewed while
researching this book were unanimous in their view that something significant
changed between 2000 and 2007 in the way Americans elected their leaders.
Opinion differed with regard to exactly what that change constituted and what
it portended, however. Political insiders believed that traditional grassroots
activists and their technologically savvy, snarky, netroots cousins had transformed the way voters gathered information about issues and candidates, as
well as the way they communicated with one another and with the candidates.
Also changed was the way contributors gave—and campaigns collected—the
money needed to run for office. But how well integrated with the political system the netroots were, or could be, remained uncertain as of late 2007.

SHORT HEADS AND LONG TAILS

In July 2007, Chris Bowers wrote an article on Open Left entitled "New
Establishment Rising? The End of the Flat Blogosphere." Bowers's argument
was that the progressive political blogosphere had "exploded" in terms of
"audience and political effectiveness" since 2002, but that it was now in danger
of moving from a "fluid, 'outsider' and 'open' form of new media [to a] new
'establishment' all its own." Bowers contrasted the "short head"—that is, "the
roughly 1 percent of progressive, political blogs that receive over 95 percent of
all progressive blogosphere traffic"—with the "long tail"—that is, "the 99 percent of progressive political blogs that receive less than 5 percent of all
progressive, political blogosphere traffic." Bowers characterized the long-tail
blogs as "independent, hobby blogs with a sole content producer, virtually no

internal community to speak of, and content that is almost 100 percent micro-punditry on current events reporting from established news sources."[8]

In contrast, Bowers described the short-head blogosphere as being dominated by group and community blogs; the emergence of "professional bloggers"; and a move away from "micro-punditry on current events" to "recruiting candidates," "commissioning of independent polls," "heavy-duty fundraising," "investigative journalism," even "writing books." According to Bowers, "barriers to entry" into the "elite" had grown since late 2005, to the point that "the composition of the 'short head' ossified." This worried Bowers:

> Simply put, the progressive blogosphere thrives on mass participation, innovative ideas, and vibrant discussion. If the barriers to entry stay too high for too long and if the people directing discussion and action remain the same for an extended period of time, then there will be a corresponding drop-off in the political effectiveness of the entire progressive blogosphere.[9]

According to Bowers, citing an August 2005 study by the New Politics Institute ("Emergence of the Progressive Blogosphere: A New Force in American Politics"), current estimates indicate "a daily audience of 4–5 million for progressive political blogs, and an occasional audience of up to 13–14 million for all political blogs." The New Politics Institute study found that, although there are "a few hundred thousand blogs in this country that talk about politics ... less than one-tenth of 1 percent of them account for more than 99 percent of all political blogging traffic." That certainly qualifies as a "long tail."[10]

The New Politics Institute study also found that, in 2003, "the conservative blogosphere was between two and three times as large as the progressive blogosphere."[11] Starting in 2003, however, the progressive blogosphere exploded, reaching double the size of the conservative blogosphere as of August 2005. And the progressive blogosphere reached a level of effectiveness far greater than that of the conservative blogosphere, as several recent Democratic electoral victories demonstrate, including Kaine, Webb, Lamont, and Tester. The question is whether this trend will continue. Or, will progressives, disillusioned and frustrated by the establishment, ratchet back their efforts and allow conservatives to get back into the game?

"THIS TRANSITIONAL ERA IS A TSUNAMI," OR NOT

Webb for Senate senior strategist Steve Jarding is highly optimistic about the netroots' ability to change American politics. Jarding believes that "this transitional era is a tsunami ... the greatest democratic movement technologically maybe ever." The power potential of the Internet is "so phenomenal," Jarding predicts, that "in one or two cycles, you're not going to have a campaign where blogging is not instrumental." This results from the fact that the

Internet can reach "a mass audience almost free of charge," allowing them to "express themselves, get involved, give money and time, get active." As a result, Jarding concludes, it's no longer "necessarily the case" that whoever spends the most money will win.

Howard Dean, writing in *Forbes* magazine on May 7, 2007, was unconditionally positive: "The Internet is the most significant tool for building democracy since the invention of the printing press." Dean added that "[p]ower is shifting away from centralized messaging and toward voters who demand that politicians listen to them before speaking to them."[12]

George Allen's former netroots coordinator, Jon Henke, offers a somewhat cautious view of the new technology's power, arguing that it "won't eliminate the traditional media, political consultants or the top-down campaign structure," but it will "help democratize the game." John Hlinko, the creative genius behind the Draft Wesley Clark movement, is characteristically more ebullient: "Voters will never have an excuse again to whine and bitch about 'bad candidates,' because someone else (like me or you) can turn to them and say, 'yeah, then shut the hell up and draft someone you *do* like.'" According to Hlinko, today's netroots activists now have the power to do that.

One effect of the rising netroots will almost certainly be on the world of advertising. The model long has been "interruption advertising," one in which you are watching television and a commercial jumps in whether you invite it to or not. Today, however, interruption advertising is dying out as people gain the ability to avoid commercials thanks to digital video recording. In its place, says communications expert Antonia Scatton, will come "permission marketing," also known as "opt-in advertising." Scatton points out that "unsubscribe" is a protocol on the Internet. Violations of this "opt-out rule" count as spam, and it's the same thing with "interruption advertising." According to Scatton, "Four years down the road, TV advertising is going to be worthless." Scatton notes that "political advertising is becoming far more expensive as it becomes less effective." Rather than repeating a simple message, future candidates increasingly will need to forge a coherent narrative that amplifies their message.

Along these lines, Joe Trippi believes that we are witnessing "a move from the phoniness of the thirty-second spot to the authenticity of what happens when I catch you on my cell phone video." According to Trippi, "The more authentic candidates are going to fare better in this medium." And, Trippi adds, "one of the reasons young people are becoming more engaged [in politics] is because [the Internet is] an authentic medium, it's their medium ... it's one of the first places they've ever seen [authenticity], or any generation has seen authenticity in a while."[13]

Paul Delehanty, also known as "kid oakland" to his readers on Daily Kos and other blogs, asserts that "[w]e are entering the era of Blogging 2.0." In Delehanty's view, "We are about to enter an era in which blogging will move from competing simply with national cable and news media" (an era he calls Blogging 1.0) "into an era where blogs also begin to merge the functions of the town hall and the local paper on the local level, a moment where local citizen journalism and local grassroots activism merge in this new media environment: Blogging 2.0." Increasingly, Delehanty argues, "the role of local blogger is merging with the role of local Democratic activist and leader ... interacting with local journalists and party organizers [and] tilting the playing field in favor of a progressive candidate that the [Democratic Congressional Campaign Committee] opposed."[14]

The question is whether modern campaigns understand what it means to put on the netroots "makeup." According to Zack Exley, campaigns have tended to "[delegate] 'the Internet thing' to staffers who are far outside of the inner circle," have believed that all they needed to do was hire a "blogger king," and have "refused to take personal responsibility for understanding the potentials of the medium on their own."[15] Campaigns still haven't put on the makeup in the sense of approaching the Internet "with the same intensity, curiosity and rigor that they apply to television, polling, speech-writing ... and debate performance."[16]

Our bet is that the first campaign to really "get" the netroots, to put on that makeup and build a genuine relationship with its online support base, will gain an advantage over other campaigns. And this advantage will be analogous to the one Kennedy achieved over Nixon in that 1960s television studio. Time will tell.

In the end, we are left with more questions than answers: Will the netroots keep rising? Will the revolution that started with Robert Reich (for governor of Massachusetts) in 2002; Wes Clark and Howard Dean in 2003; Richard Morrison in 2004; Paul Hackett and Tim Kaine in 2005; Ned Lamont, Jim Webb, Jon Tester, and others in 2006 continue in 2008 and beyond? Will something come along, perhaps regulatory changes to the current open structure of the Internet ("net neutrality"), that might derail netroots? Will the prickly relationship of the netroots and the political professionals improve, will they continue to eye each other warily, or will they break into open opposition? Will technology-powered netroots organizing become fully competitive with the top-down, broadcast media campaign model? Will netroots activists remain as an outside force, or finally "crash the gate" and take over the party? Will the Democratic political establishment embrace, cultivate, and support bloggers through buying advertising or granting stipends? Will the public keep voicing its opinions on blogs, drawn by this medium's egalitarian and connective power? Or will it be turned off by blog "echo chambers" and partisan polarization?

We agree with Jon Henke that "there will always be a place for the amateur blogger who can get good information and write with a unique voice." And we believe that once people get a taste of activist, netroots democracy it will be difficult—if not impossible—to convince them to return to mass media passivity. For candidates, the challenge will be to harness the power of the netroots or lose to those candidates who do. Either way, as the *Washington Post* concluded following the Yearly Kos convention in early August 2007, "Like it or not, the [netroots] appear to be here to stay."[17]

Notes

PREFACE

1. Daily Kos, "Memo to the Media, Pundits," November 9, 2006.

INTRODUCTION

1. Strother, *Falling Up: How a Redneck Helped Invent Political Consulting*, 2003.
2. Barlow, *The Rise of the Blogosphere*, 2007.
3. Chaudhry, "Can Blogs Revolutionize Progressive Politics?" *In These Times*, February 6, 2006.
4. Gladwell, *The Tipping Point: How Little Things Can Make a Big Difference*, 2002.
5. YouTube, "Allen's Listening Tour," August 14, 2006.

CHAPTER 1

1. Fero, interview, April 28, 2007.
2. MyDD, "The Journey with Trippi, Dean and DFA," June 29, 2006.
3. Ibid.
4. Ibid.
5. Poonawalla, e-mail interview, February 6, 2003, http://www.gwu.edu/~action/2004/cands/web0203b0.html.

CHAPTER 2

1. Internet Archive, "Howard Dean at California Democratic Convention 2003," www.archive.org/details/dean-sacramento.
2. MyDD, "Questions on the Progressive Movement and 2008," November 26, 2006.
3. Ibid.
4. *Hannity and Colmes*, Fox News, June 9, 2004.
5. Association of Alternative Newsweeklies, November 23, 2005.
6. Daily Kos, "Two Years Ago Today," February 5, 2005.

7. Howard Dean 2004 Call to Action, March 15, 2003.

8. Proctor, "Dean Is Dead, Long Live the Dean!" *Texas Observer*, March 26, 2004.

9. Ibid.

10. SEIU is the Service Employees International Union; AFSCME is the American Federation of State, County and Municipal Employees.

CHAPTER 3

1. Clark Community Network, "From the Beginning, Part II: Susan Putney's Story," August 6, 2006.

2. Ibid.

3. Dahl, *After the Revolution?* 1970.

4. Bentley College, "Bentley Study Analyzes e-Campaign for 2004 Presidential Elections and Clark Meetups," January 12, 2004.

5. Clark Community Network, "From the Beginning, Part II: Susan Putney's Story," August 6, 2006.

6. Ratan, "Draft-Clark Posse Feels Left Out," *Wired*, September 26, 2003.

7. Franke-Ruta, "Fan Friction: Hell Hath No Fury Like a Draft Clark Enthusiast Spurned," *American Prospect*, September 25, 2003.

8. DraftClark, October 8, 2003.

9. Demillo, "Maneuvers in Clark Camp Take Place on Internet," *Arkansas Democrat Gazette,* October 9, 2003.

10. Ibid.

11. Daily Kos, September 25, 2003.

12. Ibid.

13. Clark Community Network, "Meet the Press Interview Brings in New Draftees—Part I," October 8, 2006.

14. Huffington Post, "Blogosphere Day: Time to Invest in Our Future," July 19, 2007.

15. Ibid.

CHAPTER 4

1. Horwitz, "I'm Very Ashamed," *Salon*, August 27, 2004.

2. Talking Points Memo, September 1, 2004.

3. Ibid.

4. Talking Points Memo, August 29, 2004.

5. Ibid.

6. Off the Kuff, "An Interview with Richard Morrsion," December 8, 2003.

7. Matthews, KSEV Talk Radio, October 22, 2003.

8. Off the Kuff, "An Interview with Richard Morrison," December 8, 2003.

9. Ibid.

10. Ibid.

11. Daily Kos, "Corpses on the Cover," April 1, 2004.

12. Daily Kos, "TX-22: Third Party Groups Enter the Fray; And Poll," October 19, 2004.

13. Greg's Opinion, "Conventioneering 2.0—Further Thoughts," June 20, 2004.

14. Greg's Opinion, "Put Richard on TV," August 23, 2004.

15. Off the Kuff, "Still More DeLay Stuff," October 19, 2004.

16. Daily Kos, "TX-22: Third Party Groups Enter the Fray; And Poll," October 19, 2004.

17. Donald, "On the Stump: Lawyer-Candidates Try to Unseat Tom DeLay," *Texas Lawyer*, October 25, 2004.

18. Ibid.

19. Off the Kuff, "Great Article on Morrison," October 25, 2004.

20. Ibid.

21. Aynesworth, "DeLay Finds Re-Election Tougher," *Washington Times*, October 30, 2004.

22. Daily DeLay, "Breaking News: DeLay Goes Negative," October 27, 2004.

23. Carter, "Bev's Burner," *Fort Bend Star*, October 21, 2004.

24. Armstrong and Moulitsas Zúniga, *Crashing the Gate: Netroots, Grassroots, and the Rise of People-Powered Politics*, 2006.

CHAPTER 5

1. Raising Kaine, "Kilgore's Scumbag Media Advisor," January 18, 2005.

2. Waldo Jaquith, "Jerry Kilgore, Eavsedropper?" December 12, 2003.

3. Dao, "Veteran of Iraq, Running in Ohio, Is Harsh on Bush," *New York Times*, July 27, 2005.

4. Nichols, "Democratic Candidates Tout Iraq War Experience," *USA Today*, July 27, 2005.

5. Balz, "GOP Says It Will 'Bury' Name-Calling Candidate," *Washington Post*, July 31, 2005.

6. MyDD, "10/25/04: What a Difference a Day Makes," July 13, 2005.

7. Not Larry Sabato, "Top 10 Hottest Races as of 4/21," April 22, 2005.

8. Not Larry Sabato, "Who Are We?" June 28, 2005.

9. Borgmeyer, "Who's Virginia's Newest Political Star? It's Not Larry Sabato," *Charlottesville Newsweekly*, July 12, 2005.

10. Raising Kaine, "Why Jerry Kilgore Is Soft on Meth," September 2, 2005.

11. Raising Kaine, "Major Kilgore Backer Hires and Exploits Illegal Immigrants," September 17, 2005.

12. Garver, "Meet Tim Kaine," *American Prospect*, March 23, 2005.

13. The News Blog, "Tim Kaine Is a Coward," October 27, 2005.

14. Daily Kos, "Cowardice at the Kaine Campaign," October 27, 2005.

15. Shear, "References to Hitler in Kilgore Ad Criticized," *Washington Post*, October 15, 2005.

16. Kaine, "How I Won," *Blueprint Magazine*, February 9, 2006.

17. Daou, "The Triangle: Limits of Blog Power," *Salon*, September 19, 2005.

18. Grove, "Close, but No Cigar," *Washington Post*, May 15, 2003.

19. Thompson, "The Exterminator," *Salon*, September 3, 2003.

20. Reynolds, *An Army of Davids: How Markets and Technology Empower Ordinary People to Beat Big Media,* 2006.

21. Emanuel, meeting with Nate Wilcox, April 13, 2005.

22. Benjaminson, "Dems Now Eying DeLay's District for 2006," April 8, 2005.

23. Weisman, "Schiavo's Wishes Recalled in Records," *St. Petersburg Times,* November 8, 2003.

24. The Daily DeLay, "It's Time for DeLay to Go. Join Us," March 15, 2005.

25. Weisman, "GOP Leaders Seek Distance from Abramoff; Hastert to Donate Money Given by Lobbyist's Clients," *Washington Post,* January 4, 2006.

26. As of September 2007, DeLay was continuing his legal and public wrangling with District Attorney Ronnie Earle. Both sides had filed numerous appeals and counterappeals, and the case was showing every sign of dragging into 2008. Despite plentiful reason to believe that federal prosecutors had strong evidence against DeLay, no charges had been filed at the federal level.

CHAPTER 6

1. Members of the Union-Tribune's Editorial Board, *San Diego Union Tribune,* "Q&A: James Webb; Former Secretary of the Navy," October 30, 2005.

2. Raising Kaine, "Fighting Smart: Jim Webb," December 12, 2005.

3. Rasmussen Reports poll, December 9, 2005.

4. Raising Kaine, "Draft James Webb," December 20, 2005.

5. Ibid.

6. Daily Kos, "DraftJamesWebb.com," January 1, 2006.

7. Raising Kaine, "Webb Reconsiders: Never a Dull Moment!" February 3, 2006.

8. Whittington, "George Allen Torpedoed?" *Roll Call,* February 9, 2006.

9. Raising Kaine, "The Roll Call on Webb," February 9, 2006.

10. Daily Kos, "CT-Sen, VA-Sen, MN-Sen: Two In, One Out," February 7, 2006.

11. Draft James Webb, February 10, 2006.

12. Not Larry Sabato, "It's 100 Days until June 1," February 20, 2006.

13. Ibid.

14. Draft James Webb Yahoo! group, March 6, 2006.

15. Lewis, "Retired Female General to Back Miller for Senate," March 9, 2006.

16. Webb, "Women Can't Fight," *Washingtonian,* November 1979.

17. Raising Kaine, "A Warnerite's Plea for Neutrality," March 14, 2006.

18. Richmond Democrat, "What Will Harris Miller Try Next? Pork Rinds?" March 27, 2006.

19. Raising Kaine, "Harris Miller Is Washington, Jim Webb Is Virginia," April 10, 2006.

20. The Modern Patriot, April 12, 2006.

21. Daily Kos, "Paul Hackett Live Blog," April 13, 2006.

22. Raising Kaine, "Shad Planking Update—Live from Wakefield," April 19, 2006.

23. *GOTV,* "Did Webb Play Anti-Semitic Card?" May 19, 2006.

24. McDougall, "IT Confidential: ITAA's Miller Wants to Go to Washington," *Information Week,* January 9, 2006.

25. Raising Kaine, "Alice Marshall's Despicable 'Anti-Semitism' Claim," May 19, 2006.

26. Raising Kaine, "Right Wing Spreads Alice Marshall's Despicable 'Anti-Semitism' Smear," May 22, 2006.

27. Fisher, "Virginia Senate: Low Blows and the Hook(nose)," *Washington Post*, June 9, 2006.

28. Raising Kaine, "John Kerry and Jim Webb Close Out Campaign," June 12, 2006.

29. Virginia Centrist, June 13, 2006.

30. Ox Road South, "2006 Primary: Breaking It Down," June 15, 2006.

31. Not Larry Sabato, "Historic Victory," June 14, 2006.

32. Fisher, "What If the Voters Don't Care?" *Washington Post*, June 15, 2006.

33. Shear and Barnes, "Virginia Politics," *Washington Post*, June 14, 2006.

34. Ibid.

CHAPTER 7

1. Editorial, "The Jerk from Montana," *Daily Press,* August 8, 2006.

2. Adams, "Meet the Bloggers," *Missoula Independent,* August 31, 2006.

3. Biuso, "Are Voters Ready to Dump Lieberman?" *The Nation*, January 11, 2006.

4. *American Morning*, CNN, August 9, 2006.

5. My Left Nutmeg, "Cup of Irish Joe: Fair-Weather Friend to Democrats," July 10, 2006.

6. Ibid.

7. Hotline, "The Lieberman Decision," July 3, 2006.

8. Daily Kos, "CT-Sen: Winners and Loser," August 8, 2006.

9. Raising Kaine, "Lamont and Webb: Populist Reformers in Connecticut and Virginia," August 9, 2006.

CHAPTER 8

1. O'Keefe, "Webb Beats Miller for Democratic Senate Nomination," *Cavalier Daily*, June 15, 2006.

2. Daily Kos, "VA-Sen: Let's Help Jim Webb Get Elected," June 26, 2006.

3. Raising Kaine, "Note to Readers," July 7, 2006.

4. Raising Kaine, Comment by "VADem4Ever," July 7, 2006.

5. Daily Kos, "Why I Support Jim Webb," July 21, 2006.

6. Raising Kaine, "A Few More Impressions of the Debate," July 22, 2006.

7. Raising Kaine, "Webb Wagons on the Move," August 7, 2006.

8. Ibid.

9. Sidarth, "I Am Macaca," *Washington Post*, November 12, 2006.

10. Yellow Dog Strategy, "The Real Ma**ca," January 2007.

11. Ibid.

12. YouTube, "Allen's Listening Tour," August 14, 2006.

13. Yellow Dog Strategy, "The Real Ma**ca," January 2007.

14. Ibid.

15. Not Larry Sabato, "Major Senate Race Shakeup," August 13, 2006.

16. Virginia Virtucon, August 15, 2006.

17. SurveyUSA, Poll No. 10072, August 21, 2006.

18. Hotline, "Allen Campaign Shifts Gears, Seeks Help," August 22, 2006.

19. Raising Kaine, "George Allen and the CCC 'Hate Group'," August 29, 2006.

20. Pollowitz, "Schumer to the Rescue," Sixers Blog, *National Review Online*, August 30, 2006.

21. Barisic, "Giuliani Endorses Virginia Senator for Re-election," *Hampton Roads Daily Press*, August 30, 2006.

22. Virginia Virtucon, September 3, 2006.

23. Virginia Virtucon, September 5, 2006.

24. Raising Kaine, "Riley and Logic 101," September 7, 2006.

25. Shear and Craig, "Paid Bloggers Stoke Senate Battle in Va.: Campaigns Test Limits of Finance Laws," *Washington Post*, September 17, 2006.

26. Ibid.

27. Ibid.

28. "Transcript: Sen. Allen and Peggy Fox at Monday's Senate Debate," http://www.washingtonpost.com/wp-dyn/content/article/2006/09/20/AR2006092000785.html.

29. Milbank, "The Senator's Gentile Rebuke," *Washington Post*, September 19, 2006.

30. "Transcript: Sen. Allen and Peggy Fox at Monday's Senate Debate," http://www.washingtonpost.com/wp-dyn/content/article/2006/09/20/AR2006092000785.html.

31. Raising Kaine, "Peggy Fox's Jewish Question, Wes Clark, and George Allen's Anger 'Issues'," September 19, 2006.

32. Copeland, "For Sen. Allen, Questions of Much More Than Faith," *Washington Post*, September 22, 2006.

33. Continetti, "George Allen Monkeys Around: Forget the Presidential Campaign. Can He Still Win His Senate Race?" *Weekly Standard*, September 24, 2006.

34. Ibid.

35. Charlottesville Podcasting Network, "Stephen King and John Grisham Raise Money for Democrat Jim Webb," September 25, 2006.

36. Raising Kaine, "Webb, Grisham and King: It's a Good Thing to Write Books!" September 25, 2006.

37. Ibid.

38. Martin, "Shelton Responds to 9/25/06 Allen Denial," *Virginia Progressive*, September 30, 2006.

39. Not Larry Sabato, "No Apology!" October 2, 2006.

40. George Allen Campaign, "Daily Kos Gives Webb over $130,000 in Tainted Money," Press Release, October 16, 2006.

41. Mason Conservative, "Drudge: 'Allen's Revenge: Exposes Underage Sex Scenes in Opponent's Novels'," October 26, 2006.

42. YouTube, "Annandale Rally," October 28, 2006.

43. Ibid.

44. YouTube, "Real Virginians for Webb," November 1, 2006.

45. Daily Kos, "Memo to the Media, Pundits," November 9, 2006.

46. Schumer, *Positively American: Winning Back the Middle-Class Majority One Family at a Time,* 2007.

CHAPTER 9

1. Lebkowsky and Ratcliffe, *Extreme Democracy,* 2005.
2. Vargas, "A Foundation Built on Small Blocks," *Washington Post,* July 16, 2007.
3. MyDD, "Fundraising in '03 and '07," July 2, 2007.
4. Ibid.
5. Exley, "Will Obama Put on the Makeup?" Personal Democracy Forum, February 4, 2007.
6. Ibid.
7. Open Left, "The Two Anti-Clinton Strategies," September 8, 2007.
8. Open Left, "New Establishment Rising? The End of the Flat Blogosphere," July 8, 2007.
9. Ibid.
10. Ibid.
11. New Politics Institute, "Emergence of the Progressive Blogosphere: A New Force in American Politics," August 10, 2005.
12. Dean, "Wikipartia," *Forbes,* May 7, 2007.
13. New Politics Institute, "Campaign 2008: Targeting Young Voters," March 9, 2007.
14. kid oakland, "Blogging 2.0," October 30, 2006.
15. Exley, "Will Obama Put on the Makeup?" Personal Democracy Forum, February 4, 2007.
16. Ibid.
17. Cillizza, "The Net Roots' Moment in the Sun," *Washington Post,* August 5, 2007.

BIBLIOGRAPHY

BOOKS, MAGAZINES, AND NEWSPAPERS

Adams, John S. 2006. "Meet the Bloggers." *Missoula Independent,* August 31.

Armstrong, Jerome, and Markos Moulitsas Zúniga. 2006. *Crashing the Gate: Netroots, Grassroots, and the Rise of People-Powered Politics.* White River Junction, VT: Chelsea Green.

Aynesworth, Hugh. 2004. "DeLay Finds Re-Election Tougher." *Washington Times,* October 30.

Bai, Matt. 2007. *The Argument: Billionaires, Bloggers, and the Battle to Remake Democratic Politics.* New York: Penguin Press.

Balz, Dan. 2005. "GOP Says It Will 'Bury' Name-Calling Candidate." *Washington Post,* July 31.

Barisic, Sonja. 2006. "Giuliani Endorses Virginia Senator for Re-election." *Hampton Roads Daily Press,* August 30.

Barlow, Aaron. 2007. *The Rise of the Blogosphere.* Westport, CT: Praeger.

Barnes, Ben. 2006. *Barn Burning, Barn Building: Tales of a Political Life, from LBJ to George W. Bush and Beyond.* Albany, TX: Bright Sky Press.

Benjaminson, Wendy. 2005. "Dems Now Eying DeLay's District for 2006." Associated Press, April 8.

Bentley College. 2004. "Bentley Study Analyzes e-Campaign for 2004 Presidential Elections and Clark Meetups." January 12.

Bickerstaff, Steve. 2007. *Lines in the Sand: Congressional Redistricting in Texas and the Downfall of Tom DeLay.* Austin: University of Texas Press.

Biuso, Emily. 2006. "Are Voters Ready to Dump Lieberman?" *The Nation,* January 11.

Blumenthal, Sidney. 1980. *The Permanent Campaign: Inside the World of Elite Political Operatives.* Boston: Beacon Press.

Boehlert, Eric. 2004. *Lapdogs: How the Press Rolled over for Bush.* New York: Basic Books.

Borgmeyer, John. 2005. "Who's Virginia's Newest Political Star? It's Not Larry Sabato." *Charlottesville Newsweekly,* July 12.

Bowers, Chris, and Matt Stoller. 2005. *Emergence of the Progressive Blogosphere: A New Force in American Politics.* Washington, DC: New Politics Institute.

Carter, B. K. 2004. "Bev's Burner." *Fort Bend Star,* October 21.

Chace, James. 2005. *1912: Wilson, Roosevelt, Taft, and Debs—the Election That Changed the Country.* New York: Simon & Schuster.

Charlottesville Podcasting Network. 2006. "Stephen King and John Grisham Raise Money for Democrat Jim Webb." September 25.

Chaudhry, Lakshmi. 2006. "Can Blogs Revolutionize Progressive Politics?" *In These Times,* February 6.

Cillizza, Chris. 2007. "The Net Roots' Moment in the Sun." *Washington Post*, August 5.

Clark, Wesley K. 2002. *Waging Modern War: Bosnia, Kosovo, and the Future of Combat.* New York: Public Affairs.

Clark, Wesley K. 2004. *Winning Modern Wars: Iraq, Terrorism, and the American Empire.* New York: Public Affairs.

Clark, Wesley K. 2007. *A Time to Lead: For Duty, Honor and Country.* New York: Palgrave Macmillan.

Continetti, Matthew. 2006. "George Allen Monkeys Around: Forget the Presidential Campaign. Can He Still Win His Senate Race?" *Weekly Standard,* September 24.

Copeland, Libby. 2006. "For Sen. Allen, Questions of Much More Than Faith." *Washington Post*, September 22.

Dahl, Robert. 1970. *After the Revolution?* New Haven, CT: Yale University Press.

Dao, Janes. 2005. "Veteran of Iraq, Running in Ohio, Is Harsh on Bush." *New York Times,* July 27.

Daou, Peter. 2005. "The Triangle: Limits of Blog Power." *Salon.* September 19.

Dean, Howard. 2006. *You Have the Power: How to Take Back Our Country and Restore Democracy in America.* New York: Simon & Schuster.

Dean, Howard. 2007. "Wikipartia." *Forbes,* May 7.

Demillo, Andrew. 2003. "Maneuvers in Clark Camp Take Place on Internet." *Arkansas Democrat Gazette*, October 9.

Donald, Mark. 2004. "On the Stump: Lawyer-Candidates Try to Unseat Tom DeLay." *Texas Lawyer,* October 25.

Dubose, Lou, and Jan Reid. 2004. *The Hammer: Tom DeLay, God, Money, and the Rise of the Republican Congress.* New York: Public Affairs.

Dubose, Lou, and Jan Reid. 2006. *The Hammer Comes Down: The Nasty, Brutish, and Shortened Political Life of Tom DeLay.* New York: Public Affairs.

Editorial. 2006. "The Jerk from Montana." *Daily Press,* August 8.

Exley, Zack. 2007. "Will Obama Put on the Makeup?" Personal Democracy Forum website, February 4.

Ferling, John. 2005. *Adams vs. Jefferson: The Tumultuous Election of 1800.* New York: Oxford University Press.

Fisher, Marc. 2006. "Virginia Senate: Low Blows and the Hook(nose)." *Washington Post,* June 9.

Fisher, Marc. 2006. "What If the Voters Don't Care?" *Washington Post*, June 15.

Franke-Ruta, Garance. 2003. "Fan Friction: Hell Hath No Fury Like a Draft Clark Enthusiast Spurned." *American Prospect*, September 25.

Garver, Rob. 2005. "Meet Tim Kaine." *American Prospect,* March 23.

George Allen Campaign. 2006. "Daily Kos Gives Webb over $130,000 in Tainted Money." Press Release. October 16.

Gladwell, Malcolm. 2002. *The Tipping Point: How Little Things Can Make a Big Difference.* Lebanon, IN: Back Bay Books.

Grove, Lloyd. 2003. "Close, but No Cigar." *Washington Post,* May 15.

Horwitz, Jeff. 2004. "I'm Very Ashamed." *Salon,* August 27.

Ivins, Molly. 2000. *Shrub: The Short but Happy Political Life of George W. Bush.* New York: Vintage Books.

Jarding, Steve, and Dave "Mudcat" Saunders. 2006. *Foxes in the Henhouse: How the Republicans Stole the South and the Heartland and What the Democrats Must Do to Run 'em Out.* New York: Touchstone.

Kaine, Tim. 2006. "How I Won." *Blueprint Magazine,* February 9.

Karabell, Zachary. 2000. *The Last Campaign: How Harry Truman Won the 1948 Election.* New York: Knopf.

Lebkowsky, Jon, and Mitch Ratcliffe, eds. 2005. *Extreme Democracy.* Morrisville, NC: Lulu.com.

Lessig, Lawrence. 2000. *Code and Other Laws of Cyberspace.* New York: Basic Books.

Lewis, Bob. 2006. "Retired Female General to Back Miller for Senate." Associated Press, March 9.

Lind, Michael. 2004. *Made in Texas: George W. Bush and the Southern Takeover of American Politics.* New York: Basic Books.

Martin, James. 2006. "Shelton Responds to 9/25/06 Allen Denial." *Virginia Progressive,* September 30.

McDougall, Paul. 2006. "IT Confidential: ITAA's Miller Wants to Go to Washington." *Information Week,* January 9.

Members of the Union-Tribune's Editorial Board. 2005. "Q&A: James Webb; Former Secretary of the Navy." *San Diego Union Tribune,* October 30.

Milbank, Dana. 2006. "The Senator's Gentile Rebuke." *Washington Post,* September 19.

Moore, James, and Wayne Slater. 2003. *Bush's Brain: How Karl Rove Made George W. Bush Presidential.* New York: Wiley.

New Politics Institute. 2005. "Emergence of the Progressive Blogosphere: A New Force in American Politics." August 10.

New Politics Institute. 2007. "Campaign 2008: Targeting Young Voters." March 9.

Nichols, Bill. 2005. "Democratic Candidates Tout Iraq War Experience." *USA Today,* July 27.

O'Keefe, Maura. 2006. "Webb Beats Miller for Democratic Senate Nomination." *Cavalier Daily,* June 15.

Pew Research Center for People and the Press. 2005. "The Dean Activists: Their Profile and Prospects." April 6.

Pollowitz, Greg. 2006. "Schumer to the Rescue." Sixers Blog. *National Review Online,* August 30.

Pratkanis, Anthony, and Elliot Aronson. 2001. *Age of Propaganda: The Everyday Use and Abuse of Persuasion.* Orlando: Holt Paperbacks.

Proctor, Rachel. 2004. "Dean Is Dead, Long Live the Dean!" *Texas Observer,* March 26.

Putnam, Robert D. 2000. *Bowling Alone: The Collapse and Revival of American Community.* New York: Simon & Schuster.

Ratan, Suneel. 2003. "Draft-Clark Posse Feels Left Out." *Wired,* September 26.

Reynolds, Glenn. 2006. *An Army of Davids: How Markets and Technology Empower Ordinary People to Beat Big Media, Big Government, and Other Goliaths.* Nashville: Thomas Nelson.

Riordan, William L. 1995. *Plunkitt of Tammany Hall: A Series of Very Plain Talks on Very Practical Politics.* New York: Signet Classics.

Schumer, Chuck. 2007. *Positively American: Winning Back the Middle-Class Majority One Family at a Time.* New York: Rodale Books.

Shear, Michael, D. 2005. "References to Hitler in Kilgore Ad Criticized." *Washington Post,* October 15.

Shear, Michael D., and Robert Barnes. 2006. "Virginia Politics." *Washington Post,* June 14.

Shear, Michael D., and Tim Craig. 2006. "Paid Bloggers Stoke Senate Battle in Va.: Campaigns Test Limits of Finance Laws." *Washington Post,* September 17.

Sidarth, S. R. 2006. "I Am Macaca." *Washington Post,* November 12.

Strother, Raymond. 2003. *Falling Up: How a Redneck Helped Invent Political Consulting.* Baton Rouge: Louisiana State University Press.

SurveyUSA. 2006. Poll No. 10072. August 21.

Teachout, Zephyr, Thomas Streeter, and Jerome Armstrong. 2007. *Mousepads, Shoe Leather, and Hope: Lessons from the Howard Dean Campaign for the Future of Internet Politics.* Boulder, CO: Paradigm Publishers.

Thomas, Helen. 2007. *Watchdogs of Democracy? The Waning Washington Press Corps and How It Has Failed the Public.* New York: Scribner.

Thompson, Nicholas. 2003. "The Exterminator." *Salon,* September 3.

Timberg, Robert. 1996. *The Nightingale's Song.* New York: Free Press.

Trippi, Joe. 2004. *The Revolution Will Not Be Televised.* New York: William Morrow.

Vargas, Jose Antonio. 2007. "A Foundation Built on Small Blocks." *Washington Post,* July 16.

Webb, James. 1978. *Fields of Fire.* New York: Bantam.

Webb, James. 1979. "Women Can't Fight." *Washingtonian,* November.

Webb, James. 1981. *A Sense of Honor.* Annapolis, MD: Naval Institute Press.

Webb, James. 1983. *A Country Such as This.* Annapolis, MD: Naval Institute Press.

Webb, James. 1992. *Something to Die For.* New York: Avon.

Webb, James. 1999. *The Emperor's General.* New York: Bantam.

Webb, James. 2001. *Lost Soldiers.* New York: Bantam.

Webb, James. 2004. *Born Fighting: How the Scots-Irish Shaped America.* New York: Broadway.

Weisman, Jonathan. 2003. "Schiavo's Wishes Recalled in Records." *St. Petersburg Times,* November 8.

Weisman, Jonathan. 2006. "GOP Leaders Seek Distance from Abramoff; Hastert to Donate Money Given by Lobbyist's Clients." *Washington Post,* January 4.

Whittington, Lauren W. 2006. "George Allen Torpedoed?" *Roll Call,* February 9.

RADIO AND TELEVISION

American Morning. 2006. CNN, August 9.

GOTV. 2006. "Did Webb Play Anti-Semitic Card?" May 19.

Hannity and Colmes. 2004. Fox News, June 9.

Matthews, Jon. 2003. KSEV Talk Radio. October 22.

BLOGROLL

State Blogs

Connecticut

Connecticut Blog, http://connecticutblog.blogspot.com.
Connecticut Bob, http://www.ctbob.blogspot.com.
Dump Joe, http://dumpjoe.com (Keith Crane).
Lamont Blog, http://lamontblog.blogspot.com.
My Left Nutmeg, http://www.myleftnutmeg.com (Maura Keaney).
Spazeboy, http://www.spazeboy.net (Beau Anderson).

Montana

Left in the West, http://www.leftinthewest.com (Matt Singer).

Ohio

Buckeye State Blog, http://www.buckeyestateblog.com.
Grow Ohio, no longer active (Tim Tagaris).
Ohio 2nd Blog, http://blog.oh02.com (Chris Baker).

Texas

Burnt Orange Report, http://www.burntorangereport.com (Byron LaMasters).
Capitol Annex, http://www.capitolannex.com.
Clean Up Texas, http://www.CleanUpTexasPolitics.com (Fred Lewis).
Drive Democracy, http://www.DriveDemocracy.org (Glenn Smith).
Greg's Opinion, http://www.gregsopinion.com (Greg Wythe).
In the Pink Texas, http://www.inthepinktexas.com (Eileen Smith).
Off the Kuff, http://www.offthekuff.com (Charles Kuffner).
Pink Dome, http://www.pinkdome.com.
Quorum Report, http://www.quorumreport.com (Harvey Kronberg).
Texas Kaos, http://www.texaskaos.com.

Virginia

Democracy for Virginia, http://democracyforvirginia.typepad.com (Maura Keaney).
Not Larry Sabato, http://notlarrysabato.typepad.com (Ben Tribbett).
Ox Road South, http://www.oxroadsouth.com (Chap Petersen).
Raising Kaine, http://www.raisingkaine.com (Lowell Feld and Eric Grim).
The Richmond Democrat, http://richmonddemocrat.blogspot.com (J. C. Wilmore).
Virginia Centrist, http://www.virginiacentrist.com (Paul Anderson).
Virginia Virtucon, http://www.virtuconindustries.blogspot.com.
Waldo Jaquith, http://waldo.jaquith.org (Waldo Jaquith).

National Conservative Blogs

Drudge Report, http://drudgereport.com.
Free Republic, http://www.freerepublic.com/focus/f-news/browse.

Instapundit, http://instapundit.com (Glen Reynolds).
Modern Patriot, http://www.modernpatriot.net.
Q and O, http://www.qando.net (Jon Henke).

National Progressive Blogs

Daily DeLay, http://dailydelay.blogspot.com (David Donnelly).
Daily Kos, http://www.dailykos.com (Markos Moulitsas Zúniga).
Dean Nation, http://dean2004.blogspot.com (Jerome Armstrong and Aziz Poonawalla).
Eschaton, http://atrios.blogspot.com (Duncan Black).
FireDogLake, http://www.firedoglake.com (Jane Hamsher).
k/o, http://kidoaklandblog.blogspot.com.
MyDD, http://www.mydd.com (Jerome Armstrong).
The News Blog, http://www.stevegilliard.blogspot.com (Steve Gilliard).
Open Left, http://www.openleft.com (Matt Stoller).
Swing State Project, http://www.swingstateproject.com (DavidNYC).
Talking Points Memo, http://www.talkingpointsmemo.com (John Marshall).

Howard Dean Links

Blog for America, http://www.blogforamerica.com (Matthew Gross).
Democracy for America, http://www.democracyforamerica.com.
Howard Dean's March 2003 Speech to the California Democratic Convention, http://www.archive.org/details/dean-sacramento.
Howard Dean 2004 Call to Action, http://deancalltoaction.blogspot.com.
Personal Democracy Forum, http://www.personaldemocracy.com (Zack Exley).

Wesley Clark Links

Clark Community Network, http://securingamerica.com/ccn (Stan Davis).
Draft Clark, http://www.DraftClark.com.
Draft Wesley Clark, http://www.draftwesleyclark.com.
Wesley Clark 2004 Yahoo! group, http://groups.yahoo.com/group/wesleyclark2004/?yguid=134014667.
WesPAC/Securing America, http://securingamerica.com.

Social Networking, Fundraising, and General

ActBlue, http://www.actblue.com.
Association of Alternative Newsweeklies, http://aan.org/alternative/Aan/index.
Facebook, http://www.facebook.com.
Gather, http://www.gather.com.
Huffington Post, http://www.huffingtonpost.com/theblog.
Internet Archive, http://www.archive.org/details/dean-sacramento.
Juanita's, the World's Most Dangerous Hair Salon, http://www.kissmybigbluebutt.com (Susan Bankston).
Meetup, http://www.meetup.com.
MoveOn, http://www.moveon.org.

MySpace, http://www.myspace.com.
New Politics Institute, http://www.newpolitics.net.
Second Life, http://secondlife.com.
The Soapblox Network, http://www.soapblox.net.
Yahoo! http://groups.yahoo.com.
YouTube, http://www.youtube.com.

PERSONAL COMMUNICATIONS

All quotations in this work not documented by endnotes are excerpted from personal communications provided to the authors by the following individuals with their express or implied permission, gratefully acknowledged by the authors. The title and affiliation given after each individual's name is that which was obtained at the time of the personal communication or during the period discussed in the book.

Ambrose, Chris (volunteer for Clark and Webb campaigns): interview, June 22, 2007.
Armstrong, Jerome (founder of MyDD, aka the "Blogfather"): e-mails, August 16, August 20, and September 11, 2007.
Barnes, Ben (former Lieutenant Governor of Texas and former Speaker of the Texas House of Representatives): interview, February 16, 2007.
Brodnitz, Pete (Democratic pollster): e-mail, September 19, 2007.
Browner-Hamlin, Matt (My Left Nutmeg blogger, volunteer for Ned Lamont): interview, June 19, 2007.
Brundrett, Trei (volunteer on the Dean and Kerry for president campaigns): interview, July 25, 2007.
Burns, Eric (Congressman Chris Bell's communications director): interview, May 2, 2007.
Burroughs, Debby (volunteer for Clark and Webb campaigns): e-mails, April 22, August 30, and September 3, 2007.
Byler, Eric (filmmaker, Webb for Senate campaign volunteer): interview, April 26, 2007.
Chernila, Josh (co-founder of Draft James Webb movement, Webb for Senate volunteer coordinator, Raising Kaine blogger): numerous e-mails during 2005 and 2006; interview, April 26, 2007; e-mail, July 21, 2007; instant message, June 11, 2007.
Christian, Adrienne (Webb for Senate deputy campaign manager): interview, April 27, 2007.
Cobarruvias, John (leader of Bay Area New Democrats): interview, March 26, 2007.
Cofer, Rick (aide to Glen Maxey, Rick Noriega for U.S. Senate deputy campaign manager): interview, June 19, 2007.
Companys, Yosem (Clark for President national advisor on Hispanic and Latino issues): interview, April 14, 2007; e-mails, June 30, August 7, and September 15, 2007.
Coppinger, Lori Baldwin (Internet marketing consultant for Tony Sanchez for governor): interview, May 2, 2007.
Craig, Tim (*Washington Post* reporter): interview, July 24, 2007.
D'Amico, Steve (Webb for Senate research team): instant message, August 15, 2007.

Davis, Stan (moderator of the national Clark for President Yahoo group): e-mail, April 6, 2006.

DeHaas, Kyle (Tony Sanchez for governor database director): interview, April 30, 2007.

Detweiler, Mary (Webb for Senate campaign volunteer): e-mails, July 2, 2006, and April 12, 2007.

Diamond, Lee (co-founder of Draft James Webb movement): numerous e-mails during 2005 and 2006; e-mail, April 5, 2007.

Donnelly, David (director of Campaign Money Watch): interview, March 8, 2007.

Easter, Abbi (volunteer for Clark campaign, Webb for Senate Richmond area coordinator): e-mail, April 8, 2007.

Fero, Kelly (Austin-based Democratic political strategist): interview, April 28, 2007.

Fowler, Donnie, Jr. (Clark for President campaign manager): interview, August 21, 2007.

Greidinger, Marc (Webb for Senate campaign volunteer): interview, April 9, 2007.

Haskins, Conaway (South of the James blogger, Webb for Senate campaign volunteer, Senator Webb's deputy state director): e-mail, June 1, 2007.

Henke, Jon (Allen for Senate netroots coordinator): e-mails, April 25, April 27, and April 30, 2007.

Hernandez, Corey (Webb for Senate campaign volunteer, Raising Kaine blogger): numerous e-mails during 2005 and 2006.

Hewitt, Jeff (Texas Democratic political consultant): interview, January 7, 2007.

Hlinko, John (co-founder of Draft Wesley Clark movement, Clark for President director of Internet strategy): e-mails, April 2, April 8, and September 16, 2007.

Hurst, Andy (attorney, 2006 candidate for Congress from Virginia's 11th district): e-mail, July 15, 2007.

Huynh, Larry (Clark for President and Webb for Senate online strategist, Blackrock Associates): interview, April 5, 2007.

Hynes, Aldon (Lamont for Senate director of technology): interview, June 13, 2007.

Jaquith, Waldo (Virginia blogger): e-mail, May 5, 2007.

Jarding, Steve (Webb for Senate campaign senior strategist, Harvard professor): numerous e-mails during 2006; interview, April 12, 2007.

Kerrey, Bob (President of the New School, former U.S. Senator from Nebraska): e-mail, January 7, 2007.

Kreykenbohm, Barbara (Webb for Senate campaign volunteer): e-mail, April 10, 2007.

Kuffner, Charles (Off the Kuff blogger): e-mail, August 3, 2007.

LaMasters, Byron (Burnt Orange Report blogger): e-mail, August 1, 2007.

Lebkowsky, John (technologist, volunteer for Dean and Kerry campaigns): interview, July 26, 2007.

Leibowitz, Vince (Texas journalist, political consultant, and blogger): e-mail, August 3, 2007.

Lewis, Fred (Austin attorney, Texas clean campaign advocate): interview, June 25, 2007.

Lucas, Dan (Democratic political operative, advisor to Congressman Sherrod Brown): e-mail, September 21, 2007.

Mariner, Susan (volunteer for the Webb campaign): e-mail, August 8, 2006, and numerous others.

Maxey, Glen (first openly gay member of the Texas Legislature, coordinator for the Howard Dean campaign in Texas): e-mails, August 21 and August 25, 2007.

Mitakides, Jane (candidate from Ohio's third congressional district): telephone call, April 5, 2007.

Morrison, Richard (Sugar Land environmental attorney, 2004 candidate against Representative Tom DeLay): e-mails, March 17, May 25, and July 13, 2007.

Musselman, Karl-Thomas (Burnt Orange Report blogger, Dean volunteer): e-mail, August 3, 2007.

Nagler, Ellen (leader of Santa Barbara for Clark): numerous instant messages, September–December 2003; interview, April 10, 2007.

Nicholson, Mike (co-founder of Austin for Kerry): e-mails, August 19 and September 30, 2007.

Park, Annabel (Webb for Senate campaign volunteer): interview, April 26, 2007.

Parrott, Betty (Webb for Senate campaign volunteer): e-mails, April 5 and April 7, 2007.

Parrott, Ralph (Webb for Senate campaign volunteer): e-mail, April 8, 2007.

Phelan, Todd (co-founder of Austin for Kerry): interview, July 20, 2007.

Poonawalla, Aziz (co-founder of Dean Nation blog): e-mail, July 2, 2007.

Resnick, Andrew (Harris Miller for Senate campaign manager): e-mail, April 12, 2007.

Rohrbach, John (Tim Kaine for Governor Internet coordinator): interview, May 3, 2007.

Sawin, Kodi (political media consultant, constituency program director on the Tony Sanchez for governor campaign): interview, January 7, 2007.

Scatton, Antonia (Webb for Senate campaign volunteer): interview, May 1, 2007.

Singer, Matt (Left in the West blogger, Tester for Senate volunteer): interview, April 11, 2007.

Smith, Glenn (Democratic political operative, former *Houston Chronicle* reporter, Tony Sanchez for Governor campaign manager, Texans for Truth founder): interview, April 6, 2007.

Spencer, Jim (Kerry for President organizer): e-mail, September 30, 2007.

Stanley, Joe (Virginia blogger, Webb for Senate): instant message, July 24, 2007.

Stoller, Matt (MyDD and OpenLeft blogger): interview, August 7, 2007.

Tagaris, Tim (blogger, volunteer for Hackett campaign, Lamont for Senate netroots coordinator, Dodd for President Internet communications director): interviews, April 24 and June 19, 2007; e-mails, September 13, September 16, and September 24, 2007.

Tribbett, Ben (Not Larry Sabato blogger): interview, April 17, 2007.

Vanden Berg, Jessica (Webb for Senate campaign manager): numerous e-mails during 2006; interview, April 22, 2007.

Webb, Jim (candidate for U.S. Senate from Virginia, U.S. Senator from Virginia): numerous e-mails, December 2005–January 2006; e-mail, June 21, 2007.

Index

About the Authors

LOWELL FELD is a political consultant and netroots specialist. He was the netroots/blogging/online fundraising coordinator for the successful senatorial campaign of James Webb in 2006. He contributes regularly to Raising Kaine, Daily Kos, Blog Talk Radio, and Heading Left Radio. He served for eighteen years as an analyst in the Energy Information Administration of the U.S. Department of Energy.

NATE WILCOX is a political and public affairs consultant with the WebStrong Group advising clients such as Senators John Kerry and Tom Harkin on online strategy. He was online communications director for Governor Mark Warner's Forward Together PAC in 2006. He has pioneered many online political campaign innovations, including podcasting, online video, use of social networking sites such as Facebook and MySpace, blogger outreach, and aggressive online advertising.

APACK

7/08